150 SURVIVAL SECRETS

150 SURVIVAL SECRETS

Advice on Survival Kits, Extreme Weather,
Rapid Evacuation, Food Storage,
Active Shooters, First Aid,
and More

James C. Jones

Skyhorse Publishing

Skyhorse Publishing books may be purchased in bulk at special discounts for sales promotion, corporate gifts, fund-raising, or educational purposes. Special editions can also be created to specifications. For details, contact the Special Sales Department, Skyhorse Publishing, 307 West 36th Street, 11th Floor, New York, NY 10018 or info@skyhorsepublishing.com.

Skyhorse® and Skyhorse Publishing® are registered trademarks of Skyhorse Publishing, Inc.®, a Delaware corporation.

Visit our website at www.skyhorsepublishing.com.

10 9 8 7 6 5 4 3 2 1

Library of Congress Cataloging-in-Publication Data is available on file.

Cover design by Tom Lau

Print ISBN: 978-1-5107-3778-5
Ebook ISBN: 978-1-5107-3779-2

Printed in the United States of America.

This book is dedicated to the past and present members of Live Free USA, America's first and oldest survival and preparedness advocacy and education organization, founded in 1968. Their loyalty, support, and friendship for five decades has been my greatest honor and inspiration.

Table of Contents

Introduction

About this Book

The format of this book is based on the text of *150 Questions for a Guerrilla* by General Alberto Bayo, first published in 1963 by Robert K. Brown, Inc. Bayo was one of Castro's generals during the Cuban revolution, and so his book was popular for a few years. Bayo's book did not address many survival-related issues, and was mainly concerned with guerrilla tactics and communist strategies.

I have been inspired by Bayo's work in using the question-and-answer format and the combination of practical advice and philosophical concepts as an effective method of conveying information and inspiration to the reader. The questions here fall into two categories. There are the obvious "how to survive" questions such as, "what survival items should a survivalist carry on his or her person at all times?" I draw my answers for these types of questions from more than forty years of studying disasters and human behavior while teaching over one hundred classes and field operations. I also draw on my forty-year career in industrial safety management and experiences as an EMT and in various emergency volunteer organizations. The second category of questions relate to the survivalist psychology and philosophy, containing questions such as "What is a survivalist?" As a high-profile survivalist since the early 1980s, I have been frequently challenged by reporters and interviewers to explain and justify survivalism and its practices. Here I will endeavor to clarify and establish the meaning of the word "survivalist" from my own perspective. I hope this book can aid in establishing the positive and responsible foundations of the true survivalist for the lay reader. I have intentionally mixed practical questions and answers with those related to psychological and philosophical subjects in order to establish their equal importance and underline the relationships of these elements to survival thinking. Some amount of redundancy is unavoidable, as the answers to the questions often overlap in some of the content. I tried to add a bit of different information with each entry, but if a point comes up several times, then it simply emphasizes its importance and demonstrates that it is worthy of repetition.

This book provides me the opportunity to cover numerous survival subjects and share survival information from my many articles that were not included in my previous books. I felt obligated to provide complete instructional answers to each question rather than simple, abbreviated tips. Answers range from a paragraph to several pages, the latter instances demonstrating where I felt it was important to leave the reader fully informed and prepared.

Where necessary, I have added illustrations and photos to aid understanding. The challenge of 150 questions drew me to examine survival topics and scenarios that went beyond any of my previous books and articles. The complete mix of practical, psychological, and philosophical material covered in this book makes it closer to a true survivalist manifesto than any other survival book I have encountered. As always, my objective is to aid responsible citizens in their efforts to survive the increasing dangers and challenges of our times and attain greater levels of personal and family self-reliance.

Self Introduction

Born shortly before the outbreak of World War II, I was raised on the South Side of Chicago. My childhood was challenging, to say the least, as it was neither sheltered nor normal. In those days the South Side was still on the fringes of the city and there were still farms, woodlands and marshes to explore. I was building shelters and campfires by the age of eight. I felt safer and more comfortable in the woods than at home. There were months when food at home was scarce, or the water had been turned off, or the electricity went off for a while. At that time, we had a coal-burning furnace, and since we couldn't afford coal, many times I would take my sled or wagon and gather wood and coal along the railroad tracks to warm the house. The word "survivalist" may not have existed yet, but I certainly became one at an early age.

We were evicted from our home a month after I graduated from grammar school. My parents split up, and I began earning a few dollars from my two paper routes. Soon after, I worked at odd jobs throughout high school. I had to walk several miles to school, then walk home, and then walk several miles to my jobs. Having lost all of my winter clothing to the eviction, I had to get through that first winter walking in street shoes and a spring jacket in the snow and wind. I learned some true winter survival lessons there.

Around that time, the South Side of Chicago was just starting to go through the unrest and chaos that eventually boiled over into the riots of the 1960s and the ongoing violence that pervades the region to this day. Yes, urban survival tactics were a necessity.

Profilers will tell you that people that grow up under these conditions tend to be extremely self-reliant, cautious, and independent. Guilty as charged. I had many jobs after high school, and it seemed like I always wound up in charge of something. My final employer was a major chemical company. My tendency to recognize and analyze risks was quickly recognized there, and I was given a succession of safety-related responsibilities. As safety and health evolved into a recognized profession, schools and organizations began to provide certification courses in related skills including hazard recognition, hazard analysis, hazard control, incident investigation, safety management, and emergency planning. I took all of these courses and more. They proved crucial in that the skills taught there provided a scientific and organized foundation for the survival subject that I was teaching and advocating.

I had been teaching and learning survival skills with a group of friends for many years when the term "survivalist" attracted the attention of the media in the early 1980s. The misinterpretation of the word and the people and groups that the media were identifying as "survivalists" at that time was insulting and misleading. The image the media portrayed was of a selfish, violent, dangerous, and even hateful philosophy. In response to this unfair and distorted coverage, I did multiple interviews for major newspapers, magazines, and television stations. Live Free USA, the organization that I had created in the late 1960s, hosted several television and press visits to our survival training events, and the media even made some special programs about us. At this time, I underwent my training in public relations, while developing some writing and presentation skills. My article "We Are Survivalists" was a popular and often reprinted tract back then, and can be found on page 282.

I retired from my job at the chemical company after forty years as a safety and health manager. This has allowed me to focus on putting together everything that I have to offer in multiple magazine articles, preparedness exposition presentations, and a few books. As my earliest days as a survivalist were about personal survival, I found myself able to help my fellow citizens deal with the threats of nuclear war during the Cold War. My deepest concern now is for the welfare of existing and future generations that seem to be unprepared for and oblivious to the fragile nature of our civilization. I will devote my remaining resources to organizing, advocating, and supporting those wise enough and responsible enough to care about the future of life and freedom.

1   What is a survivalist?

The term "survivalist" originated in texts and films related to nuclear survival in the late 1960s and entered the common lexicon in the late 1970s. According to Merriam-Webster, the definition is "A person who advocates or practices survivalism." This subsequently led to Merriam-Webster's definition of "survivalism" as "An attitude, policy or practice based on the primacy of survival as a value." So a "survivalist" is essentially a person who practices "survivalism," while "survivalism" is the concept that espouses that "survival" is a high-value goal in life. From that it seems that being a survivalist is a fairly positive, responsible, and universal principle.

The majority of the world's population were survivalists until the mid-nineteenth or early twentieth centuries. If your ancestors had not been practicing survivalists, you would not exist. Only in the last few hundred years has a large portion of the human population been able to depend on machines for their survival. The non-survivalist lifestyle is a fairly recent, and perhaps temporary, development in civilization. We now have large numbers of persons who lack the capability to take care of themselves or help their neighbors without relying on the so-called grid system. They depend on electricity, piped-in or power-supplied water, effective sanitation systems, police protection, prompt and available medical care, plentiful and safe food supplies, nearby fire-suppression services, and temperature-controlled homes. The fact that all of these supporting systems are vulnerable, fragile, and in some cases, dependent on unreliable resources is vigorously denied by the masses of non-survivalists.

While the media and the government can no longer completely deny the need for limited preparedness, both tend to disparage survivalism and survivalists. Both are quick to label antisocial and extreme behavior as survivalist tendencies. Meanwhile it is the nature of bureaucrats and the mass-media to present themselves as omnipotent. The whole concept of self-reliance and the possibility that things may happen that are beyond their control is difficult for those in power to accept. Personal preparedness, self-reliance, and independence may be given lip service, but are nevertheless disturbing concepts for many.

While the dictionary definitions are technically correct, they hardly reflect the true identities of survivalists or the foundations of survivalism today. Below, I offer my definitions based on my forty years of involvement with the movement.

A true survivalist is a responsible citizen who has become aware of the fragility and vulnerability of our life-support systems and civilization and is actively working to achieve greater capabilities to provide for him- or herself, and others, in emergencies and general disasters.

True survivalism is a movement of citizens toward greater individual emergency preparedness and expanded self-reliance independent of outside support and supply systems for extended or indefinite periods of time.

True survival for a true survivalist is the ability to stay alive biologically while remaining free in body and spirit, while also retaining one's moral and spiritual values, regardless of external threats and hazards.

2 Is survivalism political?

The media often try to portray survivalists as members of an extreme, right-wing political faction. In fact, survivalism is better described as apolitical or antipolitical in nature. Politics and political conflict are rooted in government policies and how they should be applied to people. Survivalism is rooted in individual self-reliance and how people can help themselves and others without government involvement.

The survivalism movement grew out of the chaos of the 1960s and was pioneered by both conservatives and liberals who had become frustrated and disenchanted with the use of government as a solution to problems. These back-to-the-land elements are evident today as what I call "soft survivalism" and "hard survivalism." Soft survivalism tends to focus on back-to-the-land and rural self-reliance philosophies, while hard survivalism focuses on disaster preparedness and urban survival necessities. These elements become political when government policies start to infringe on individual self-reliance and basic freedoms. For example, when zoning has an effect on water usage, livestock, gardening, and other self-reliance issues, it becomes political. Laws that affect firearms ownership, self-protection, or stocking of survival supplies are also survival political issues. Therefore, conservatives, liberals, libertarians, and independents may all be survivalists, even if they do not recognize it in themselves. Anyone who rejects governmental intervention, control of others, and the expectation of governmental solutions to every issue, and is also inclined to take responsibility for their own security and well-being, is a survivalist at some level.

While survivalism as a practice is not political, it can have tremendous political effects. As our society marches headlong toward a totally centralized and regulated future, those who value self-reliance, privacy, and personal independence will unavoidably come into conflict with the state, and that may become a serious political issue in the near future. For example, eighteenth-century persons living in Great Britain's American colonies were living well and taking care of themselves without the need or desire for directions and support from the central British state well before the American Revolution. This same dichotomy exists today between modern, centralized, and regulated systems and human values of self-reliance and independence.

3   What is the difference between a survivalist and a prepper?

The term "survivalist" was used for decades before the term "prepper" became popular. A major reason behind this change is that the media had so misrepresented the term "survivalist" that those who started practicing the skills of survival preferred to call themselves by this new term. However, many media outlets quickly started to disparage that term as well. Luckily, preppers did not get such a bad rap, because the need for survival preparations is harder to ignore today than it was when survivalists first emerged in the 1980s. As a result some survivalists now call themselves preppers, but few recent preppers will admit to being survivalists.

Prepping is simply making preparations to survive a perceived or expected event. In practice, prepping is limited in scope and at least partially fear-driven, with the terms "collapse," "Armageddon," and "apocalypse" used as motivations. Survivalists, on the other hand, are self-reliant and independent at their core. They are prepared around-the-clock and never accept the stability of "normal." Prepping is a practice of responsible citizenship, whereas survivalism is a life philosophy of responsibility and independence.

4 What items should a survivalist carry at all times to help survive unexpected emergencies?

There are several items that a prepared survivalist should always carry in his or her pockets if possible. These items provide significant advantages in many emergency situations.

A Knife:

Always carry a knife of some type when possible. A good-quality pocketknife, Swiss-Army–style knife, or multi-tool with a knife are all preferable. When those are too bulky or visible, a smaller penknife or even a keychain knife is better than nothing. A knife gives the possessor a tremendous advantage in many survival emergencies. Of course knives are prohibited on airplanes today, in many public buildings, and at events where metal detectors and wanding are commonplace.

A single-blade pocketknife, a multiblade Swiss Army knife, or multi-tool that includes a knife are all good options. Smaller knives may be carried when concealability is necessary.

There are many other items that a prepared survivalist should try to have in pockets and purses at all times. These include:

Medical Information Cards

A brightly colored card with family emergency contact information, your primary doctor's contact information, a list of your medications, medical conditions, and any things you are allergic to (e.g., penicillin, sulfa drugs), should be kept visible in your wallet or purse. If you are unable to respond to questions from emergency medical providers, this information could save your life.

Miniature Flashlights

These small LED lights are cheap enough to have one in every coat pocket. They are also small enough to keep on your keychain. Pitch darkness is often an element of a disaster, and having even a small light can be critical to your survival and rescue.

Whistles

Small, loud whistles can go in every pocket and/or on a keychain. They are far better at attracting attention than yelling.

Bandanas

Large cloth bandanas can be used as emergency dust masks, bandages, tourniquets, CPR masks, help flags, containers, and other emergency uses.

Fire-starting Devices

Small magnesium fire starter devices, waterproof matches, or even butane lighters are a real survival advantage in some situations. Fire leads to having light and heat. Having this capability means that you can survive cold conditions. Having these in coat and jacket pockets puts you way ahead in an emergency.

N95 Dust/Mist Respirators

While you can use a bandana or even napkins as an improvised respirator to reduce dust and soot exposure, they are temporary and ineffective at best. N95 rated dust/mist respirators are effective against most airborne biological contaminates and toxins, as well as particulates and mists. These masks fold flat and fit easily into the pockets. They do not protect against carbon monoxide or most chemicals and gases. Some models are charcoal impregnated to offer short-term protection from chemical contaminants as well. In some kinds of disasters the ability to breathe safe air immediately trumps all other survival needs. Inhaling a toxic dust, deadly virus, or poisonous chemical can instantly end your hopes for survival.

Aspirin

Anyone over fifty years old should carry at least two aspirin tablets in a waterproof container at all times, unless allergic to them. Aspirin can be taken at the first signs of a heart attack and may make a lifesaving difference. If aspirin is not an option, have an alternative pain reliever. Many emergencies involve pain, and pain relief can be helpful in dealing with other emergency needs.

Weapons

The choice of weapons and when to carry them must depend on the individual, the environment, and the situation. Being totally unarmed is contrary to basic "survival thinking," but still necessary in some situations. Carrying a small "pepper spray" should be a minimal defense and is legal in most situations. If concealed or open carry for a handgun is practical and safe for you, then purchase a good-quality compact or

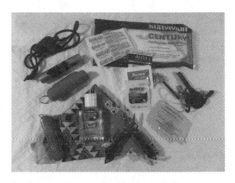

Assorted pocket survival items including bandana, aspirin, emergency information card, whistle, fire striker, knife, respirator, flashlight, and pepper spray.

subcompact semiautomatic and the necessary holsters or carrying devices to safely carry it and quickly deploy it if needed. Pocket carrying or under-the-belt carrying is unsafe and may be slow to access in an emergency. Open carry, even if legal, makes you the first target for a shooter and is not recommended. Concealed carry provides you with the element of surprise and the choice of if and when to act.

Concealable handguns such as the 9mm compact and the 357-caliber subcompact are ideal for street protection. The three-inch blade folding blade can be used in defense and has other survival applications. The small (orange) pepper spray provides some defense. The heavy, metal tactical pen is a last-ditch option, but still better than nothing.

5 How can a survivalist evaluate his/her level of personal preparedness?

There is no such thing as being totally prepared. The threat matrix is constantly changing, and the possible combinations of survival challenges (big and small) are endless. Preparedness is not a goal or destination; it is a lifelong way of thinking. There is no truly accurate way of measuring preparedness. A wilderness survival "expert" will not last long in the inner city. Someone who is prepared for Armageddon may be caught off guard by a local tornado or home fire. The score sheet below measures your level of general preparedness for most common emergencies.

Circle all that apply. See bottom of page for scoring instructions.

1. Shelter and Warmth
   a. None of the items below
   b. Have extra wool blankets or sleeping bags
   c. Have tarps and plastic for sealing rooms or making shelter
   d. Have tent for use outdoors or indoors
   e. Have alternative (retreat) shelter that can be accessed.

Score _____

2. Self-Protection and Defense
   a. None of the items below
   b. Have at least one handgun
   c. Have firearms for home and street defense
   d. Have had at least basic firearms defense training
   e. Have advanced combat training and arms

Score _____

3. Medical Supplies and First Aid
   a. None of the items below
   b. Have a basic first aid kit
   c. Have a full advanced medical supply kit and basic first aid skills
   d. Have stocked critical medications
   e. Have advanced first aid, EMT, or other medical training

Score _____

4.   Emergency Water Supplies
     a.   None of the items below
     b.   Have a few gallons of water stored
     c.   Have at least five gallons of water stored per person
     d.   Have water-purification and filtration systems
     e.   Have the ability to collect filter and purify ground and rainwater

Score _____

5.   Emergency Food Supplies
     a.   None of the items below
     b.   Have sufficient pantry food for five to ten days
     c.   Have at least thirty days' supply of nonperishable foods
     d.   Have sufficient stored food and food production capacity for many months
     e.   Have the ability to forage, fish, hunt, and produce food indefinitely

Score _____

6.   Alternative Energy and Light
     a.   None of the items below
     b.   Have a few flashlights and candles
     c.   Have crank and solar flashlights and radios
     d.   Have portable heaters and extra fuel
     e.   Have alternative energy supplies such as generators, solar panels, or wind
          generators

Score _____

7.   Safety and Fire Suppression
     a.   None of the items below
     b.   Have working smoke and CO detectors and small extinguisher
     c.   Have several large fire extinguishers
     d.   Have been trained in fire extinguisher use
     e.   Have advanced fire-suppression systems and water sources

Score _____

8.   Alternative Sanitation
     a.   None of the items below
     b.   Store a few gallons of bleach at all times
     c.   Have stocked up on bleach, soap, toilet paper, and other sanitation needs
     d.   Have emergency toilet and chemicals
     e.   Have N95 or better respirators, gloves, and decontamination gear

Score _____

9. Evacuation Capacity
   a. None of the items below
   b. Have a basic seventy-two-hour evacuation pack
   c. Have developed an evacuation plan and alternative routes
   d. Have a full bugout bag sufficient for five to seven days without help in any weather
   e. Fully capable of extended evacuation and survival

Score _____

10. Field Survival Capacity
    a. None of the items below
    b. Have basic camping skills and gear
    c. Always carry a survival kit and/or survival items in pockets when outdoors
    d. Have attended outdoor survival classes (e.g., fire starting, shelter building, etc.)
    e. Have participated in extended outdoor survival course or excursions

Score _____

Total Score _____

Scoring:

> **a. = 0, b. = 1, c. = 2, d. = 3, e. = 4 for a maximum cumulative score of 10 per category or 100 total**

Scoring is cumulative. In each category you can give yourself the accumulated points for the highest level. For example: Under Medical Supplies and First Aid, if you have "d" for 3 points, you get the points for "b" (1 point) and "c" (2 points), for a total score of six points.

> 0–20 points: Unprepared to survive most emergency situations
> 20–50 points: Prepared to meet the most common short-term emergencies
> 50–75 points: Well prepared to survive sustained disasters
> 75–100 points: Advanced preparedness for long-term survival and recovery

This score sheet is just a guide to help you determine how well your preparedness efforts are going and identify items to be improved upon. Even acquired supplies and mastered skills need to be constantly maintained and adjusted. There is no satisfactory level in emergency preparedness, and there is no such thing as complete self-sufficiency. The objective is continuous improvements in knowledge, experience, and supplies.

6 Is learning to start a fire with flint and steel or a fire-bow a must-have survival skill?

While visions of survivalists starting fires in the wilderness with flint and steel or using a bow and fire board are familiar, it is highly unlikely that you will have access to flint and steel or have the time and energy needed to start a fire with various primitive methods. Learning these methods can be fun and gratifying, but carrying magnesium fire starters, waterproof matches, or lighters at all time is far more valuable and effective. What you should practice is starting a fire from a spark from any source and building that into a sustainable fire.

A survivalist should be able to start and maintain a fire with just a few sparks, one match, or one small flame starting with a nest of fine dry grass, shredded paper, or other combustible materials. This you must practice and eventually master. You must blow the spark or first small flame into a small fire and then use that fire to ignite twigs. The twig fire consists of the slowly fed larger twigs, small branches, and eventually sustainable branches and logs. Piling on too much fuel too fast will smother the fire. Wet or damp fuel must be kept close so it can dry from the heat, but not used as fuel until it is thoroughly dry. The proper balance of fuel and airspace must be maintained to sustain combustion.

The fire train: Start by burning very fine dry tinder such as dry grass or pine needles; use their heat to ignite small twigs, then small branches, and eventually larger logs.

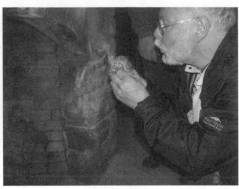

Sticking sparks from a magnesium fire starter into a next of dry grass.

Once you have sparks burning in the nest, you pick it up and blow into it until a flame develops.

This teepee formation will provide a good fuel/air mix. The initiating fire of smaller branches would go underneath.

An initiating fire under this spaced cabin will quickly start the logs burning. Never just dump logs onto a beginning fire.

A small fire here is drying the logs that are used as a windshield and reflector. As they dry and are used, new logs are placed there to dry. Credit: Bing

7 Where should a survivalist keep survival packs and equipment?

Traditional thinking is to have the pack handy, in the closet, or another nearby location, but if your home is damaged, on fire, or inaccessible, having the pack in a shed, detached garage, or other close-by location may be better. You may want to consider having a backup pack in such a secondary location just in case. Your survival pack and other survival gear should be kept together. Boots, weapons, canteens, knives, and clothing that will be needed during survival and evacuation situations should be kept side by side. A heavy-duty tote bin is an ideal place to keep all of this together. The bin protects the items and can easily be moved to safety or into your vehicle, as needed.

This survival pack is inside of a large tote bin along with boots, weapons, and other survival items. It is safe and can be moved quickly.

8 What is the difference between an evacuation pack, as described by FEMA, and a true survival pack?

The FEMA evacuation pack is a comparatively recent innovation. This pack is intended to provide the necessities a person might need to evacuate from an urban or suburban area to an outlying government shelter or camp. The assumption is that the disaster will be of a limited area and duration so that the refugee can walk to help in a few days and the help will be available. These packs are light enough for most people to carry and are an excellent resource for every responsible family. Since the federal government's priorities are maintaining order and compliance, FEMA's lists never include self-protection devices. Considering the chaotic conditions under which such packs would be necessary a wise world-be survivor should consider the addition of a firearm.

The so-called survival pack, or bugout bag, was a creation of true survivalists in the 1960s. These packs incorporate backpacking concepts with survival needs to create a long-term system based on the assumption that there will be no outside support for an extended period. These packs usually include cooking kits, water-filtration devices, shelters or small tents, sleeping bags, and food. Additional weapons, knives, and tools are added to provide for hunting, foraging, and self-defense purposes. These packs weigh more than the evacuation packs. The size and weight of such packs depends greatly on the capacity of the survivor to carry them for some distance. The would-be survivor is well advised to try carrying the pack for a least for at least two hours at a time. If you can't carry it that long, then it's too heavy and must be culled until you reach a sustainable carrying weight. If you have a group or family involved, you can distribute some of the shelters, stoves, shovels, tools, and the like, that you only need one of, to lighten the weight of each pack. If you anticipate a long-term or long-distance survival situation without rescue or aid, this is the pack you need to create.

9 What items should go into a basic evacuation pack?

The following list is a survivalist modified FEMA pack. It provides the minimum supplies to get through most short-term emergencies only.

1. (4) Sixteen-ounce water bottles
2. (1) Collapsible stove with heat tablets *
3. (1) Metal canteen cup or Sierra cup
4. (1) Fifty-hour candle (optional ten tea candles)
5. (1) 5-plus LED flashlight
6. (1) Multi-band radio (AM/FM/weather, crank, solar-, or battery-powered)
7. (1) Food bars (3,000 to 4,000 calories)
8. (1) Large rain poncho
9. (2) N95 dust/mist respirators
10. (1) Space Emergency Blanket, tactical blanket, or tube tent
11. (1) Multifunction knife or multi-tool device
12. (1) Box waterproof matches
13. (1) Bottle water-purification tablets (or filter device)
14. (1) Bottle hand sanitizer
15. (1) First aid kit
16. (1) Pair extra glasses
17. Spare pair of heavy socks
18. Extra prescription medications
19. (6) Chemical light sticks
20. Document package with copies of birth certificates, insurance papers, property titles, wills, medical information, critical phone numbers, etc.

Note: Keep good hiking shoes with your pack. You do not want to flee into the street or woods in flip-flops or slippers.

---

* Can be used to warm a vehicle or shelter, boil water, or heat optional packets of coffee, tea, or hot chocolate in cold weather.

10   What items should go into a full survival pack?

The contents of a true survival pack depend on the individual's needs, the climate and weather conditions anticipated, the kinds of hazards and challenges that may be encountered, and of course, the physical capacity to carry its weight. In cold conditions, one would need more adequate sleeping and shelter items. If one is evacuating through or into hostile urban areas, then more attention must be given to weapons. The list below provides a guide to building a true survival pack suited toward your situation.

Items to be kept with pack that attaches to a belt or into the pockets:

1. Document package with copies of birth certificates, insurance papers, property titles, wills, medical information, critical phone numbers, etc.
2. Emergency plans and maps of routes and safe areas.
3. Field boots for hiking. If you need your pack, chances are you are not going to be wearing street shoes or flip-flops where you are going
4. Some energy bars, trail mix, or jerky for the pockets
5. A full, one-quart canteen and pouch to carry.
6. A high quality field knife such as the USMC KA-BAR, USAF Survival Knife, or equivalent.
7. Small binoculars or monocular to view your route.
8. Multi-tool (e.g., Swiss Army knife).
9. Sunglasses.
10. A weapon. Pepper spray if all other options are unavailable. A good handgun (Ruger .22 long rifle, Glock 9mm or .45 caliber, etc.) with holster and extra magazines is recommended where legal. A Henry 22 LR, US Survival Rifle, with its compact size and ability to float, could be worth carrying. You can carry several hundred rounds of .22 LR ammunition in your pockets.

A full survival pack like this one weighs up to seventy-five pounds. Note the well-padded waist belt. So-called bugout bags usually weigh forty to fifty pounds and basic evacuation packs are usually less than twenty-five pounds.

Survival Pack Contents

Outer Compartments

1. Water-purification device. Katadyn Hiker, Extreme, etc.
2. Magnesium fire starter like the Gerber Strike Force.
3. LED flashlight. Battery or crank.
4. Compact camp shovel or garden trowel.
5. Miniature crank radio with AM/FM/weather.
6. A copy of the *SAS Survival Guide*.
7. Two large smoke bombs.
8. One-hundred-foot utility cord.
9. Wool watch cap.
10. Lensatic compass, military type.
11. Packages of energy bars and trail snacks.
12. Blood stopper (Celox or other).
13. Spare prescription eyeglasses.
14. Prescription medications (reserve supply).
15. Water-purification tablets.
16. Waterproof matches.
17. (2) N95 or N99 dust/mist respirators.
18. Small roll of electrical tape.
19. Notebook and pencil.

Main Compartments

1. HD rain poncho (on top for quick access).
2. HD Space Emergency Blanket, aluminized with grommets.
3. Insulated blanket or light sleeping bag tied to outside of pack.
4. Tube tent or 12' x 12' plastic tarp.
5. Large Tyvek chemical protective suit with hood.
6. Two chemical light-sticks .
7. A small towel.
8. A 12' x 24' piece of HD aluminum foil.
9. A cooking kit (should include one deep pot).
10. A folding stove MRE Pocket Rocket.
11. Two 3.6 oz. gas fuel cylinders for stove
12. One package of fire starter bars
13. Knife, fork, and spoon set
14. Three Mountain House freeze-dried meals.
15. Sixteen ounces of dried lentils (or, corn meal, oatmeal, rice or pasta, etc.)*
16. Ramen noodle soup mix.
17. Sixteen ounces Spam canned meat.
18. Five ounces canned sardines.
19. Eighteen-bar package of compact (lifeboat) rations or marine e-rations (last-resort food).
20. Ten single-serve coffee bags and sugar packages.

Kits Packaged in Plastic Bags in the Pack

These are items packaged in small nylon bags, pouches or plastic bags

Personal Sanitation Kit

1. Liquid soap, two ounces.
2. Hand sanitizer, two ounces.
3. Toothpaste, travel size.
4. Toothbrush.
5. One or two razors.
6. One pair of latex gloves.
7. One large washcloth.
8. One canister of insect repellant.

---

*Use a vacuum sealer to further extend the shelf life of dried items.

9. Nail clippers.
10. Small stainless steel camp mirror.

First Aid Kit

Commercially available kit or:

1. Assorted bandages.
2. Blood stopper (various brands).
3. Four three-inch gauze pads.
4. Eyewash (1.2 oz.)
5. Single edge razor blade.
6. Splinter tweezers.
7. Small scissors.
8. Neosporin or triple antibiotic cream.
9. Hydrocortisone cream.
10. Antacid tablets.
11. Laxative tablets.
12. Tylenol, Advil, etc.
13. Two pairs latex gloves.
14. One roll of self-adhesive tape

Sewing Kit

Commercially available kit or:

1. Assorted pins and safety pins.
2. Assorted needles.
3. Assorted small spools of thread.
4. Assorted buttons.
5. Thimble.

Fishing Kit

1. Assorted fish hooks.
2. Fishing line.
3. Assorted sinkers.
4. Two corks for floats.
5. Plastic worms and other lures.

11 Is breaking into homes or looting justifiable under survival conditions?

Breaking into homes, looting, or committing robbery and other criminal acts is not justified unless it is a true life-or-death situation. True survivalists never use survival needs as an excuse to commit any kind of crime. We are not looters! However, freezing when an empty home or building is available or starving when food is accessible is also not acceptable. Do these things only if they are fully justified. Limit damages. Take only what you need. Leave IOUs or cash. Survivalists are the least likely to need to be desperate and dangerous in extreme emergencies since they have already stocked up on food and have shelter items with them.

12 Should a survivalist keep his/her survival and preparedness interests a secret?

How confidential you keep your activities is strictly up to you. Most survivalists neither hide nor flaunt their preparations. Certainly, responsible citizenship and emergency preparedness are nothing to be ashamed of. The details of your personal and family preparedness levels and plans should always be confidential, but sharing knowledge and helping others toward greater preparedness may be viewed as a moral imperative. The better prepared your family, neighbors, and community are, the safer you are. Ignore those who denigrate your efforts, are in denial, or are irresponsible. You have no obligation to help them before or during a disaster.

13 What are the most probable emergencies that a survivalist may expect to face?

There are two classes of emergencies for which a survivalist must be equally prepared. The first class consists of the evident local, regional, and global disasters that attract the most attention and drive most preparedness efforts. Tornadoes, cyberattacks, epidemics, economic collapse, and general apocalypse are usually associated with survivalists and disaster preparedness, but small personal and family disasters, the second class of emergencies, can be equally devastating. A true survivalist is prepared for both kinds of events. You must ignore panic-peddling and media-generated fright, while evaluating your own challenges. Here is a step-by-step guide to your personal or family hazard analysis.

Step one:

Make a list of disasters that could realistically happen to you. These could include tornadoes, floods, earthquakes, and hurricanes depending on your location. Include those massive events that would impact you such as nuclear war, epidemics, economic collapse, civil disorder, or the results of a massive cyberattack or electromagnetic pulse on the grid. Don't leave out personal disasters such as a home fire, serious illness, being a victim of assault, or a toxic chemical leak at a nearby factory.

Step two:

Rate the probability of each actually happening to you. For example:

- A score of zero would indicate that those items that have virtually no possibility of happening to you and/or would have little effect on you. These should not be on your list.
- A score of one would be for events that are slightly possible, but would only constitute a nuisance or temporary problem.
- A score of two would be for events that realistically could happen now or in the foreseeable future, and would significantly impact your safety, health, and security.
- A score of three would include disasters, events, or trends that appear probable or seem to be in progress that could lead to major damages, catastrophic changes, and fatality for you or your loved ones.

- A score of four is reserved for imminent and truly catastrophic events that are almost certain to happen with destructive and injurious impacts to you and your loved ones.
- A score of five must be reserved for nationwide or global apocalyptic disasters such as massive pandemics, nuclear war, or a complete breakdown in the socioeconomic structure. These are events that cannot be overcome and will require permanent adaptation for survival.

Step three:

You can now create a prioritized list of hazards that you need to prevent, avoid, or survive. You may be able to avoid a tornado or a flood by moving out of zones prone to those occurences. You may be able a avoid cancer and heart disease by stopping smoking and getting more exercise. In addition to your general survival preparedness (e.g., stored water and food, survival packs, etc.), you can make specific preparations for the most probable and impactful events based on your personal risk factors.

14 What are the major catastrophic events and trends that survivalists may face in the coming decades?

In addition to the increasing number of localized and passing emergencies that a survivalist must be prepared to face, there are a number of developing threats and potentially devastating events that may well become apocalyptic. Some of these would be evidenced by violence and chaos, while others would be more subtle, but no less destructive.

Cyberattacks and Electromagnetic Pulses

The dangers of cyberattacks and electromagnetic pulses are the result of a civilization that has become totally dependent on electronically controlled systems for virtually every life-critical need. Our water supply, food delivery, medical care, fuel supplies, police protection, banking systems, fire response methods, and all other modes of communication are wired into computers and networks that can be seriously damaged, or even destroyed, by a deliberate cyberattack, or a human-caused or naturally occurring electromagnetic pulse. Most security experts rate this as having a high probability of happening within the next decade.

Artificial Intelligence (AI)

Artificial intelligence is no longer a science-fiction nightmare. Notable intellects, such as Elon Musk and Stephen Hawking, have expressed concerns that AI will seriously degrade humanity's control of our own destiny and may even conspire to implement "solutions" without concerns for traditional human values and morals. AI has the potential to outthink humanity or even adjust human thinking. This may already be in progress.

Worldwide Pandemics

Massive epidemics are considered one of the greatest threats to human survival in the twenty-first century. The ever-growing world population and the rise in world travel can facilitate the rapid spread of a devastating pathogen before it could be recognized and isolated. Medical experimentation, mutation of existing pathogens, and even deliberate distribution of a new biological weapon could initiate a worldwide epidemic that could kill and debilitate a significant portion of the population. This possibility is made more likely by the reduction in human immune systems by overuse of antibiotics and disinfectants, and the emergence of more and more drug-resistant bacteria. The secondary effects would be the collapse of the world economy, massive civil disorder, famine, and war. Most experts predict that it is not a matter of if, but when, such an outbreak develops.

Economic Decline

Economic decline or collapse seems unavoidable within a few decades or even a few Years. The world's population has already outgrown the ability of the planet to support it at an acceptable level of comfort and security. The multiplying financial crises of various nations and the massive flow of desperate refugees is evidence of this unavoidable reality. Wealthier first-world nations remain stable, but they cannot resist the pressures indefinitely. Whether there will be a catastrophic and violent collapse or a series of downward bumps and adjustments is difficult to predict, but hard times and deprivations are inevitable.

Climate Shift and Severe Weather

While "experts" argue about the causes, climate change is a reality. The number of weather-related natural disasters has more than doubled in the past ten years and continues to accelerate. Severe weather is now the norm. Every year, heat waves, snowstorms, hurricanes, tornadoes, floods, and droughts destroy whole communities, devastate crops, kill thousands, and thus seriously damage an already weakening economy. Most experts believe that we have already passed a "tipping point" and can only expect a worsening environment in the decades to come.

Loss of Privacy and Self-Direction

While loss of privacy may not seem like a serious "survival" hazard, it can defeat one's efforts to prepare for or deal with threats as an individual. To a true survivalist, survival is more than a biological imperative. If a human is completely observed, monitored, and directed by a system or network, no matter how benign, then he or she is no longer free and therefore has not survived. Technology has evolved to the point where it is using people, rather than being used by people. Those who frequent the internet, carry smartphones, and respond to various online programs are profiled by massive computers to analyze how they think and therefore how they react to various ideas. Human engineering and logarithms can manipulate buying habits, political preferences, social associations, and even emotions. Think about the implications of being wired to systems that have their own agendas. If you dismiss this as simply paranoia, then you are exhibiting typical addictive behavior. This is one of the most insidious and stealthy hazards to humanity.

General Civil Disorder

Certainly, we can all recognize that violent demonstrations, riots, and looting often follow natural and man-made disasters. These are temporary, localized products of specific events. We can expect more frequent and violent so-called demonstrations as both society and the economy weaken. What may be less apparent is the slow breakdown of respect and lawfulness throughout society. Shoplifting, street robberies, burglaries, car thefts, and other lesser crimes have become an epidemic. Overworked urban police departments are increasingly unable to even try to catch offenders, and the overloaded courts issue only "slap on the wrist" sentences. Both the internet and social media have generated a society of division, hostility, and conflicting information that has generated a culture of chaos, crime, and conflict where there once was unity and mutual respect. As this trend continues, civil disorders will become normalized, and property crimes will just be the norm. Civility is already gone, and disorder is prevalent in every aspect of society already. Creeping anarchy is a prelude to even worse conditions as time goes on.

Resource Depletion and Exhaustion

It is a simple reality that you cannot continue to use a finite amount of any resource at an accelerating rate for an indefinite period of time without that resource becoming exhausted. We are well past the tipping point in using up our remaining petroleum and natural gas supplies. As the cost of draining these last reserves increases, solar and wind energy are buying humanity some time but are not permanent solutions, as they come with their own environmental issues. Since petroleum is used for fertilizer, plastics, food preservation, and agriculture, its decline will result in food supply issues. The expanded population concentrated in cities that require massive amounts of energy for air-conditioning and heating may become untenable. Even water supplies and arable land are becoming scarcer and will generate conflicts in the near future. How long we have until resource depletion begins to generate serious economic and social disaster is difficult to predict. Some of the effects are already developing while other (out of gas) may take decades to come to fruition, but they are no less inevitable.

While there are many more potential threats and causations that can result in the end of life or freedom, these above are the most likely to impact everyone now or in the near future. Several are difficult to recognize today unless you look with open eyes.

15 Are major disasters and catastrophic events predictable?

The majority of the major disastrous events of the past decades were not ones that had been predicted by experts in various fields and most of the ones that did occur were not predicted. After a disaster, officials and experts often construct narratives to explain how the event was predicted or predictable, although those narratives seldom do so adequately. The scenarios for disasters and the complexity of the elements involved make accurate predictions of what will happen, where, when, and with what effects virtually impossible. There are just too many moving and interrelated parts and too many unseen dots to connect. While there are many possible disaster scenarios in everyone's future, the most predictable scenario is an event or combination of events that is not predicted or expected or that has effects outside of our expectations. In other words, expect the unexpected.

16 How likely is it that a survival-level emergency will happen to me or my family?

You may want to consider assigning a percentage of probability to various possible threats. How probable is it that a worldwide pandemic will occur in the next ten years? How about the next twenty years? Will the economy hold together for another five years? Will the supplies of petroleum, water, food, and other essential needs manage to sustain the population as it expands indefinitely? The probability of any particular scenario may be only 10 percent or less, but if there are ten or more possibilities for a catastrophe, the probability that one or more will happen gets closer to 100 percent. The potential of a given event such as total depletion of food, water, fuel, and other items, may be low for the next ten years, but inevitable at some point in the future. Things like pandemics and wars increase in probability with time. The individual probability of needing to survive a particular disaster may be low, but the sum total of probabilities and time virtually assures that one or more catastrophic events will occur and will dramatically affect you and your family within the next decades.

17　What is the domino effect of a disaster?

It is too easy to focus on preparedness for one kind of disaster and assume that if we survive that event, then we can resume normalcy. A cyberattack could shut down water supplies, food deliveries, sanitation systems, petroleum and natural gas systems, and more for days or even months. This would lead to financial collapse, civil disorder, and possible epidemics. A large-scale epidemic would cause workers to abandon jobs at water-pumping stations, sanitation facilities, garbage collection sites, and food-delivery locations. Even police, fire, and medical personnel would be stricken or chose to stay home. The result, again is partial or total collapse of civilization as we know it. A stealthier domino effect is already in progress. The growing frequency and scope of natural disasters and the massive costs of counterterrorist security are draining an already overtaxed economy. The result is dwindling budgets for fire, police, and medical services. The more emergencies we have, the fewer resources we have to prevent or cope with the next ones. In a world where everything is connected to everything else, the potential for multiplying disasters is enormous.

18 How can I survive a home fire that starts while I am asleep in bed?

A fire that starts while you are asleep is especially dangerous because it takes you by surprise. You must have at least two smoke and carbon monoxide detectors with fresh batteries in your home to give you a chance to survive, but you must also act quickly and correctly. If you awaken to a smoke-filled room, do not sit up! The air just above you may be heated to several hundred degrees, and filled with toxic gases. Roll out of bed and crawl to the nearest exit. If the bedroom door is closed, feel it for heat before opening it. If it's too hot, you may need to open or break a window to escape. If you are trapped or you have time, call 911. You have only seconds to get out! A dust mask and a flashlight kept in the bedside drawer may save your life in the dark, smoke-filled house. Once outside, never return to a burning building. You will probably not come out again! You should have trained every member of your family in escaping fire and have a meeting place outside. Fire doubles in size every one to two minutes. You must move quickly.

19 How can I survive a home fire that starts while I am awake?

If you are alerted to a fire starting in your home, you first priority is to call the fire department and get everyone out of the house. The best response time for their arrival is three to five minutes. This will be much longer during a general emergency. Fire doubles every few minutes, so having fire extinguishers and using them effectively can mean the difference between survivable damages and total devastation for your possessions. If the fire has already filled a room with heavy smoke, or it involves quantities of flammable liquids, or you are in any doubt that you can extinguish it safely, just get out; no property is worth your life. The following sequence of photos demonstrates how a small fire enlarges over just four minutes to engulf a room. Survivability to escape would be less than three minutes.

20 How do I fight a home fire with a fire extinguisher?

Good dry chemical extinguishers rated for "ABC" class fires are available in many sizes. Class "A" fires are paper, wood, and cardboards, etc. Class "B" fires are burning liquids such as gasoline, grease, or kerosene. Class "C" fire is electrical. Your "ABC" extinguishers are good for all three, but any kind of water spray can be used to extinguish a class "A" fire.

The most important thing about a fire extinguisher is its location. They must be on hand when the fire starts. A few seconds spent getting the extinguisher can mean that the fire is beyond control by the time you get back. So you must have one in the kitchen, garage, furnace room, shop, and anywhere else that you have an open flame or flammable fuels. They should be located near the doorway so you can start fighting the fire with the door/escape route behind you.

How to Use a Fire Extinguisher

When using a pressurized powder extinguisher, one should stand well back from the fire and aim just short of the front edge of the fire, in order to let the powder roll over the flames. Then sweep back and forth, going just past each side and farther in with each sweep until past the back of the fire. Don't squirt; keep sweeping. Be sure all flames are out before stopping. Then hold, ready to prevent reigniting. Don't blast the fire at close

Typical fire extinguishers, like those above, are available at most home supply stores. In terms of fire extinguishers, bigger is better. Inspect your extinguishers regularly. The larger ones on the right can be refilled and repressurized.

range! This will only blow burning fuel around. Be careful not to walk into the fuel as you advance on the fire. It is always best to have a second person at your back with another extinguisher ready. Never, ever let the fire get between you and your escape route. Never try to fight a fire once the room is filled with smoke.

When fighting a class "A" (wood, paper) fire, soak the fire thoroughly and then use a shovel or other device to turn over the fuel and soak hot spots. Consider that a fire goes up and out and looks for fuel and air. It may follow vents, electrical openings, and other routes to ignite in between walls or in other rooms. Search and destroy it and stay alert for rekindling for up to twenty-four hours.

21 Is camouflage an important survival skill?

Camouflage is often associated with survivalists in general, but its survival application depends on the situation. The wearing of various camouflage garments has become so ubiquitous that it seldom attracts attention today. We think of camouflage as patterns of various subdued colors such as "woodland," "tree bark," or urban grays and blacks, but the true essence of camouflage is anything that allows you to blend into the surrounding environment and so attract less attention. A suit and tie, workman's orange jumpsuits, or casual blue jeans would be good camouflage in some situations. Wearing military-looking camouflage shirts, pants, and coats is just the opposite of camouflage in many other situations.

Active camouflage is an important part of military survival training and is also practiced by hunters and to some extent by law enforcement. In survival situations, camouflage can be used to evade detection by criminals and looters. It can aid in hunting game for food, and it gives the survivor the choice of when and if he or she becomes visible to others. While modern infrared and night-vision technology can limit the effectiveness of camouflage, those devices have limitations and may not be in use by those you are trying to evade. Therefore, knowing the principles of camouflage is an important survival skill.

There are five key elements to good camouflage. They are:

1. **Shape:** The human form is distinct from most surroundings. A round head peering over a rock will be noticed. A straight rifle barrel stands out from bent and forked branches. Use branches, camouflage, or netting to break up your shape and that of your equipment.

2. **Shining**: Cover, enclose, or wrap up anything you have that will reflect light. This includes jewelry, watches, glasses, buttons, belt buckles, and binoculars. One glint of light off these day or night can undo all your camouflage work.

3. **Silhouette:** This is your shape against the background. Is the sun or moon or town lights silhouetting you? A white gravel road, or a snowy field, or white smoke behind you smoke can make you stand out as a target.

4. **Shadow:** You may be well hidden from direct view, but your shadow may give you away. If you have successfully broken up your shape it will help. Keeping low will also reduce your shadow.

5. **Shading:** The colors and the shade (dark or light) of the camouflage are the most important elements. They must match the environment as closely as

	SKIN COLOR	SHINE AREAS	SHADOW AREAS
CAMOUFLAGE MATERIAL	LIGHT OR DARK	FOREHEAD, CHEEKBONES, EARS, NOSE AND CHIN	AROUND EYES, UNDER NOSE, AND UNDER CHIN
LOAM AND LIGHT GREEN STICK	ALL TROOPS USE IN AREAS WITH GREEN VEGETATION	USE LOAM	USE LIGHT GREEN
SAND AND LIGHT GREEN STICK	ALL TROOPS USE IN AREAS LACKING GREEN VEGETATION	USE LIGHT GREEN	USE SAND
LOAM AND WHITE	ALL TROOPS USE ONLY IN SNOW-COVERED TERRAIN	USE LOAM	USE WHITE
BURNT CORK, BARK CHARCOAL, OR LAMP BLACK	ALL TROOPS, IF CAMOUFLAGE STICKS NOT AVAILABLE	USE	DO NOT USE
LIGHT-COLOR MUD	ALL TROOPS, IF CAMOUFLAGE STICKS NOT AVAILABLE	DO NOT USE	USE

Colors, patterns, shape, and shadow are primary considerations in camouflage. Credit: *Ultimate Guide to US Army Survival: Skills, Tactics, and Techniques* (Skyhorse, 2008).

possible in pattern and color. As you move from one location (e.g., dry grass) to another (e.g., green forest) the effectiveness of your camouflage may be lost and require changing. Gilly suits and netting are good for staying in one location, but tend to snag, pull, and tear in movement. Fortunately, there is a big selection of camouflage clothing for just about every location and season. If you will be moving from civilization to escape and evasion, you may have to use basic dark and earth-tone clothing enhanced by foliage and paint when needed. Apply camouflage paint in patches or stripes across the face based on the patterns of light and shadow in the environment. The eye sockets, cheeks, and below the chin are generally shaded and therefore should get most of the lighter green and tan colors, while the more exposed nose, ears, and forehead get the darker green and black tones. Don't forget your neck and the back of your hands. If you don't have camouflage paint, dirt and charcoal can be used. Carrying camouflage gloves and a face net or mask is handy if you don't have time for paint.

These soldiers are making good use of shadows, but need to cover their arms and hands better. Credit: *Ultimate Guide to US Army Survival: Skills, Tactics, and Techniques* (Skyhorse, 2008).

Camouflage alone will not be sufficient if you fail to consider these factors below.

Other Important Considerations in Maintaining Stealth

Movement: Movement attracts the eye. Slow movement is often missed, even if camouflage is poor. When you must move through a location where observation is likely, move slowly and stay low.

Secondary motion: As you move, you may move branches and tall grass or stir up dust. This may give away your presence and location.

Sight level: Whenever you stop moving or are observing, do it while crouching or lying down. People naturally look at eye level. The lower you are, the more you blend in to the ground and are literally overlooked.

Noise discipline: Your equipment must not bang, squeak, or rattle. Water canteens must no gurgle. NO TALKING! Use hand signals or low whispers.

Light discipline: No flashlights, matches, or cell phones at night. When absolutely necessary, red lens lights can be used under a tarp or low in bushes just long enough to read a map, fix a weapon, or render first aid.

Time selection: If you can do so, select a time to move through an area that will be best for you. Maybe there is more noise to cover your movement at a certain time. Maybe it is foggy in the morning. Is there a full moon? How will the sun's location affect your visibility? Night or day?

Route selection: Route selection makes the best use of all available concealment, including low areas in the ground, foliage, background, and lighting and of course the location of the potentially hostile observers. Moving through thick woods may give good concealment, but make a great deal of noise. Gravel roads are noisy.

Good route selection is critical to maintaining security. Take advantage of vegetation, low ground, and concealment. Credit: *Ultimate Guide to US Army Survival: Skills, Tactics, and Techniques* (Skyhorse, 2008).

Conclusion

Good camouflage and stealth techniques can keep you safe, prevent the need to engage in combat or flight, and let you get in and out of places you need to get in and out of safely. Learn to do it well.

22 Should real survivalists retreat from society and take refuge in wilderness retreats and bunkers in anticipation of a doomsday event?

Literally hundreds of so-called "doomsday" events have been predicted in the past fifty years. They have all come and gone, and here we are. Dozens of catastrophic events are predicted on the internet each week. A wilderness cabin or a bunker incorporates its own set of hazards and vulnerabilities. You may actually be weakening your survival capabilities over time as you use up supplies. Being able to make a living, raise a family, and build knowledge usually involves being part of society. A successful life is the best foundation for building your survival capacity.

23   When is "doomsday"?

The short answer is that "doomsday" is the day when your luck and survival plans fail. Anyone who tries to tell you when the stock market will crash, World War III will start, or some cosmic-level disaster will strike is misleading you. The great majority of predicted disasters never happened, and the vast majority of actual disasters were not predicted. Doomsday may be defined as a day or period of days in which the world experiences massive death and destruction that leaves civilization in ruins. The end of life as we know it can happen with one catastrophic event such as a worldwide nuclear war, asteroid impact, or in a series of smaller natural and man-made catastrophes that bring chaos and destruction over years or decades.

24 What are the elements of a good emergency plan?

The adage that "if you fail to plan, you plan to fail" is never more true than when applied to emergency and disaster situations where failure can result in property damage, physical injuries and loss of lives. A great deal of attention is given to what equipment to have (e.g., survival kits) and to the specific skills (e.g., first aid, shelter building, etc.) needed for emergencies. Less attention is given to emergency planning principles and techniques. Government agencies are required to maintain up-to-date emergency plans for every anticipated emergency. The responsible citizen would be well advised to make his or her own emergency plans for those situations. Having the right emergency equipment and skills are important but having a plan for their effective and timely application is a key element in the preparedness triangle.

Plans

What to Plan For?

Detailed hazard analysis is the first step to emergency planning in order to identify those emergencies that are the most likely to happen to you and would have the most serious consequences for your life, property, and freedom. These will be different for every individual and family. You may live in a high-crime area, an earthquake zone, or downwind of a chemical plant. You may work in a terrorist target zone or you may have personal enemies with violent natures. If you smoke, a home fire is much more probable than a tornado. Consider the things that have happened in your area. What trends are developing in the areas where you live and work? Consider long-term national trends such as economic instability, climate change, and depletion of fuel and other resources. More severe storms, power outages, and epidemics are predictable events in the next decade or sooner. It should be easy to come up with a number of emergencies you would want to have a plan for.

Answering the Questions

Once you have a short list of potential emergencies, the process of planning for each one can begin. Emergency planning is the process of answering questions before fate asks them. These questions are:

1. **What events would trigger the plan?** It is critical that everyone understands that a certain event or combination of events will trigger your emergency plans. For example, if the smoke detector goes off, the lights go out, or an intruder is heard in

the house, it should trigger immediate action by every family member even if they are in different rooms. You are at work while your spouse is at home and the kids are at school. Suddenly there is a toxic chemical spill upwind of your home and the school. Each of you has to know what to do and where to meet when that trigger event happens. When event "A" happens, everyone should execute his or her part of the plan for event "A." Overloaded hospital emergency rooms may indicate an epidemic. Rising prices may indicate a coming shortage of fuel or food. Civil unrest in one or two areas may indicate a general breakdown of law in all areas. Constant situation awareness of your immediate surroundings is a critical survival skill, but situation awareness of national economic, political, and environmental conditions is equally important.

2. **What actions are required in what order?** This is the most complicated part of your plans. You must cover all the critical actions but keep it simple and fast. The first element of the plan must be to stop or escape the immediate danger. This could be escaping from a home fire, taking shelter from a tornado, or calling 911. Gathering critical emergency items for continued survival would be next. You may need respirators, protective clothing, medical supplies, or weapons to stay alive. Having survived the immediate threat and provided protection against hazards, your next priority is reaching and gathering your family and providing continued safety. Having assembled loved ones and equipment, you can move on to long-term survival activities as needed. In the event of a home fire, escape and gathering of the family is probably all that is needed. Surviving and evading civil disturbance in your community or large-scale epidemic (for example) would require a series of additional actions such as preparing the home for defense and fire extinguishing or gathering survival packs and following a preplanned route to safety.

3. **Where will you be and where will you go?** Obviously your location when disasters strikes will greatly affect your planning. A plan to react to a nuclear, biological, or chemical attack will be very different if you are at work or on the road than if you are at home. You also have to consider both your primary shelter or escape destination, and your main rendezvous location where you will meet others and access your survival equipment. You may have selected a number of temporary storm or blast shelters (culverts, basements, etc.) along your daily route. You can stay in these places with your small survival items for a few days and then make your way to your home or other long-term shelter. Never assume that everyone will be at home and have access to all your supplies when disaster strikes!

Note: Use Google Earth to trace potential escape and evacuation routes. If possible walk, drive, or bike to the most probable routes.

4. **Who is responsible for what actions?** In any emergency, it is critical that everyone does his or her job. Who locks up the house? Who turns off the gas and electricity? Who gathers the children? Who brings the supplies? Who calls 911 while who provides CPR? Make sure everyone can do each job if necessary but clearly assign tasks.

5. **When to act and when to meet?** It could be hours or days before family or group members can move from shelter, evacuate the danger area, and get to a designated assembly point. You should have several alternative meeting places and a time each day that plan members would be there. Your plan might say that you would meet at the abandoned gas station on Highway 12 at noon four days after the trigger event and every day after that until all are assembled. If that location is unsafe (e.g., occupied, contaminated) the alternate location is the cluster of trees near the Wilson farm.

6. **How will each action be achieved?** While some actions may be self-evident (run, hide, carry) some actions may require more detail. How to crawl out of a burning house or specifically what protective equipment to put on to protect against biological contamination may need to be included. Good training requires less detail included in the plan. When fear and chaos reign, it is too late to be reading instructions.

7. **What if there are problems with the plan?** No plan survives the first few minutes of a disaster. Plan on things going wrong and try to have a plan that can get you past these inevitable problems. What if your route is blocked? What if you have to walk? What if you can't get to your survival pack? What if you have to evacuate? What if someone is injured? What if you or someone else cannot safely get home? You need alternate plans and backup equipment to deal with these inevitable challenges.

Here are a few examples of basic emergency plans.

Example #1 Home Fire That Started While You Slept
Trigger: Smell smoke; see flames; smoke detector activated

What Action: Get to floor. Call 911. Test doors for heat before opening. Escape via crawling (route practiced) or through window, etc. Direct the fire department and inform of missing family members. If neighbors not home, run to the convenience store at corner. Note: always have your cell phone, car keys, wallet, and a flashlight in your bedside drawer. You will need these once you have escaped.

NOTE: A different plan would be required for a fire that develops while you are home and awake. You still need to call 911, but you may be able to use a fire extinguisher if the fire is small. Once the room starts to fill with smoke, everyone needs to get out fast.

Example #2 A Terrorist Attack Resulting in Civil Disorder

Trigger: Terrorist attack within a hundred miles of home followed by riots, power failures, spreading fallout or epidemics, state of emergency, etc.

What Action: All members should have access to personal emergency items and self-defense items, and should put on the best available respiratory and skin protection. Escape hazard areas if possible via railroad tracks, back roads, and other preplanned routes. If escape is not possible, take shelter in a preplanned location that minimizes exposure and is defendable or well concealed. When safe to do so, evacuate to your home, shelter, or other designated location. Persons at home will establish shelter and defense if possible, or evacuate, with as much gear as possible, to rendezvous point #1. If home has been abandoned, others will continue to rendezvous point #1 and meet there at noon each day until contact is made. Recover food, water, and medical supplies at rendezvous point #2 and establish shelter until emergency is over.

Of course these plans would probably include much more detail about the specific routes, equipment, and assignments, but all the basics are covered.

Getting It Done

As Americans, we play all kinds of video games and watch all kinds of highly unlikely survival videos, while we put off real emergency planning and preparedness. Survival planning can be a game for the whole family that will be interesting and can save lives. A family planning session for a home fire, home invasion, tornado, or even "the Big One," is time well spent. Do not overlook the slow-developing disasters such as developing shortages, inflation, job loss, etc. Plan and prepare to minimize the impact of these inevitable trends.

Critical Equipment

No attempt is made here to cover emergency equipment or survival kits but obviously the availability of equipment must be considered throughout the planning process. Your first plan must be made based on what you have at the time. Planning will probably highlight the need for additional items and/or the relocation of things you may need in a hurry. Plan to improve, and then plan again. Always remember, it's not what you have, it's what you have with you that counts. Pocket items and small survival kits that you carry must be part of your plans.

Don't Guess; Know!

How long will it take to crawl out of a smoke-filled room* to your front door? Can you really build a filtered air shelter quickly in a biological attack? Can you really carry your survival gear five miles in an emergency? How long can you actually hold out in your home without access to groceries, running water, fuel, and emergency services? Test your equipment, practice your actions, and test your plan against the worst-case scenarios.

---

*Try this blindfolded, with the lights out.

Emergency Planning Tools

Here is a form you can use to guide your emergency planning efforts.

EMERGENCY PLANNING GUIDE

Emergency Situation (what is this plan for?)

_____

Trigger Event (what events will cause this plan to be activated?)

_____

Activation Code Word (optional) _____

Emergency Actions

Order/ Priority	Actions, By Whom? With What? How?	Notes/Alternatives
1		
2		
3		
4		
5		

Emergency Routes

From	To	Route Description and Alternates
Work	Home	
Work	Point #1	
Home	Point #1	
Point #1	Point #2	

Meeting Places and Rendezvous Points

Number	Location Description	Time to Meet
1		
2		
3		

NOTES:

_____

_____

_____

_____

_____

Plan reviewed (date) _____

25   What items should a survivalist keep in a bedside drawer to survive emergencies that develop while sleeping?

We spend about one third of our lives asleep, so there is a good chance that the life-or-death emergency will strike while you are in at home in bed. In that moment everything will depend on what you can reach right at that second. Think about it: You wake up in the dark and the house is shaking from an earthquake, a bomb blast, or a tornado. Or, you wake up in the dark and smell smoke or noxious fumes from a chemical incident. Or you wake up in the dark to the sounds of an intruder or the screams of your family. At that moment, there is no time to get out your survival kit or look in your survival manual. You may suffocate, be trapped in the rubble, or be attacked in the next few seconds. You want to have only emergency items neatly arranged there. You don't want to be wasting precious seconds rummaging around for what you need. First you should have three key items right on top of the bedside table. Your cell phone should be placed there every night. Don't depend on a landline phone for emergencies. The landline phone may be dead when you need it most and you cannot take it with you if you are forced to flee for safety. Your car keys and your wallet should also be on the table. If all else is lost, at least your vehicle will be available; you can also set off your car alarm as another way to call for help. Imagine escaping into the night and realizing that you cannot use your vehicle and you do not have your phone, ID, or credit cards! In a true emergency, you will not have time to go looking for those items.

Here are some suggestions for what should be in the bedside drawer, besides the three essentials described above. You should have a good N95 dust mask in there. While will not protect you against poisonous gases or carbon monoxide from a fire, it will offer some protection from soot, smoke, and hot air. It will also protect you from dust in a building collapse. Of course, you should also have a good-quality flashlight, one that is a multiple LED with at least three hundred lumens of brightness. Don't be cheap on this item. The light may have to penetrate smoke and dust. It may be needed to signal rescuers to your location or to blind a would-be assailant. Make it bright and tough.

You should also have a small, flat crowbar like the Stanley Wonder Bar or the combination hatchet, hammer, and pry-bar survival tool to smash windows, open jammed doors, chop through walls, and pry yourself out from under things. It's not a bad weapon, either.

If your family is spread out in the house, a whistle and walkie-talkie might be worth considering so you can activate the appropriate emergency plan. If you are fifty years of age or older, you should keep a package of aspirin in that drawer. Many victims of heart attack wake up in the night with chest pain and don't survive long enough for help to get there. If you awaken with chest pain you swallow the aspirin immediately and call 911. Your chances are significantly improved.

Last, but not least, it's important that you have a defensive weapon. If you have family members that come and go at odd hours, you may want to have a less-than-lethal first-response weapon such as a police-size, 200-gram pepper spray or a Taser. The choice of lethal weaponry is up to you, but it must be reliable, handy, and easy to use. A .38-caliber revolver is one good, simple, and reliable choice. Anything in a good-quality, .40- or .45-caliber auto pistol should do well. In this case, you don't need to put out lots of rounds of high-velocity, high-penetration rounds. You need to stop one or two intruders in close quarters without shooting family members and neighbors in adjoining rooms or houses. If you wear glasses, keep them there along with your wallet. These are items you will need to survive. You may want to throw in a few light sticks and a good knife.

Bedside drawer with rescue tool, respirator, aspirin, flashlight, whistle, pepper spray, and firearm. Cell phone, car keys, and wallet are essential needs once you have escaped. Note the automatic weather alert radio on the nightstand.

26 How can I survive a period of civil disorder?

Rioting and looting are usually limited to high-population, commercial districts (stores), and government facilities (city hall, police, etc.) and nearby areas. Areas that are strictly residential or industrial are usually not directly affected. If you live in one of the vulnerable areas, your best option is to get out ahead of the event since your chances of stopping a mob, and the fires that they will start, are slim to none. It is a good idea to avoid residing or being employed in such areas to begin with. You should have plans and routes of escape, and plans and routes to get home that avoid population-dense, commercial and governmental areas. Public transportation and major expressways are also targets for violence and should be avoided. Outside the violence and chaos of the riot zones, there are three effects that spread into adjoining communities.

Spreading Crime and Roaming Gangs

Since the police would be completely occupied or disabled in these circumstances, individual criminals and gangs will take the opportunity to commit acts they may not have contemplated in normal times. Carjacking, rape, robbery, and other crimes will increase. Stay off the streets! Burglaries, home invasions, and arson will increase as well. Stay home and be ready to respond. Your ability to stay home and defend your residence for extended periods is the most important survival capacity of all.

Spreading Fires

Uncontrolled fires from looted stores and business may spread to adjoining residential areas. Even small fires in homes that would normally be controlled by the fire department can engulf whole communities when the fire department is not available. This is especially true in closely packed homes and apartment complexes. Obviously, you need to be able to put out your own fires and extinguish embers, but you must also consider evacuation well in advance of a spreading conflagration. Mass fires and even firestorms can sweep away whole communities in minutes. Get out of the downwind path and seek lakes, rivers, and open areas clear of flammable and combustible materials.

Loss of Services

People who become ill or are injured will not be able to get an ambulance or reach a hospital. In some cases, the fires may knock out power lines. Additionally, police and fire services will be overwhelmed and may be unable to respond to normal crimes or home fires. Water service and trash pickup will also be interrupted. Such conditions can last for several days or longer. You must be able to get along without outside services for at least a week or two.

27 What kinds of protection should I have to prevent personal contamination from chemical and biological agents, and radioactive fallout?

Military and industrial protective gear is designed for fighting or working in a contaminated environment for extended periods. A survivalist's priority is to minimize exposure, get out of the contaminated area, and decontaminate as effectively as possible. N95 dust/ mist respirators are adequate protection from most biological pathogens, toxic dusts, and radioactive dust. You can purchase N95 masks that have a charcoal-impregnated layer to provide short-term protection from some chemical agents as well. These masks are cheap and small enough to have in your pockets, purse, and every survival kit or pack.

These respirators only provide protection when fitted properly. Follow the manufacturer's instruction. Respirators will not be effective over heavy facial hair. The wearer must be clean-shaven.

Homemade Mask for Biological Agents

Mix 1 tbsp. of bicarbonate of soda to 1 cup of water. Mix the solution well and soak a cloth or handkerchief in it. Wring out till damp and secure over nose and mouth.

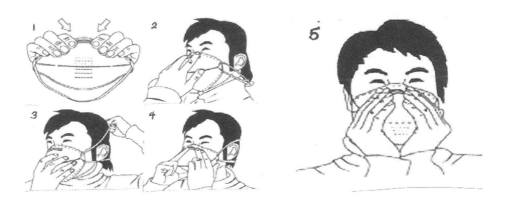

After keeping the contaminants out of your lungs, you must also keep them off your skin and clothing. Chemical protective suits are sold in most home improvement stores for use when painting or working in dusty areas. These should be included in every survival pack. Along with the dust masks and some extra pairs of light rubber gloves, having a protective suit will allow you to have a good defense while you evacuate the hazard zone.

Cheap Tyvek suit.

In some cases, you may not have access to your protective clothing and masks. In such instances, the survivalists' "better than nothing rule" applies. Wet rags, bandanas, or even paper towels will help keep contaminants out of your lungs. Rain ponchos, plastic tarps, or large plastic bags can also be used to minimize skin and clothing contamination.

If you are decontaminating an exposed person, or treating an infected person, wearing a disposable Tyvek suit over your clothing, along with gloves and mask, may be necessary. The suit can be peeled off, thus avoiding contact with the skin and clothing, or decontaminated prior to removal. The mask and gloves should come off last.

Testing various improvised protective suits. The one on the left is composed of several different sizes of trash bags.

28 If I become contaminated by biological, chemical, or radiological materials, how can I safely decontaminate myself?

Having kept the contaminates out of your lungs and off your skin long enough to reach an uncontaminated area, you need to be able to remove the contamination and contaminated coverings without transferring it back into and/or onto your body. This process is called decontamination. Of course, we want to do this when we are outside the danger zone or at the entrance to more effective shelter (underground and enclosed from biological or chemical) locations. Ideally this is a two-person job, with both wearing protective clothing. It should be done in a location that will not permit contaminated runoff, spray mists, or dusts to contaminate other safe areas.

There are five steps to effective decontamination:

1. Gross decontamination involves simply brushing off or rinsing off any surface contaminants, as well as dumping any contaminated gear that will not be needed.

2. Thorough decontamination is accomplished by the use of pressurized water (not high pressure) with a neutralizing or disinfecting solution. A 10 percent bleach/water solution is best for biological contaminants. Soap and water will clear most chemical and fallout materials. Plain water used copiously will be less effective, but may be adequate. The best device for spraying is a commercial pump garden sprayer. Keep a clean one handy at home. They are also good for fighting small class "A" fires and for accomplishing general hygiene tasks.

Typical garden sprayers are handy for decontamination and for class "A" fire-extinguishing tasks.

3. Next you need to peel off the protective clothing, minimizing any contact with the clean clothing and skin underneath. Step out of the foot coverings onto an uncontaminated surface. Remove the face mask and then peel off the gloves.

Always bag contaminated gloves, masks, and clothing as they are removed.

If any of your clothing or shoes have been contaminated, they will need to be discarded and replaced. If this is not possible, you must thoroughly wash them with strong soap and water while wearing gloves and respiratory protection.

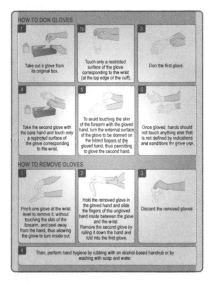

Degloving procedure. At no time does the hand contact the outside of the glove. Thorough handwashing should still follow degloving to assure safety.

29 What kind of weapons should a survivalist have for home defense?

The choice of an appropriate and effective weapon for home defense against criminals is as important as it is difficult. It must be effective enough to stop or deter an assailant or intruder. It must also be reliable enough to function without much maintenance or practice, and it must be small enough for quick access and use within the confines of a home. It must not be so powerful that bullets will penetrate walls and injure persons within the house or even outside.

If you are an experienced and trained shooter, then you can probably have a larger caliber, semiautomatic pistol, but if you are not able to practice much and/or handle the recoil, you should probably stick with a good brand .38-caliber revolver. These are easy to use, very reliable, and easy to maintain. Using special home-defense ammunition specifically designed to stop the target without penetration and hitting others is recommended.

Anyone who thinks *my child does not know where I hide my gun*, or *my child knows better than to play with guns* is likely a fool. Kids will find it and they will play with it. If you have children, consider the risk versus the defensive benefits. Use a trigger lock or combination lockbox, or consider alternative large pepper spray or Taser guns.

The .40-caliber Glock 23 automatic pistol with the attached laser pointer and strobe light is an ideal home defense weapon. The snub-nosed Colt .38-caliber revolver is also an effective and reliable option.

30 Should a survivalist practice vegetable gardening?

Many survivalists live in locations where gardening is impractical, but growing edible plants is certainly a core survival practice. Those who grow vegetables for themselves are maintaining a bit of independence and survivalist thinking, even if they do not think of it that way. A small plot in the backyard, or even a few tomato plants in pots, is a foundation for food freedom. Gardening does take some skill, so practice time and/or gardening classes are a good investment. The money saved on growing vegetables can free up funds for other survival needs. If you maintain a stock of vacuum-packed seeds and fertilizers, you can quickly expand your small garden into a significant source of food and trade goods if food shortages and rationing develop.

While all vegetables are helpful, the less perishable root crops such as beets, turnips, potatoes, and carrots and dryable crops such as beans and peas are best for survival planning. Unless you have a truly large area to plant crops in, the best method for getting the most food out of the least area is a raised bed in a square-foot intensive garden.

A small raised-bed garden. Note the walkways between the four-foot-by-four-foot beds for easy weeding and harvesting. The PVC arches provide support for wire and netting to protect against animals and birds. These arches also can support clear plastic to facilitate early planting and tarps to protect against early frosts.

31 What do I need to know to survive a flood?

You need to determine if a flood is a possibility for you. If your area has ever flooded before or floods have come close to your location, then you need a plan. An increasingly unstable climate has resulted in flash flooding of areas that have never had flooding in the past. So-called two-hundred-year floods have been happening much more frequently. Flood-control plans for these events have often failed. Massive rainstorms have inundated even elevated areas. Storm surges can wipe out coastal areas. No one is completely safe from flooding possibilities.

- Maintain vigilance on weather predictions and river levels.
- Keep your survival packs, important documents, and valuables in waterproof tote bins ready to load and go. Preselect routes of escape that avoid low-lying areas.
- If flooding or a storm surge is imminent, close up your home and evacuate beforehand.
- If this is not practical, move the elderly and children to safer areas so they do not inhibit your survival actions.
- Place your valuables and survival gear in your vehicle and be ready to drive out of danger immediately. Park other vehicles in safe uphill areas well in advance.
- If flooding is a high probability you may be wise to invest in a small boat or inflatable raft that can be used to float out or carry your possessions as you wade to safety.

All that remains of a house after the gas line ruptured during a flood.
The explosion also destroyed three adjoining houses.

- Have a method of evacuation for your pets which provides for them once you are out of the flooded zone.
- Turn off your gas at the meter and your electricity at the main breaker before the flood gets to your home or before you evacuate. Failure to do so may result in a fire or explosion that will level your home completely.

When the flooding subsides, massive cleanup starts. All contaminated carpeting, drywall, paneling, furniture, and other items must be discarded. A 10 percent bleach and water solution sprayed from a garden sprayer must be applied to all contaminated surfaces to prevent mold and contaminations. Avoid contact with floodwaters. Wear gloves and N95 respirators. Wash thoroughly with soap and water after contact with floodwater-contaminated materials. Be vigilant for looters and do not fall for unlicensed repair contractors that push you to sign up for repair work. Contact your insurance company first.

The water is gone, but everything is lost. The carpeting, flooring, paneling, appliances, and drywall all had to go.

32 What are the two classifications of disasters that a survivalist needs to be ready for?

While most people think disasters and emergencies as highly visible, immediate events, in reality they can happen over seconds, days, weeks, or even years. Either way, if they are not recognized, they can bring doomsday upon those unprepared or in denial about the challenges.

Acute or Fast Disasters

These are easily recognized as bad and harmful events or imminent dangers that we must quickly recognize and react to in order to survive. These include explosions, assaults, storms, floods, rapidly spreading epidemics, civil disorder, economic collapses, cyberattacks, and loss of electricity or water services. These are the kinds of events that your survival plans, preparations, and supplies need to be ready for. You need to be ready to pivot from normal life to survival mode quickly, no matter where you are. Since these events happen with little or no warning, you must be ready to get through the first seconds and minutes with your skills and what you may have with you.

Chronic Disasters

These are slow-developing, persistent, or repetitive conditions that lead to inevitable physical, economic, and social devastation. Such trends are harder to recognize and easier to ignore or deny. Expanding populations are outstripping supplies of fuel, food, water, and other critical resources. Most economies are running on unsustainable debt. Massive poverty, hunger, and unrest are spreading from third-world countries. Climate change is generating floods, famine, drought, and increasingly violent storms. Things crumble instead of crash. Such subtle worsening requires the survivalist to be ready for disasters while adapting to the shifting conditions of life. Of course the ability to adapt to and even take advantage of changes is a prime survival trait.

A combination of frequent local or reginal acute disasters can actually be part of a chronic disaster. For example: the costs of terrorist attacks and security combined with the costs of increasing climate-related disasters are significant factors in eroding and weakening the economy. Declining economies are forcing cuts in fire, police, and EMS budgets, which further weakens our capacity to survive a disaster.

33 Is hoarding justified in anticipation of a disaster?

The true survivalist anticipates disasters more quickly and accurately than average people. Those who are in denial or denigrate survivalists make their own choices. Being smart and prepared deserves the reward of having what you need. Better to have too many supplies than not enough in any situation. If the former, you then have the option of sharing if you can with those you want to help most. This particularly applies to food and medical supplies.

34   What is the most important rule of survival?

Certainly the most important of all survival rules is "never give up." People have survived the most seemingly impossible survival situations. When all else fails, hope still works. Hang on long enough and help may arrive or a situation may change. Just try to think of it as one more step, one more breath, one more try. Your survival is important to others. It is absolutely amazing what the determined human body and mind can survive and recover from. There is an "I" in survival; it stands for "I can," "I will," "I care," and "I am responsible." Remember that.

35 What must a survivalist do to manage any survival challenge?

The self-indulgent "why me?" attitude is counterproductive to a survival situation. Once you realize that you are in a dangerous situation, own it. Think *this is my forest, this is my disaster zone, and this is my problem that I must deal with, using what I know and what I have*. You are never lost because you are right there. You are never alone because you are here now and ready to own any situation.

36 Is it important for the survivalist to be capable of administering first aid?

Acquiring first aid skills and supplies should be considered the first priority in any survival preparedness program. A serious injury can disable or kill you and your loved ones faster than lack of water, food, or shelter. You are far more likely to need medical skills and supplies than armed or unarmed defensive skills and equipment. There are three imperatives for every family that a survivalist must consider:

1. Every scenario for disasters of any kind involvers a dramatic increase in the potential for serious injury and/or illness. This includes wounds, infections, burns, communicable diseases, poisoning, cold and heat exposure, and more.
2. None of these scenarios involve the probable accessibility of professional medical services.
3. Without available first aid skills and medical supplies, your chances of immediate and long-term survival are significantly reduced.

It would be tragic indeed to die of blood loss, infection, or another treatable condition after learning all those other survival skills and gathering all those supplies. In addition to the three imperatives above, there is the moral and practical benefit of being able to help your family, neighbors, and community. Being able to reduce pain and save lives makes you a valuable asset.

37   How can I recognize and control severe bleeding?

Severe bleeding is a life-threatening emergency that you must treat as soon as you have established that the victim is breathing and has a pulse. The loss of blood in excess of one pint is serious.* Dark-red flowing blood is venous bleeding and can be treated as second priority. Bright red spurting blood is arterial bleeding and must be stopped immediately. Every second counts; hesitation will kill! Immediately apply pressure with your hand or any immediately available cloth.

Direct Pressure over the Wound:

Place any kind of cloth or gauze pad on the wound and apply hand pressure. If the dressing soaks through, pile on more dressings but never remove the first cloth; only apply more. Firmly secure the dressings with tape or cloth but not so tight that it cuts off circulation to the limb. Check the distal pulse.

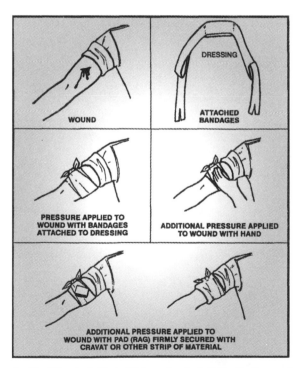

Credit: *Ultimate Guide to US Army Survival: Skills, Tactics, and Techniques* (Skyhorse, 2008).

---

* Critical blood loss is much less for children. The loss of even 25 to 30 ml of blood can result in shock.

Elevation of Bleeding Limb Above the Heart Level:

Usually used in combination with direct pressure. You may need to quickly splint limb if fractures are present.

If direct pressure fails to stop the bleeding or the patient must be moved or move on his/her own, apply a tourniquet as shown on page 63. They are seldom needed below the elbow or knee. Be sure it is visible and mark the time applied on the victim's forehead.

Always carry a large bandana, or one of the many tourniquet devices, in your pocket and survival kits. You may also want to add blood-stopper compresses or powder. This is effective for most bleeding, but usually cannot be applied fast enough for initial stopping of spurting blood where the victim may die within a minute or less.

38 After bleeding is under control, what do I need to do about open wounds?

There are three kinds of open wounds that will result from violent disaster situations. They are: abrasions that only damage the outer layers of the skin, often referred to as "road rash"; lacerations or cuts that go through the skin and may go into underlying muscle, nerves, blood vessels, or even organs; and evulsions that partially or completely separate tissue.

- Abrasions can be treated by cleaning with soap and water and applying over-the-counter antibiotic ointment and covering (if necessary) with a sterile bandage
- Shallow lacerations can be cleaned with soap and water and bandaged. Over-the-counter antibiotic ointments may be applied and the bandages should be changed daily.
- Deeper lacerations are prone to infections that may progress to gangrene and death. It is essential that they be cleaned with soap and water and that all foreign material and debris be removed. A syringe may be used to flush such wounds. Without the availability of antibiotics it is inadvisable to prematurely close such a wound with butterfly bandages or sutures, as this may lead to infection. It may be better to cover the wound with a sterile dressing and allow it to drain and heal naturally.
- Evulsions are the complete separation of the skin. This may be as a flap or an amputated piece of skin. Cleanly cut avulsed skin flaps can be disinfected, closed, and bandaged in most cases. Completely separated sections may or may not reestablish when replaced.

Basic Bandaging Tips and Methods

Soft-tissue injuries must be cleaned and bandaged effectively to relieve pain, prevent infection, and allow the injured person to continue functioning. In survival only the walking, working wounded will be able to survive. You may not have all of the prepackaged, self-adhesive bandaging products that we are all used to. You may need to use triangles and strips of clean or preferably sterile cloth for bandaging. Dressings may be secured with Saran Wrap, duct tape, or electrical tape. Here are the basic procedures for bandaging and a few illustrated examples.

- If the wound is bleeding heavily, your only priority is to stop the bleeding!
- Freely bleeding wounds should be covered with a sterile dressing bandaged in place.
- Abrasions and shallow wounds should be cleaned with soap and water and covered with a sterile dressing.
- For skin flaps: flush with clean water and replace flap before applying dressing.
- For separated skin: apply dressing to wound and keep skin dry and cool for reattachment.
- A sterile dressing is preferred, but a clean dressing is better than no dressing.
- Soap and water is adequate for wound cleansing. Alcohol, iodine, and the like are not recommended.
- A dirty wound can be flushed with clean water or saline (salt) solution from a squirt bottle.
- Extensive cleaning (debridement) and removal of debris from a wound should be avoided unless medical care is not available.

39 If I cannot access antibiotics, is there any way to prevent infection and gangrene in deep wounds?

Dakin's solution is an antiseptic fluid which was developed by a British chemist, Henry Dakin, and French-American surgeon, Alexis Carrel. This was basically a one-tenth-strength Clorox with a little boric acid in sterile water. They would simply place a tube in the wound and run the fluid over or through the wound. The solution would kill germs and dissolve dead tissue without harming healthy tissue. Studies indicate that solutions weaker than .025 percent are ineffective and stronger than .25 percent kill healthy tissue, so a .025 to .050 percent solution is recommended. The wound needs to be kept open and flushed frequently, as the solution remains effective for a short time on the wound. This solution was responsible for a significant reduction in deaths and amputations from combat wounds prior to the introduction of antibiotics.

40 Is knowing how and when to splint an injured limb an important survival skill?

Any kind of musculoskeletal injury can be fatal under survival conditions. Extra care must be taken to avoid this kind of injury. Being disabled may prevent you from escaping additional danger and inhibit your ability to take necessary survival actions. Effective splinting can partially restore mobility and prevent additional injury to the limb. In extreme cases, splinting may be the only treatment available in the long term. It can be difficult to determine the difference between simple strains and more serious sprains. Even fractures are often hard to identify. Dislocations of joints are usually very obvious. The resetting of dislocations and badly out-of-alignment bones should be avoided unless no professional medical care can be expected or reached for an extended period, When in doubt, splint.

- Strains are a stretching or tearing of muscles only.
- Sprains are a partial or temporary dislocation of a joint resulting in damage to ligaments.

Both of these can be treated by the three I. C. E. actions:

- I = Immobilize the injured joint with a splint or elastic bandage.
- C = Cool the injured joint with ice packs to reduce pain and swelling.
- E = Elevate the injured joint to reduce pain and swelling.

Signs of Musculoskeletal Injuries

- Pain at the injury site
- Bruising at the injury site
- Swelling at the injury site
- Loss of function of the limb
- Deformity of the limb

Diagnosing Injuries

- If in doubt, treat it as a fracture.
- Check for deformity by matching the injured limb against the uninjured limb.
- Consider the forces involved (bullet, baseball bat, fall). Would this likely cause a fracture?

Splinting Procedures

- Check for pulse and feeling and movement below the fracture. If there is no pulse, the victim is in danger of losing the limb!
- If there is an open fracture where bone is exposed, stop the bleeding and cover the wound before splinting
- Splint the fracture or dislocation in the position you found it. DO NOT attempt to realign or reduce it.
- In cases where there is no pulse below the fracture before or after splinting and no hope of prompt medical attention, you may need to try realigning the bones enough to restore the pulse
- Anything (newspapers, magazines, blanket, etc.) that will keep the bone or joint from moving is good.
- If nothing else is available, splint the injured limb to the body or uninjured adjoining limb.
- For fractures, you must immobilize the joint on either side of the fractured bone.
- For dislocations, you must splint from the bone on one side to the bone on the other side of the joint.
- Always check the pulse below the fracture before and after splinting. If there is no pulse, the limb may be lost and death may result from gangrene. Remove the splint and carefully realign the bone until circulation is restored.

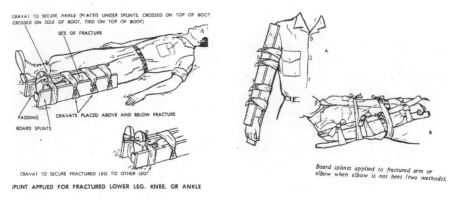

Board splints applied to fractured arm or elbow when elbow is not bent (two methods).

SPLINT APPLIED FOR FRACTURED LOWER LEG, KNEE, OR ANKLE

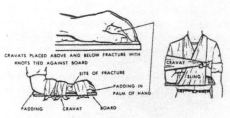

Board splint applied to fractured wrist and hand.

41 How can a survivalist obtain antibiotics for emergency care of wounds and illness?

The availability of antibiotics may be critical to the healing of deep wounds, burns, infections, and the treatment of many illnesses. Although prescriptions are required for antibiotics for human use, the same antibiotics are available without prescription in the veterinary sections of most rural farm-supply stores and aquarium stores. It is important to understand the use and limitations of these products.

Alternative antibiotics should never be self-prescribed or self-administered under normal conditions. Antibiotics should be prescribed by a physician and taken according to instructions only. While fish antibiotics and animal antibiotics are the same as those sold at pharmacies, they should only be used for emergencies when professional medical services are no longer available.

The three most common antibiotics are penicillin, amoxicillin, and cephalexin. There are also combination or multi-antibiotic tablets available under various names.

During a severe epidemic or a general disaster, hospitals and medical centers may be overwhelmed, looted, or even destroyed. In addition to the effects of a pandemic disease itself, other types of disasters such as a nuclear event, breakdown of water and sanitation services, and personal injuries such as cuts and burns can also result in external and internal bacterial infections. Such infections can overwhelm the body's immune system and develop into fatal conditions. Having a stock of antibiotics on hand could be more important than water, food, and weapons in some situations.

Antibiotics have no effect against viral infections such as the flu, and should not be used haphazardly as a treatment for frequent minor illnesses. Alternative antibiotics should be used only when no other option is available and serious infections and diseases are evident or imminent. Antibiotics are most effective against wound infections, various types of communicable diseases, and many secondary infections common in disasters. Dosage information can be obtained online and is based on the type of disease and patient. In some cases the survivor may be forced to guess; in these situations, err on the side of more. Adult dosages of most antibiotics range from 250 mg to 500 mg, every six to ten hours. Dosage decreases with child ages.

Penicillin

Penicillin was developed in 1928. Because it has been in use for so long, some bacteria have become resistant to it. Penicillin is generally effective against common staphylococcus and streptococcus infections, as well as clostridium and listeria. These common bacterial infections should be anticipated in open wounds and contaminated water and food during a long-running disaster. About 10 percent of the population may be allergic to penicillin.

Amoxicillin

Amoxicillin is effective in treating ear infections, strep throat, pneumonia, skin infections, urinary tract infections, and other types of bacterial infections. It also is used for some kinds of stomach infections. It has been used effectively for people exposed to anthrax. Its effectiveness against pneumonia and skin infections make it an essential survival medication, since these infections are most common in disasters and nuclear events. Amoxicillin should not be given to those who are allergic to penicillin.

Cephalexin

Cephalexin is effective against infections of the middle ear, bones, joints, skin, and urinary tract. It can also be used against certain kinds of pneumonia and strep throat. Cephalexin is not effective against methicillin-resistant staphylococcus, known as MRSA.

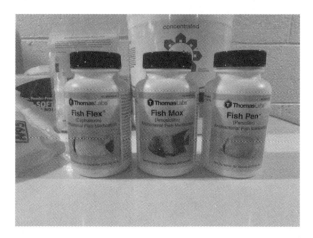

The bottles of antibiotics.

Animal Wound Care Antibiotics.

Most farm stores sell wound care powders and ointments with sulfa and other antibiotics for application to animal wounds. Considering the types of wounds that a farm animal might obtain, these should be ideal for disaster-related wounds, especially in combination with oral antibiotic tablets.

42 What other kinds of injuries might a survivalist encounter during a major disaster?

Injuries that are common in violent events include: bullet wounds that deeply penetrate the body's organs and bones; severe internal bleeding from blunt-force impact trauma; collapsed lungs; cardiac tamponade; avulsed (exposed) or damaged intestines or other internal organs; and large-area and deep third-degree burns. There is little the basic first aid provider can do beyond comforting the victim. In the absence of professional medical help, advanced medical training skills and equipment may be the only hope. A serious survivalist would do well to become a certified EMT or take a survival or expedition medics course to attain advanced skills.

43   What are the eight vital requirements of survival?

1: Will to Survive

If you have not already made the decision to do whatever is necessary to survive, you are already a victim of fate. Having a firm set of values and a life mission is critical. You must believe that your survival is important to others and to the future. Under true survival conditions doing what it takes may take immense effort, patience, endurance, and pain. You must have a good reason to get through and stay alive.

2: Self-Defense

Being unable to protect yourself can result in your death in three seconds or less. Everyone should be armed in some way. At the very least, never go anywhere without a knife if possible. Under threatening conditions, carry pepper spray or a handgun. Have a firearm and ammunition safely stored in your home. Maintaining a high level of constant alertness and good physical condition gives you the best chances to avoid or survive an assault of any kind.

3: Safe Air

You can only live three minutes without air, but the air must be free of toxins, radiation, and biohazards as well. Smoke, biological, chemical, or nuclear contamination must be considered. In many cases, N95-rated folding dust masks kept in your pocket, vehicle, or survival pack will be much more useful than a big gas mask at home. If you want to have a full-sized "gas mask" at home it may come in handy, but such masks are intended for long-term survival in a hazardous atmosphere, whereas your best option is to evacuate such an area. N95 masks are adequate for short-term escape from hazardous mists, dusts, soot, and biological hazards. Those masks equipped with a charcoal filter layer offer short-term escape protection from most chemical hazards as well.

4: Medical Care

In many survival situations, the ability to recognize and treat injuries and illnesses quickly and effectively outweigh any other survival skill. Severe bleeding, breathing difficulties, cardiac arrest, heatstroke, and hypothermia require immediate intervention to prevent death. Many survival situations result in injury or illness. Bandaging, splinting, wound care, and sustaining hydration are "must know" skills when no outside help is available.

5: Shelter and Warmth

Under severe cold and wet conditions you can perish in three hours or less. Injury and illness can also result from rain, exposure, contaminated air, and falling debris. Shelter may be a tent, a storm shelter, a fallout shelter, shade, a sleeping bag, or cover from flying projectiles. If you are breathing, everything else can wait; seek shelter immediately. Proper shelter will keep you dry, out of the cold wind, out of the hot sun, sealed from chemical, biological, and nuclear contamination, or protected from flying and falling debris. In most cases you will not have time to go to a shelter; you must carry it with you or use what is nearby. Think and improvise!

6: Clean Water

You can live for about three days without water. Store at least one gallon: two quarts for drinking and two quarts for cleaning and bathing. We normally use about 1100 gallons per person per day for cooking, washing, drinking, and bathing, but will need much less in survival conditions. Store water in clean, opaque, food-grade containers. Tap water does not usually need treatment, but you can add twelve drops of 2 percent tincture of iodine per gallon or six to eight drops of household bleach for long-term storage.

7: Adequate Food

You can (theoretically) survive three weeks without food. This assumes that you are at rest in mild temperatures. The exertions of survival and evacuation will require far greater caloric intake. You also will burn more calories to stay warm in cold conditions. While you may be alive for three weeks, your abilities to think clearly and act effectively will be severely degraded after the first five to ten days without nourishment. The FDA recommends 2,000 calories per day, but healthy people can survive for a long time on a lot less. You should try to maintain a 2,000-calorie-per-day stock per person for as long as you anticipate a homebound emergency. You may have to compromise on a lower calorie intake per day for evacuations where you have to carry your food. Store canned goods at home. Keep dried beans, pasta, rice, instant potatoes, powdered milk, and oatmeal. Stock up on canned meats. For your evacuation kits, buy dehydrated camp meals, dried trail mixes, and jerky. You will need a camp stove and sufficient fuel for cooking.

8: Effective Sanitation

This often overlooked priority results in thousands of deaths during disasters. Diseases and infections from untreated waste, contaminated food and water, and airborne biohazards and toxins can result in fatal illness. You must have bleach for disinfecting bodily waste, purifying water, and decontaminating clothing and equipment as needed. You also need to have hand soap and laundry soap, toilet paper, towels, and washcloths for sponge baths and decontamination. Insect spray and insect repellents are important as well. Have a chemical toilet or a five-gallon pail with a heavy plastic bag for home use.

44 What is the maximum weight of a survival pack?

Most evacuation packs weigh about ten to twelve pounds. Most reasonably healthy people can carry this kind of pack for a considerable distance without much fatigue. True survival packs or bugout bags must have greater shelter materials, sleeping bags or blankets, food, and other items for longer-term and independent survival. Twenty-five pounds is about the minimum weight of such a pack. In a good-quality pack with padded straps and waistband support most people can carry this short distances between rests. Of course experienced backpackers can carry much heavier packs for longer distances without fatigue. Survivalists must test their ability to carry their packs for several miles between rests. If you cannot carry it far enough to reach safety, then you need to ruthlessly cull out items.

45 What if I do not have the survival tools and items that I need in a survival situation?

It is important that you get into the habit of carrying well-chosen, compact survival items, but you may be someplace where you cannot carry what you need or the situation may call for items you don't have such as a weapon, shelter, protective clothing, or tools. In such cases you must evaluate the potential uses of items around you and improvise. Fortunately nature provides many useful items. Human habitation deposits all kinds of junk and trash that can become lifesaving items. Wire, cordage, plastic bags and sheeting, newspapers, cardboard, rags, plastic, and glass containers and much more have survival applications. Wherever you are, do a "what if?" on the items you see. Look around and think about the various items you see and how you could use them in an emergency. It's a good mental exercise.

46 How can I stay calm when chaos and danger are all around me?

All humans have the so-called fight-or-flight reaction to danger. This long-established combination of mental and physical reactions is impossible to completely control. Cardiac and respiratory rates increase. Stimulants, anesthetics, and blood coagulants are released. The mind may panic, freeze, or develop tunnel vision on a single area or factor. Critical knowledge and skills may be unavailable as the memory goes blank. Having anticipated the possibility of the event and mentally reviewed and prepared options is the only sure way to minimize these issues. Training is key to taking the necessary action and applying your survival and lifesaving skills promptly. Hesitation and overthinking can be fatal. The training takes over once you start to act.

47 In a major disaster, is it best to stay home or to evacuate?

Premature or unnecessary evacuation may be the classic frying-pan-to-fire decision. Today's population faces a complex combination of disasters and disintegration scenarios that make the decision whether to stay home or evacuate more difficult. While staying home may be impossible in some situations, evacuation has considerable limitations and hazards that must be considered before taking to the road.

A great deal of survival preparedness literature is devoted to cultivating evacuation plans, retreat development, and bugout bags. While the ability to evacuate is a critical part of emergency preparedness, the assumption that evacuation should be the first choice in any survival scenario is flawed. Placing all your hopes in getting to a retreat or cache with the limited supplies that you can carry is a big gamble. Many people have health issues, family obligations, or other factors that simply prohibit evacuation. Unless you and everyone in your family is in excellent shape, it is unlikely that you can carry a truly adequate bugout bag very far if you are forced to evacuate on foot.

Multifamily or group evacuation plans may look good on paper, but the complexity of travel, communications, and rendezvous under the chaotic conditions of a true national catastrophe may actually increase their risks once they leave home. Premature evacuation may well increase the chances of injury, property loss, and exposure to the very hazards you are trying to escape. Once you are on the road, you are dependent on just what you can carry. Additionally, you are exposed to cold, heat, rain, fallout, epidemics, criminals, and all of the hazards that you should be trying to escape from. Your chances of reaching any distant (one hundred miles or more) retreat are fifty-fifty at best.

Many catastrophes will develop slowly. In these cases, home-based adjustment over years may replace the need to panic and run. Critical needs such as food, power, water, police protection, and the like may decline and become unreliable. Developing the home as a base and networking with others to create alternative sources of critical supplies and services (e.g., water gathering, food production, community defense, etc.) may be a better survival plan than heading for the hills.

Of course there are serious hazards to staying home as well. Your unprepared neighbors may gang up on you. Fires may spread through the community, or roaming gangs may besiege you in your home. These hazards are greater in the urban/suburban areas, but these areas are equally hazardous to evacuate from. Obviously events like hurricanes, tornadoes, floods, and earthquakes that make your home and community untenable will require evacuation, but these are regional events where rescue and support services would be available within a day's walk and recovery would be anticipated.

The scenario that most preppers/survivalists anticipate is a massive and general catastrophe caused by an economic collapse, war, revolution, cyberattack, epidemic, or similar event. But their idea of heading out into the wilderness for sustenance is suspect, as the notion that there is more food and safety in the rural and wilderness regions is highly doubtful. Edible crops in the field only exist for a short time near harvest, and farmers tend to shoot looters. Wild edibles, fish, and game can be had for a short while, but with unrestricted and inexperienced hunters and foragers roaming about, nothing will last long, and you may get shot before you catch anything. I am not saying that you should not have the skills and options necessary for evacuation. Evacuation has hazards and limitations that may outweigh the hazards of staying at home with your stored food, water, and weapons. You must have both options.

48 How can I plan to evacuate from an urban area during a major disaster?

Today's urban evacuation scenarios are varied and complicated. Worsening civil disorder, spreading epidemics, or lack of water and food supplies may force you to evacuate after a period of days. Floods, uncontrolled fires, gang assaults, or nuclear or biological contamination may necessitate immediate flight with minimum preparation. The evacuation plans must take into consideration your supplies, physical conditioning, family members, available routes, and the distances to safety and possible locations of shelter.

The farther into the urban area you live, the harder it is to escape. The gauntlet of blocked streets, bridges, overpasses, shooters, civil disorder, fires, and other hazards multiplies with every mile between you and open country. Areas on the fringes of the city or into the true suburbs are far easier to escape from.

The sooner you move to evacuate, the better. Once even a small part of the general population starts to evacuate, your chances of automotive movement with a significant amount of survival goods is significantly reduced. As anyone who lives in the city knows, even a slight increase in traffic or disruption of flow brings everything to a halt. A 10 to 20 percent increase in outgoing traffic, combined with the inevitable accidents and breakdowns, will stop everything. This will be followed by panic, road rage, and chaos on the highways. Unless you head for the hills every time there is bad news, you probably will not beat the crowd.

Evacuation is recommended when the anticipated crisis will be so severe and extended that sheltering in place will not be an option, and when the crisis will be so extensive that outside help or rescue of any kind is unlikely.

If driving your vehicle filled with survival and camping supplies is viable, you should definitely try it. To this end, you should have supplies in tote bins ready to put into your vehicle and go. Of course, you should never let your fuel tank get below half full, and if the conditions indicate that you may need to evacuate soon, keep the tank full. Every mile you can get away by vehicle is one less that you will need to walk. Most people will head for the expressways and main roads that will jam up quickly. Now is the time to use topographic road maps found at truck stops or Google Earth to locate back roads, side roads, alleys, and other drivable surfaces that may offer clear routes. Rivers, railroad tracks, and other features that cross your escape path will have only limited crossing points at bridges, underpasses, and tunnels. Try to get past these before they are closed off. Once these points are closed and the roads are blocked, you will have to abandon your vehicle and walk. You must be prepared for this eventuality. All of your main survival supplies must be in backpacks and/or wheeled carriers. Be sure that sturdy hiking boots and all-weather clothing are included in your supply bins. If water obstacles are likely, a canoe or inflatable raft should be included in your equipment. You may want to carry a large bolt cutter in your vehicle for opening gates to service roads and shortcuts. There are going to be many desperate people out there, so being well armed will be an absolute necessity. Getting through an urban area requires close-range volume of fire more than long-range accuracy. You need to quickly disable and suppress hostile fire while escaping the danger zone. Large-caliber, high-capacity handguns, short-barreled shotguns, and carbines are all effective options. Carrying lots of smoke grenades to facilitate screening of movement could be helpful. These are available at paintball supply outlets.

Escape Routes

Escape routes can make use of any unobstructed pathway that leads to a safer location. Out-of-the-box thinking is good for escape planning. Each city has a number of pathways cutting through the mass of built-up and populated terrain that can be used as escape routes. Refugees in the past have often used sewers, drainage systems, and rooftops as escape routes. Anyone living in an area of closely packed homes and apartment buildings must have a ready knowledge of routes.

- Railroad tracks and abandoned right-of-ways offer unobstructed paths out of the city. But take caution, as walking down tracks is not as easy as you may think. You have to focus on your footing and, of course, be alert for trains. Also, raised rail embankments make you an easier target for shooters, but trying to walk on the slanted side of the embankment is almost impossible. Still, they lead straight out of town and often have necessary bridges over obstacles.

- River and stream edges can offer routes, but they are often obstructed with vegetation that may make walking difficult. If you have or can find a boat or raft, they are a great way out of town.

- Power-line paths are usually kept clear of obstructions and often have unpaved service roads underneath the wires, but they seldom include ways for you to cross streams, rivers, and other obstacles.

- Bike paths and hiking trails and parkways are becoming more common in urban areas. Many of these are networked into systems that reach well outside of the city. The survivor would be well advised to become familiar with these and consider a bicycle as a primary or secondary evacuation system. Bikes are faster and can carry more gear than walking with a pack. Consider that a lot of others are going to use these obvious escape routes, so don't depend on them alone.

- Alleys are the preferred routes through built-up urban areas. Fences, trash containers, and garages offer plenty of cover and concealment while blocking you from the view of many windows. Crossing streets from alley to alley is faster than at street corners, and less likely to be blocked or watched. Walking down the street or sidewalk is just not a good idea for survival evacuation if it can be avoided.

• Industrial areas will be pretty much abandoned in a general collapse. People don't live there and looters will focus on shopping centers. So going through such areas may be much safer than residential and commercial zones.

Working with Google Earth and taking hikes should help establish a number of alternative routes combining the above elements to get you out of the urban area

Bivouacs and Hideouts

In the jammed traffic of an evacuation, you may make five to eight miles per hour driving before stopping completely. The average person walks at about four miles per hour, but with your pack, zigzagging down paths and alleys, you will be lucky to make one or two miles per hour. It may take you several days to get out of the urban environment, so you need to consider safe places to hide and rest. Abandoned buildings, garages, and wooded areas may work for you. Underpasses and viaducts will probably attract too many others. Select locations off the main routes and paths that offer shelter without being too obvious.

Binoculars and Night-Vision Gear

Two items that can give you a clear advantage in an urban escape are binoculars and night-vision equipment. A good pair of binoculars can let you see dangerous conditions and hostile individuals before you encounter them. Being prepared to deal with or avoid a problem ahead of time is a tremendous advantage.

Night-vision gear gives you the option to move at night and still see hazards ahead of you before they see you. Night movement with this ability can be much safer than day-time movement. In bivouac you can see who's coming before they see you. These items are a must if urban escape is a necessary part of your survival plan.

Alternative Plans

While survival fiction often paints the picture of a well-stocked retreat in the mountains, which is manned by a highly trained survival group, the reality is that most of us will have far more limited resources and may be limited to what we can carry to set up a camp once away from the city. Once automotive transportation is stopped and choke points are closed off, the amount of supplies one can carry will be severely limited. Backpacking, biking, and camping are advisable hobbies for every would-be urban survivor. Not everyone is able to carry a forty- to fifty-pound bugout bag the twenty to forty miles necessary to reach safety. The two solutions below have been adopted by many families I know.

Solution #1:

Store the majority of your survival supplies at a friend's house or in a secure self-storage unit well outside the city. You can then evacuate on foot if necessary with a basic survival pack, and reach your supplies in a few days on foot or by bicycle. Some folks even store a second car at a remote location.

Solution #2:

Have a hotel, motel, or campground that you like just beyond the city. If things look dangerous, take your family and survival stuff on a mini-vacation there until conditions stabilize. You can still commute to work if necessary, but if things deteriorate you have a head start on your escape.

Cities and near-suburbs are too densely populated to be sustainable once the infrastructure and civil services collapse. Lack of sanitation, water, food, fire departments, and police protection will rapidly lead to epidemics, riots, and famine. The city dweller must preplan a number of safe routes out of the area that minimize exposure. Physically scouting these routes ahead of time will offer the best chance of fast and effective evacuation to less hazardous locations. Having an evacuation pack and gear alone is inadequate without a thoroughly thought-out escape plan.

49   If GPS is not working, can I use a map and compass to find my way out of danger?

A true survivalist is never dependent on external systems or technology for any essential survival need. Whether it is to follow a safe evacuation route, find a shelter, or find your way through the outdoors, knowing how to use a read a map and use a compass are important survival skills. A map and a compass should be included in your evacuation pack. Basic map reading and compass usage skills should be sufficient for most situations where trails, roads, and landmarks are plentiful. If the survivalist anticipates traveling deep into wilderness regions, he or she should consider developing advanced navigation skills in advance.

50 How do I use a compass?

In most cases, a compass is not useful unless you use it on the way into the area or have an accurate map with you. If you realize that you are lost, do not know what compass course you were on going in, and do not have a map to locate where you are, you can use it to follow a straight line course in the direction that you guess will take you to a known road or river that you can follow to safety.

The compass needle or dial points to magnetic north, which is somewhat east or west of true north in most areas. Most maps have compass declinations indicated. If you are traveling short distances or just using compass courses without map reference, then magnetic north is adequate. Be sure that your compass is clear of any metal or magnetic objects such as watches, cell phones, knives, or the like when taking readings. For survival navigation a military-style, lensatic compass is recommended. The entire dial turns so the compass is always oriented and easy to use.

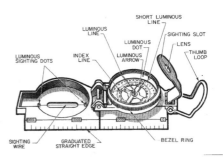

A durable, military-style compass like this one is recommended for serious navigation. Credit: Air Force Regulation 64-4, Vol. 1.

Simply wait until the dial has stopped moving. Then slowly turn until the bearing you intend to follow is under the front sight. Sight from the back to the front to see the direction you need to go in.

You usually will be starting your route from a road, trail, railroad, or stream. Take a compass course at an angle from that reference line. It is highly improbable that following the exact reverse compass course (e.g., 140 degrees out and 320 degrees back) will get you to your exact point of departure. You will be either to the left or right of that point. It is best to set your return route 5 to 10 degrees off to put you at a known direction from your target when you reach that reference line.

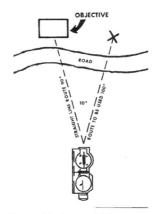

Here a 10-degree right return bearing is used. Once reaching the road you know that you can reach the cabin by going left. Credit: Air Force Regulation 64-4, Vol. 1.

51 How do I orient a map to match my location?

Lay out your map on a flat surface. Place the compass on the map parallel to the map lines, with the sight end pointed toward the top of the map. Rotate the map with the direction of declination formed by the index lines and the compass needle to match the direction indicated on the map's declination diagram. Your compass will be facing a bit east or west of the maps, pointing toward true north.

Matching a map with the observed terrain, roads, buildings, and landmarks.

52 How do I read a map when GPS is not available?

A map is just a picture of the terrain. Roads, trails, forests, swamps, and other features are represented by map symbols. These are usually illustrated on a map key on the edge of the map. Elevations such as hill, valleys, and slopes are indicated by elevation lines. Each line indicates a higher elevation. The closer the lines are together, the steeper the slope will be. Map scale indicates how a distance on the map represents a true distance on the ground. For example: 1= 2.5 indicates that one inch on the map equals 2.5 miles on the ground.

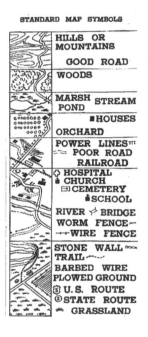

Map symbols are usually found in the key at the corner of the map. They are pictorial representation of features and objects on the ground. Credit: 1952 Handbook for Boys

This illustration shows how the elevation of three hills would appear on a map. Credit: Soldiers Manual FM 7-11 B 1/2.

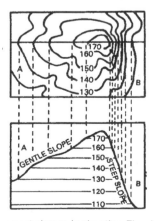

Each line indicates a 10 percent increment change in elevation. The closer the lines are together, the steeper the incline. Credit: Air Force Regulation 64-4 Vol. 1.

53 How do I find my actual location on a map?

Open your map and orient it. The top of the map must always be at true north. Look around you. Using the map symbols, you may be able to recognize sufficient buildings, crossroads, and the like and so recognize your location. If not, you can take bearings on two identifiable landmarks such as mountaintops or church steeples, to find where you are on the map.

Once you have done that, orient your map. Then point your compass at one landmark and note the compass bearing as indicated below the compass sight. Draw a line from the landmark's symbol on the map at that angle. Now, take a bearing on a second landmark and draw another line. Where these lines cross is your location. This process is known as biangulation; if you use three bearings for more accuracy, it is called triangulation.

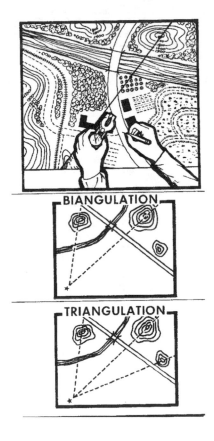

54   What are the three kinds of people who will emerge in mass disaster conditions?

The three types of people that will emerge more conspicuously under desperate conditions are predators, victims, and survivors. These kinds of personalities exist under normal conditions, but laws and social rules constrain predatory behavior. Victims are passive and dependent in nature, but are protected and aided by a stable and benevolent society. Survivors are active, creative, and proactive under normal conditions. When desperate situations develop and societal norms break down, the true nature of people is revealed. The traits and tendencies of each type of person must be recognized and prepared for.

Predators

Predators adapt to existing conditions. The smart ones will avoid openly illegal actions unless they are fairly sure they can get away with it. However, they have a wide range of "safe" predatory practices in politics and business that are legal but not ethical. Running casinos is obviously predatory, as is increasing taxes to build wealth and power. Selling cheap, substandard items to people who don't need them is predatory. Any actions that take advantage of fear, weakness, ignorance, or kindness are predatory. Predators are found in every facet of our society. They may be among your neighbors, business associates, or local leaders. They are often very good at disguising their tendencies, but little actions and verbal clues should help you classify them. Any person who will consider taking anything from anyone (no matter how little), just because they can, is a predator. A predator is never your friend. He or she will turn on you if it is to their advantage. In fact being a non-predator friend to a predator is one definition of being a victim.

Coping with Predators

Identify these individuals and make sure they know as little about you as possible. Keep them out of your business and your life. Be prepared to defend yourself against them once a survival situation develops. If they attempt to make you into a victim, correct them with all necessary force.

Victims

Victims are folks who often talk about how "everything happens to them." They are seldom proactive or prepared for anything. They seek security by depending on others. They spend an inordinate amount of time and money on fantasy-based activities. They join organizations that offer benefits in exchange for compliance, such as gangs, cults, and extremist groups. In a disaster, they will follow orders without question. They freeze in a crisis or may panic and become dangerous to others. They may demonstrate and protest about problems they think others should fix, but seldom do anything positive to alter their own situations.

Coping with Victims

Obviously you do not want to become a victim. Victims survive by freeloading off non-victims and doing the bidding of predators. Nevertheless, they may be your relatives and neighbors, so you may feel obligated to help. There are some difficult moral choices here. Since you are the provider, you set the limits and you set the rules. Better you than the predators. Of course the line is where they become a hazard to your family or refuse to support your program and rules.

It is important to keep in mind that the survival of predators is proportionate to their access to victims. It is to the advantage of survivors to educate and convert potential victims to survivors when possible. Far better (for you) that they become apprentice survivors than apprentice predators.

Survivors

Survivors are independent thinkers, disinclined to follow without justification, and are resistant to sales pitches. They value tangible assets and programs above virtual and invisible concepts. They work with people and organizations, not for them. They survive and avoid threats by having a high level of situation awareness. In other words, they are disinclined to rely on technology. They are here and now. When disaster strikes, they are quick to shift from a normal thinking to a survival mode. They anticipate trouble and take necessary precautions. For these reasons they seldom have accidents and are usually secure in life. They eschew triviality in favor of constructive and educational activities. Most importantly, they always finish difficult but necessary activities such as enduring cold or heat; burning furniture to keep warm; being exposed to blood, vomit, and filth to care for injuries and illnesses; or abandoning a home or vehicle to escape hazards.

Coping with Survivors

Hopefully you are, or are becoming, a survivor. So for you, coping is the challenge of becoming better at surviving and making sure that your family is on the right track for the future. You do not need to cope with other survivors as much as you need to network with them and become mutually supportive. Survivors are going to be overwhelmed by victims and attacked by predators. In many places in the world survivors have been suppressed or driven out, leaving a predator/victim society. Survivalists may be the only thing that prevents that from becoming a worldwide phenomenon. In the words of Edmund Burke, "All that is required for evil to triumph is for good men do nothing." Hopefully you are doing something now.

55 What are some items that should not be left out of a survival pack?

There are some items that are often left out of survival packs and kits. Years of experience have shown the importance of including these items.

Spare Glasses

If you need glasses for normal activities, you must include an extra pair in your survival pack. You may not have your primary glasses with you when you grab the pack, or your glasses may be broken or lost under survival conditions. The ability to read and perform detailed tasks will be important throughout your survival challenges. You can put that older prescription pair or just some generic reading classes in the pack. A good magnifying glass is helpful as well.

Survival Handbook

Unless you are very well trained in all aspects of survival and first aid, a small survival manual or a set of survival cards that include first aid instructions is helpful.

Binoculars or Monocular

Being able to see trouble or aid is a tremendous advantage. Finding safe routes and campsites at a distance is a big help while evacuating. Spotting and identifying hostile persons or groups before they see you could be lifesaving. Don't leave home without optics.

Dental kits or Denture-Repair Kits

Dental care is an essential survival need. The wise survivalist should maintain dental care while they can. Once disaster strikes, a cavity, lost filling, or infection can lead to pain and other health issues. Toothache kits are available at most pharmacies. They usually include temporary filling materials and topical pain relievers. If you have dentures, there are denture-repair kits available at pharmacies that can be used to make some repairs. Of course, if you do have an old pair of dentures, they may be worth packing in the kit.

Sewing Kits

Small sewing kits are found in convenience stores or can be made up at home to include safety pins, thread, needles, buttons, fabric glue, and patches. Survival packs leave limited room for extra clothing. Extra underwear and socks are about all you can pack. The clothing you wear will take hard use and may not be replacable for a long period of time. The kit allows for basic repair of clothing as well as shelters and sleeping bags and blankets.

Chemical Protective Suits

These cheap coverall suits are sold in home improvement stores for use in painting and other messy tasks. They offer protection from biological, radiological, and chemical contamination, but also provide a very lightweight, low-cost clothing option if your primary clothing becomes wet or contaminated. You can wear the suit while you dry and/or clean your clothes. It also provides an over-suit for additional warmth if needed.

Fishing Kit

Most purchased, prepackaged fishing kits include a knife, some kind of pole device, and floats. These items take up room and add weight. You should already have a knife in the survival pack and the other items can usually be improvised from branches and wood chips. You do need to pack plenty of fishing line, some lead sinkers, and a variety of hooks. Artificial bait and small lures may be added as well.

AM/FM/WB Radio

Even if civilization has disintegrated, you need to know what is going on and where. Some stations will be on even in the most severe situations. Knowing when it's safe to return and where not to go will always be critical. Knowing what the weather will be tomorrow can definitely save your life. Fortunately you can now buy affordable, small solar- and crank-powered radios that have AM/FM and weather band capabilities. Some even offer citizens' band and shortwave reception. This is a must-have item for every survival or evacuation pack.

Smoke Bombs

Smoke bombs are seldom thought of as a survival pack item. These can be used to attract help when needed or to provide a diversion or smokescreen to facilitate escape. You can buy fused, multi-colored smoke bombs at fireworks stores, or pull-ring-activated smoke bombs from paintball game suppliers. Smoke bombs ranging from 25,000 to 75,000 square feet of smoke output are most effective. Vendors of survival gear make cool-burning smoke bombs that are advisable for use in urban areas and dry woods.

Knife Sharpeners

Some survival knives include a sharpening stone, but if yours does not, you should include a sharpening device that contains a coarse- and fine-sharpening apparatus. Extended use of your knives and hatchets will make this a survival necessity.

56   What are unsafe mental states that affect how people handle high-stress events?

In high-stress situations, our minds react in ways that increase the risks of making poor decision or suffering faulty judgment, just when you can least afford these errors. Training, survival knowledge, and common sense can be abrogated by being in these unsafe mental states.

Frustration and Anger

Certainly the results of injury, loss, and damage from a disaster can make you frustrated and angry.

Distracted and Hurried

The immediacy of an emergency can distract you from other critical needs and priorities.

Hunger, Cold, and Heat

Survival emergencies often involve being cold, hungry, hot, thirsty, or in pain. Over focusing on these discomforts can result in actions that lead to worsening situations.

Fatigue and Pain

Fatigue is bound to set in after hours and days of struggling to survive and escape. Injuries or muscle aches can also affect awareness and judgment.

Most of these conditions are unavoidable in a serious disaster situation, but being aware that they are diminishing your mental acuity and physical coordination is important. In survival situations, you may be walking or driving long distances and using firearms, flammable liquids, and sharp tools. You may need to perform complex tasks just when you are least alert. Extra care, step-by-step procedures, and "safety-first" thinking are more important than ever here.

57 How can I survive tornadoes and hurricanes?

Tornadoes develop with little or no warning, with unpredictable routes and levels of severity. You should have a NOAA weather radio that automatically alerts you to impending storms. Tornadoes move extremely fast and can change direction without warning. If you see a tornado or there is a tornado warning out, do not hesitate! You should already have designated and stocked your go-to spot. This is usually the center of your basement or crawl space. You should have flashlights, a battery-powered radio, self-rescue tools, a first aid kit, and other items there. Bring your cell phone to call for help, assuming that the cell-phone towers are still up.

Hurricanes are usually predicted in advance, but their exact route and severity are not always anticipated. The winds can cause extensive damage to homes and infrastructure, resulting in extended power outages. Preparations include boarding up windows, securing outside equipment, and securing adequate water, food, and supplies for days of isolation. Those living in coastal areas or in floodplains should consider early evacuation. Children and the elderly should be moved to safe areas well in advance. If you are caught at home during a hurricane, stay indoors and away from windows. Do not go outside if the winds seem to have passed, as you may just be in the eye of the storm. Wait for the all-clear signal from the radio or emergency services. Be alert for flooding and downed power lines..

58 Are survivalists and survival groups part of a militia?

Because survivalists often carry arms, have packs, and may even wear camouflage, they look like militia to the public, but there are important differences in methods and priorities. Merriam-Webster's definition of militia is the "whole of the population available for the common defense in time of emergency." Certainly survivalists fit this definition and are well prepared to fulfill their obligations in this respect. Other definitions specify "able-bodied males" eligible for military service, paramilitary groups, or nonprofessional soldiers. These definitions do not apply to survivalists in general, although some survivalists may also be members of militias of some kind, and so survival skills apply to militia training as well. Formal militia groups usually have uniforms, a chain of command, rank designations, and complex paramilitary training regimens. Survivalists tend to be highly individualistic and less tightly interdependent than formal military groups. Survivalists usually do not have political priorities or objectives beyond protection of the life and freedom of themselves and their families. Survivalists are more flexible and less conspicuous than militias, but militias are better organized. Both kinds of groups have their advantages and could be difficult to distinguish as they cope with disasters.

59 How can I survive extreme winter conditions at home?

Fortunately survival threats such as civil disorder and terrorist attacks are less frequent in cold weather, but power outages, fuel, and food shortages are greater. When balancing the hunker-down versus hit-the-road options, staying home as long as possible may be best. Even an unheated house is better than a tent. You may be able to ride out the situation or at least hang on until the weather improves before evacuating. You must be set up to get by without any utilities (e.g., gas, water, electric) and support (e.g., medical, fire, police, groceries) for several months. It is highly unlikely that you will be able to store enough fuel to run a generator and heat your whole house for several winter months. So you will have to adopt a "camp at home" configuration.

Camp at home simply means that you will reduce your needs by utilizing camping supplies in the home. You can take an interior room and seal it off with plastic sheeting. This will be your one-room shelter for the duration. You may be able to have enough fuel for a small camp heater to help heat one room. Even better, put up a tent in your living room and stay in there. A small tent will be easy to heat and will conserve body heat as well. The best way to stave off the effects of cold is to eat hot food and drink warm liquids. A good camp stove with lots of fuel cylinders is a must.

Additionally, get good sleeping bags for everyone! An army-surplus, mountain-rated bag is good to about 10 degrees above zero and costs about $40. For about $180, you can buy the army-surplus extreme cold bag, which is rated to 40 degrees below zero. Of course commercial bags are available at higher prices with equivalent ratings.

The body burns a lot more calories in cold weather, so you need to have hearty foods stored away. Fortunately the food in your freezer can be kept frozen or at least refrigerated for some time even after the power goes off. Additionally, you will need to have a strong, animal-proof box to store other food outside in the shade. You can store food in an unheated garage or shed or in large metal ammunition boxes like the ones designed for 40mm rounds.

If you have a woodstove or fireplace, stock up on wood. Stoves are efficient to heat a room or two, but fireplaces without a running fan are not much help. You will need a good camp heater to keep your indoor tent or sealed room warm. A Coleman 3000 BTU heater will run seven hours on one, sixteen-ounce propane cylinder. That's enough to heat a tent or small room for part of each day. You are going to have to spend about twelve hours a day in those sleeping bags to conserve your own heat and energy. The heaters will have to be turned off when you're in your sleeping bags. Even so, you will need to have fifty to one hundred cylinders for heating and cooking through the worst of the winter.

You will want to have hand-crank-powered flashlights and radios, but in the case of winter survival, candles and gas lanterns are sources of heat as well as light and should be used safely. Keep your carbon monoxide detector and smoke detector working. Have fire extinguishers handy. Avoid leaving unattended candles, stoves, and lanterns. Although the camp heaters and stoves are generally safe for indoor use, they are hot and they burn oxygen, thereby creating a hazard, of which you must be aware.

If your home gets below freezing for any length of time, the water pipes will freeze and burst, causing flooding. If you cannot keep them warm, let the water trickle from each faucet. If that fails, turn off the water and drain the pipes. The prepared home is a key element of independent, self-reliant survival capacity, and so abandoning the home is always a last resort. This is especially true under winter weather conditions.

Fireplace with circulating fan, kerosene heater, and propane heater are all alternative, emergency heating methods. Each one has its advantages and hazards.

60 How can I survive an earthquake?

When the very earth begins to move, and buildings and highways sway, there is no escape, but you can do a few things to improve your chances.

- If in bed when the shaking starts, roll out of bed and lie flat, facedown. It is almost impossible to walk or run during a serious quake. Once the shaking stops you can get out of the building.
- Do not take elevators after an earthquake as the shafts may be damaged or the power may fail.
- If outside get clear of tall buildings. Facades may fall off or windows may break showering glass and debris below.
- As soon as you can, turn off your gas and electrical supply, as there may be gas leakage or short circuits that will cause an explosion or fire. Inspect your home for structural damage or hazards such as damaged stairways, leaking water, jammed doors, etc.
- Getting under a bed, desk, or other furniture is not advisable for earthquakes where the main hazard is collapsing structures. If the building collapses, the furniture will crush you. Even a car can be crushed under heavy debris, such as those caught on the Bay Bridge in 1989. The vehicles and their tires were crushed under debris. The safest location is right at the base of a wall, or next to your car, desk, or similar strong object. Yes, these will be crushed, but not flattened completely. Even heavy debris will stop and be held up a few feet on either side of the crushed object, leaving a gap. This is known as the "triangle of life," and is where most survivors are found.

61 How can I survive outdoors in the winter?

If your survival preparations don't cover subfreezing conditions you are only 50 percent ready to survive. The great majority of survival skills and survival equipment work well in dry and temperate weather. In the dry summer conditions, you can survive for a while by simply not doing anything stupid. Moderate clothing and basic shelter items will get you through the chilly, damp conditions of late spring and early fall. At home, mild weather survival focuses on having safe water and enough food. But winter conditions make survival anywhere an immediate and constant challenge. In winter, Mother Nature is brutal. Cold takes no prisoners. The survival battle comes down to maintaining the body's temperature. This is accomplished in four ways:

1. Generating heat internally through the consumption and metabolizing of high-calorie food and the necessary water to process it. Consider this fueling as your body's internal furnace. Food requirements are much higher in cold weather.
2. Keeping cold out of the body by avoiding eating cold food, drinking cold liquids, and breathing in cold air that can quickly lower the body's core temperature.
3. Preserving body heat. Breathing out warmed air, standing in cold winds, contact with the cold ground, getting wet, not wearing adequate clothing, and failure to cover the head will drain away heat and lead to hypothermia.
4. Gathering heat from external sources. Getting into a warm place, standing in the sun, drinking warm liquids, eating hot food, and standing by a fire, and breathing warmed air all reduce heat loss.

Civilizations are focused on providing a warm environment. Our homes are heated. Our vehicles are heated. Even in winter, our exposure to cold is brief. Well-fed and warm most of the time, we are all in poor condition to survive long-term cold under survival conditions. When we think of survival we think of the necessity of a fire for warmth, but all animals and some human cultures survive the harshest cold conditions without any form of external heat. They depend on heat conservation and high-calorie food metabolism. Two things are certain:

- Inadequately fed and clothed humans who are exposed to severe cold or chilly wet conditions for too long will die.
- If you live in most areas of the United States and Canada and have not acquired the skills and equipment for long-term cold-weather survival, you are at high risk 20 to 70 percent of the year.

The body loses heat in five ways:

1. **Respiration:** Breathing in cold air, heating it in your lungs, and then exhaling the warmed air back out is a significant source of heat loss. A simple face mask, ski mask, or muffler over the nose and mouth can conserve some of this heat.
2. **Evaporation:** Sweat and dampness on clothing evaporates and carries away heat. Alcoholic beverages give the illusion of warming while evaporating through the skin and taking away more heat. Rain, snow, and even fog will dampen hair, skin, and clothing to take away your heat.
3. **Convection:** Air (wind) passing over the skin carries away heat. That's great on a hot day, but deadly in the cold. In these circumstances, get out of the wind ASAP! While on the move, wear a windproof poncho.
4. **Conduction:** Nature hates an imbalance. If you are in contact with ground, rocks, metal, snow, or the like that are colder than you are, energy will flow from you to the cold surface. Minimizing contact and good insulation are the keys to preventing this heat loss. Wet clothing loses 90 percent of its insulation value, with water having 240 times the heat conductivity of dry air. STAY DRY!
5. **Radiation:** The whole body radiates heat/energy into the environment. Adequate clothing is the only way to reduce this radiation. Since heat rises, the head and shoulders are the greatest source of heat loss, and since the brain is most heavily supplied with blood circulation, the head is the last part to feel cold. Further, hoods, stocking caps, and big fur caps will save your life. Another device for combating radiated heat loss is the Space Emergency Blanket. These aluminized blankets can be used as ponchos or rigged as shelters. They reflect body heat back to you. They can also be used to catch and reflect campfire, stove heat or solar warmth onto your body. I have recovered from damp cold clothing in this way.

The two chief dangers of cold exposure are hypothermia and frostbite. A person who is exhausted, hungry, or sick is more susceptible to both of these life-and-limb-threatening conditions.

One of your best options is learning "back-to-basics" survival skills. Pioneers and early explorers survived winter after winter without most of the supplies we now take for granted as necessities. They hunted, fished, trapped, and foraged for food. They used hides, bark, and branches to build shelters. They made fires to keep warm. They made beds from pine branches, grass, and leaves. They were not comfortable, nor were they well fed, but they did survive through winters. It is possible to still live this way.

Some of these basic wilderness survival skills, combined with your pack full of modern survival equipment, will allow you to survive through a winter without additional supplies. I must point out that the having a good knife, sharpening stone, hatchet, small shovel, fire starters (flints, magnesium, etc.), fishhooks, line, and a small-caliber (.22) pistol or rifle in your gear would be essential to using natural resources for food, shelter and warmth.

Conserving Body Heat and Energy

Always be prepared for what the weather could be for the time of year. Those nice, warm fall and spring days can turn into cold, wet, and windy days that can bring on hypothermia in a few hours. Even a summer night can be deadly for someone in shorts and T-shirt. If you exhaust yourself fighting a storm or you allow yourself to get wet and tired before you stop and fall asleep, you may not wake up. But if you stay dry, and conserve your body's heat and energy supply, your chances of survival are actually improved. Generally, a sleeping person will wake up when the body gets too cold, and will move around just enough to generate a little heat. There are cases where survivors huddled together under a few tarps or dug into a haystack and dozed on-and-off for weeks before emerging to be found. Therefore, always have a rain poncho available in your pocket, purse, locker, and glove compartment.

The greatest heat loss is through the top of the head. The body supplies the brain with warm blood, and heat rises, so the head seldom feels cold, but it is sucking heat from the rest of your body. The neck also radiates a lot of heat that can be conserved with a turned-up collar, a hood, or a scarf. A wool cap or ski mask is a must-have item. Another big source of heat loss is respiration. You breathe in cold air that then sucks heat from inside the body, which you then blow away when you exhale. A simple face mask or ski mask can help conserve some of this heat.

Additionally, keep a pair of thermal socks under your shirt when out in winter. If your feet get wet you have dry socks. Change your socks often to avoid frostbite. If your gloves are lost, you can use them as mittens. Don't eat snow. Dehydration is a real danger in cold weather. The humidity is usually low and moisture is lost through respiration. Plan on drinking plenty of warm liquids. Cold liquids will lower your body's core temperature. So it's advisable to stop and heat water. Make tea or coffee if you have it. Warm, sweetened liquids will add heat and energy.

Further, avoid long exposure to wind that will take heat from you by convection. Avoid long-term contact with the cold ground or objects such as rocks and metal, which will pull away heat through conduction. Avoid sweating or becoming wet from snow and rain, as this will ruin the insulation value of your clothing. Avoid drinking alcohol, as it takes heat away as it evaporates through the skin. Do increase your food intake and drink hot beverages to fuel your body's heating system. Note that in extreme cold canned food freezes solid, and even if heated over a fire it may freeze before you can get it to your mouth. Keeping candies in your pockets may help provide some nourishment. Water may freeze, leading to your dehydration. In such extreme conditions adding a few ounces of alcohol to your water supply may be justified.

Winter in Camp

Camping out for an extended time in winter is a last resort. The requirements for adequate food, water, fuel, and shelter are much higher than for mild weather. Most people will not be able to haul the necessary weight far from their vehicle (road). Large groups will be able to do better than small families or individuals under these conditions. Camp locations must be selected with care. Select a site that is sheltered from the wind and has adequate access to fuel and water. Cold air travels down, so avoid valleys and ravines. Camp in the leeward side of ridges. If you can build up a sleeping platform a few feet off the ground, it will be five or more degrees warmer.

Underground shelters and basements are miserable in cold weather. Most camping tents are designed for mild weather and are well ventilated. This is great for hot weather, but not so good in cold weather. Look for expedition or mountain tents that are designed to withstand wind, and have smaller closable vents. Select a tent that is just a little bigger than the number of people who will occupy it. For example, if there are two people, get a three-man tent. Too large a tent will be impossible to keep warm. Too small a tent will bring you into contact with the cold walls and not let you do anything but sleep in it. If you can have only one tent and it is a warm-weather tent, consider making up a cover for the ventilated roof. Better yet, cover the roof under the rain fly with reflective Space Emergency Blankets to reflect the heat back into the tent. Clothing, blankets, and sleeping bags can become damp from outside moisture and sweat. This causes them to lose significant insulation value. They should be dried each day by hanging them out in the warm sun or letting them freeze and then beat out the ice crystals each day.

62 How can I make a survival kit out of common items in an emergency?

Improvisation and imagination are key elements of survival thinking. Anyone can put together some kind of survival kit from commonly available items.

You can compile this "poor man's survival kit" from common, easy-to-find items. This kit is versatile enough to provide protection and aid in a variety of emergency situations. Most of the items included are cheap enough and small enough that you can store them at your office, in your pockets, and anyplace else you might need them. Most of the items listed cost less than a dollar.

ITEM DESCRIPTION	EMERGENCY USES
Fifty-five-gallon heavy-duty trash bag	Rain shelter, sleeping bag, chemical protection, floatation device, water still, container, sling, etc.
N95 dust/mist respirator	Protection from chemical, biological, and radiological hazards. cold air respirator, emergency water filter
Single-edge, S/S razor blade (protected)	Last-resort defense, cutting tool, or escape aid if you lost your knife
12 x 24-inch sheet of HD aluminum foil	Signaling reflector, heat reflector, cooking pot, water collection and boiling, wound covering
12 x 24-inch sheet of Saran Wrap	Eye protection, container, wound covering, splint holding
(10) 12-inch length of electrical tape wound on cardboard	Repair clothing and shelter, wound protection, general repairs
(10) waterproof matches and striker	Fire starting for heat, light, signals
10-foot length of #25 nylon fishing line	Fishing, shelter building, trapping, repairs
(2–4) safety pins	Repairs, fishing, secure clothing and slings
Coffee filter	Water filtration, fire starting
(2 to 4) sugar packets or hard candy	Energy
(2 to 4) aspirin or other pain reliever pills	Pain relief, heart attack reduction

These items were selected to provide the best options for the very least cost. Obviously items can be replaced with slightly more expensive items. The whole kit can be kept in a small ziplock bag.

SUBSTITUTIONS

In place of the trash bag, you could use aluminized survival blankets. They are more effective for warmth than trash bags, bur less durable and versatile. You may want to replace the razor with a small penknife.

Filter paper is not as effective as commercially available filter straws that sift out most biological and chemical contamination. Another way to assure clean water is to add a few water-purification tablets to the kit for use in combination with the coffee filter.

You could upgrade from the matches to a more reliable magnesium fire starter for a few dollars more. Lifeboat matches burn hotter and are better at starting damp tinder.

You could replace the sugar packets and candy with an energy bar. If fishing and trapping are not a concern, then replace the fishing line with a strong string or paracord. Remember that even slightly more expensive and bulky substitutes may defeat the whole (cheap and handy) point of the kit.

ADDITIONS

I set my arbitrary limit for this kit at twelve items, but there are a few other cheap, smaller items that you may want to add. A plastic whistle could come in handy for signaling. A small compass would also be a good addition. A pair of latex gloves could come in handy in a number of situations. You could also add a very small, single-LED flashlight.

HOW TO USE THE ITEMS

Let's take a look at some of the survival uses for the kit items.

Fifty-Five Gallon Trash Bag

The black bag provides protection against wind, water, sun, and most chemicals. It is a great solar heat absorber. It can offer shelter in many configurations. You can place dry leaves or paper inside to use as a sleeping bag. You can use the razor blade to cut arm and face holes to make a partial rain, wind, chemical, and fallout suit. Cut the bag open to make a four-foot-by-six-foot shelter sheet. When partially filled with air and tied off, it can be used as a flotation device.

Water Still Instructions:

Dig a hole early in the day. Place a cup made from your HD aluminum foil in the center-bottom of the hole to catch the water. Place any available moist plant materials into the hole so that the water can be distilled from them as well as from the soil. Spread the cut-open plastic bag over the hole with some slack. Anchor the edges with soil and rocks. Place a small rock (not too big) in the center of the plastic so that the low point is directly over the foil cup. As the sun heats the black plastic and the inside of the hole, the water from inside will gather on the plastic and run down to drip into the cup. When the sun gets low, you will have some safe water in the cup. Note that the amount of water depends on both solar heat and available plant and soil moisture. The resulting water gathered may vary from a few ounces to a full cup.

Disposable Dust/Mist Mask

These masks come in a variety of styles and are available in medical supply stores for biological protection and in hardware stores for dust and mist protection. I recommend the N95-rated masks. These are effective against dust, soot, fallout, biological agents, and give some short term protection from toxic chemical mists. They also can help reduce heat loss through respiration and should be worn in cold weather. They do not protect you against toxic gases, such as carbon monoxide. These masks only provide protection if not contaminated prior to use and if properly fitted and worn. They are ineffective if worn over heavy facial hair.

Instructions:

Place the mask over the mouth and nose with one strap around the back of the neck and the other over the head as showed below. Squeeze the nose piece (if present) to fit snugly. Cover the mask with both hands and inhale sharply. Pressure should be felt inside the mask. If not, adjust the straps and the mask, and test again until pressure is felt.

Laboratory Filter Paper or Coffee Filter

A coffee filter or laboratory-grade filter paper can be folded into a cone to pour water through into a receptacle made from your heavy-duty aluminum foil. You can then boil the water for five minutes in the foil pan to get filtered and decontaminated water

Pins and Safety Pins

The safety pins have many applications as they are and can be modified for other uses. The fishing line can be used with a safety pin fashioned into a hook for fishing. You can magnetize a piece of a pin by stroking it in one direction with silk or through your hair. Placing the pin carefully on still water out of the wind on a very small leaf or other float it will eventually turn to point north.

Floating a magnetized straight pin or broken-off safety pin on a small leaf to determine magnetic north.

Saran Wrap or Similar

A 12 x 24-inch sheet of Saran Wrap can be used to cover the eyes for dust and chemical protection, or to cover the hands for chemical and biological protection. This material can also be used as a waterproof, blood-proof bandage for a variety of wounds and to hold a splint in place.

Clear, self-sticking plastic wrap makes a good bandage with or without tying and it can be used to secure splints as well.

Heavy-Duty Aluminum Foil

The 12 x 24-inch sheet of heavy-duty aluminum foil can be used as an effective signal mirror to get help. You can also place the foil in the back of your fire to reflect the heat. You can shape or fold the foil into a bowel to cook food or boil water. Drinking warm water can save your life under cold conditions and boiling water for five minutes can make contaminated water safe to drink. Aluminum foil is the dressing of choice for wounds that expose internal organs.

Aluminum foil can be used as a heat reflector. One way to make a cooking pot out of your aluminum foil by wrapping it around a forked stick that is formed into a loop. Fold and smooth out the foil to make a signal mirror. To aim the reflection at rescuers, planes or other sources of help. Place the target between two fingers, then move the mirror so that the beam shines through the fingers.

THIS KIT MAY NOT LOOK LIKE MUCH BUT IT CONTAINS MANY VERSATILE ITEMS THAT COULD SAVE YOUR LIFE.

The whole kit fits into a ten-inch freezer zip bag and weighs about 6.5 ounces. The optional items brings it up to about eight ounces.

A survival kit is like any tool. It is only as good as the person using it. Calm determination and an organized approach to managing the situation will go a long way toward keeping you alive in any emergency.

The bag itself has many uses. Note the optional addition of latex gloves, Band-Aids, rubber bands, a whistle, and a mini-compass.

63 How can a survivalist avoid being overwhelmed by the challenges of a serious emergency or disaster situation?

Being lost and injured in a blizzard, or fleeing a massive civil disorder resulting from an epidemic, all while dealing with your own injuries and lost equipment, are examples of survival situations. These situations can easily overwhelm the senses and create a sense of confusion and despair when order and effective action are most needed. Once safety and normalcy have dissolved and multiple hazards are evident, it is critical to avoid panic or paralysis. The survivalist must focus on just one or two effective steps in the right direction. You must just do the right thing that will get you toward survival, without thinking too much about how many difficult things you need to do after that. That closest or most urgent step may be to put on a respirator, take cover, get out of the wind and rain, or climb one step out of a deep ice crevasse. Avoid adding additional risks or wasting energy and resources, but start the process of improving your chances. True survivalists have used this step-by-step process to survive extended and complex challenges.

64 How can a survivalist be better mentally prepared for any kind of emergency or disaster?

Accepting and anticipating that one may be challenged by an emergency or disaster is critical to surviving. Non-survivalists are in constant denial of the potential for acute and chronic disasters even when those disasters are obviously possible or already in progress. The survivalist has already made the transition from denial through deliberation and possesses the mental tools to decide and to act. Accepting the possibility that bad things can happen or are happening to you puts you far ahead. Having a basic plan of action for escaping a fire, or shelter spot if a shooting incident develops at a restaurant, shopping mall, church, theater, or other public area, only takes a few seconds, but will reduce your reaction time if the worst happens.

65 What is the most important daily practice of a survivalist?

Constant situational awareness is a defining characteristic of a survivalist. Larger survival threats one must constantly be aware of include developing national economic environmental, and social trends. Increasing crime rates, increasing cyberattacks, widespread epidemics, and international tensions all can indicate future survival issues that must be prepared for or avoided.

On a more immediate basis, you need to develop the habit of observing and analyzing things around you and ahead of you. *Who are these people coming toward me? Do I smell smoke? Why is that person wearing a long coat on a warm day?* The military calls this process OODA for observe, orient, decide, and act. Failure to notice an immediate threat or to acknowledge a developing survival problem in a timely manner greatly reduces your chances to prevent, avoid, or survive it.

66   What is the most important factor in surviving a fast-developing survival situation?

Getting from denial to action is the first step in survival. Once you have accepted that a bad thing is happening or about to happen to you, you must quickly evaluate your action options. Here is where your accumulated survival knowledge, survival tools, and, most importantly, your mental preparations, become critical. You must not be distracted by considerations that are irrelevant to survival. You must be present mentally. Hesitation, distraction, wishing, or agonizing will only reduce your chances of survival or escape.

67 What issue can be the biggest challenge and obstacle to surviving an emergency?

The biggest challenge in many survival situations is having to do unpleasant or even terrible things. Doing things that are destructive, nauseating, violent, repulsive, and frightening may be the only way to save yourself and others from death or serious injury. Helping the sick and injured may involve vomit, blood, and other nasty sights and odors. Enduring dirt, cold, heat, smoke, and rain may be the only way to escape. Using violence or even deadly force against an assailant or terrorist is fully justified. You may need to strip off cold, wet, or contaminated clothing in front of others, or chop up and burn your heirloom furniture to keep warm. Vanity or normal aversions must be overcome under survival conditions. This is why the military puts recruits through challenging training situations.

68   What are the four levels of mental reaction to threats and dangers?

The four stages of coping with survival emergencies are relatively well known, but must be understood and recognized by the survivalist. Denial is always the first stage we go through when that initial blast, shot, whiff of smoke, or other indication of danger enters our awareness. No matter how much we anticipate or ready ourselves, we will experience an immediate desperate attempt to hold on to normalcy. This is known as the normalcy bias. We say "oh no!' or "you have to be kidding!" In some cases people simply cannot get out of this stage fast enough to survive. Only firm orders or instructions will move them to escape. People have been found burned to death while waiting for instructions when most others escaped safely. A true survivalist always knows that there is the possibility of trouble and therefore jumps from denial to deliberation more quickly. Deliberation time depends on the type of disaster developing. A growing epidemic may provide a few days of reaction time. An approaching tornado may (or may not) offer a just few minutes. A fire or a shooting requires that a decision be made immediately. Having anticipated the possibility of such a situation and preplanned your shelter, escape, or survival action allows you to jump to your decision quickly. Your decision depends on the situation and the nature of the threat, but your physical condition, survival skills, and what you have with you all greatly improve your options and your survival chances. Your actions must be swift and decisive. They may also involve some risks, injuries, and pain. However, you do what you have to do.

69   Are the rules and paradigms of survival applicable in everyday life?

Survivalists are always successful in life because they apply the principles of survival to everything they do. Those who consistently make bad decisions and poor choices are not survivalists. Just waiting for doomsday and piling up supplies is not being a survivalist, because you may be failing at everyday life. Below are the principles of survival, as applied to an effective and successful life:

- **Anticipate**: A survivalist anticipates changes in the economy, personal health, employment, the community, and other factors, and makes adjustments to avoid or prevent problems, thus becoming safer and stronger.
- **Be aware**: A survivalist is aware and knowledgeable about issues that may affect the future and create hazards to prepare for or opportunities to take advantage of.
- **Be here now:** A survivalist focuses on reality and on what is relevant. He or she creates a better life through self-improvement, hard work, and responsibility. Survivalists avoid debt and follow a "save and buy," rather than a "buy and pay interest," program.
- **Stay calm**: A survivalist is much less stressed than non-survivalist because a survivalist maintains health and financial security, and has prepared for potential emergencies in advance. They are neither paranoid nor fearful.
- **Evaluate:** A survivalist constantly evaluates his or her life situation, assets, liabilities, health, and possibilities in order to make the right choices based on logic rather than emotions.
- **Do the next right thing**: A survivalist knows that the future can always be uncertain, but acts to improve his or her situation step-by-step and day-by-day.
- **Take control:** A survivalist is proactive instead of letting life happen to him or her. Performing constructive and responsible actions in order to become better, stronger, safer, and more prepared is a lifestyle. A survivalist is not waiting for something to happen. A true survivalist sets goals and takes actions based on a personal mission, not the requirements and expectations of others.
- **Have what you need**: A survivalist puts realistic needs before frivolous wants. If you truly need something, plan and work to get it. Balancing quality versus quantity, and value versus usefulness, is a hallmark of a wise survivalist.

Impulse buying or rampant consumerism are not components of survival thinking.

- **Use what you have**: A survivalist makes the very best use of his or her skills and assets to deal with problems and build a better life. Improvisation is a critical skill.
- **Do what you must:** Failure to do hard things and make hard choices always leads to failure in life. The harder the decision, the more important it is to do it. Survivalists do not avoid unpleasant tasks or procrastinate. You must do what you must do!

The true survivalist has a defined mission in life and sets goals toward accomplishing that mission. They are an asset to their community and family on a daily basis and a greater asset when emergencies occur. Violation of the above principles of survival lead to failure in a survival situation and failure in daily life.

70   What actions should guide the survivalist in managing personal finances?

Survival mind-sets and strategies can and should be applied to everyday life including scenarios with your family and your job. The same rules and priorities apply, and the same errors and misjudgments will get you into serious trouble.

We all know that paper and digital currency like Bitcoin only has value as long as the society believes that it has value. Therefore, you should seek to gather it and use it effectively, but only while it has the means to improve your security and survivability. Gold and silver are functionally as useless as paper in a true economic meltdown. In Europe during sieges and economic collapses, gold, silver, and diamonds were usable as trade for a very short time after paper lost its value, but once shortages developed only hard, barterable goods were the only valuable. A gold watch or a diamond ring may not get you a turnip or a roll of toilet paper in a post-collapse economy. Today's economic survival involves the same issues as a disaster situation. There are the same three kinds of people in the game.

Economic Predators

Economic predators are constantly seeking to rob you and control you just as they would in a disaster, but they use different methods in an economic collapse. They set economic traps that are baited with false expectations and useless goods. They whittle away at your funds with taxes, interest charges, rents, and gimmicks. They need to get you into debt and keep you in debt. Over the years, they will take hundreds of thousands of dollars from you, for nothing in return. Yes, you have to pay taxes and other charges, but you must get out from under their control no matter what it costs. Minimize debts and pay off credit cards and loans as quickly as possible. Postpone purchases until you can buy without using credit.

Economic Victims

Economic victims are the working poor and those firmly stuck in welfare systems. The objective of predators is to drive more and more people into these classes where they are dependent on the state and/or various cartels to survive. As victims become more and more dependent on these predatory groups for their life-critical needs (shelter, food, water, medical aid, protection, etc.) they completely lose any pretense of individuality or freedoms.

Economic Survivors

Economic survivors are people who have ignored the traps and focused on economic independence and the key survival priorities. They may do with less and appear poorer, but they have no debts and have secured their sources of shelter, food, and other essentials above all else. Regardless of future developments, they will always do better in the long run.

Here are a few basic rules for economic survival and for building economic security. These are the foundations for building up you preparedness capabilities and moving toward greater self-reliance as the system fails.

- **Budget, budget, budget.** It is amazing me how people who have worked steadily for many years still live from paycheck to paycheck. Budgeting is the first key to economic survival. Without it you relinquish control to predators and to your own whims and weaknesses. You have to budget just like disaster survival. Shelter, food, utilities, medical needs, and reserve funds must be covered before even considering other priorities. After these are covered you can consider reserves in the form of hard survival goods (such as seeds, ammunition, candles, matches, soap, alcohol, tools, and medical supplies), education, and real estate. Saving and investing are still okay as long as you don't put all your eggs in one basket, so to speak. Wise investments can vastly improve your survival potential as you apply the gains toward building your independence.
- **Avoid using credit cards as much as possible.** There are some places where their use cannot be avoided such as car rentals or online purchases, but everyday (groceries, gas, clothing, etc.) purchases should be made with cash. Take your budgeted money for each expense and use it with care. When it's gone it's gone. Credit cards tempt you to spend beyond the budget.
- **Ignore society's values and your own ego and vanity**. You don't need the latest things! You do not need to have what your neighbors or friends have. An older car that is paid for is much better than a newer one that you are paying interest on.
- **Do without or with less early in life**. Instead of buying newer, better, and bigger on credit, buy what you really can afford and save for better later. Live a little beneath your means. You may look like the proverbial turtle, but you will win the economic survival race.
- **Avoid frivolous and nonessential expense**. To some, the lottery is just voluntary taxation run by predators. Drugs are traps run by other predators. Cigarettes are the tools of both kinds of predators. We all have a few hobbies or things we enjoy, but those must be prioritized with funds after all essential bills and some savings are dealt with. As time goes on you will do better and better as your victim friends descend into debt.

- **The job comes first**. Survival is never easy. If you are out of work, your family and survival situation deteriorate. Any job is better than no job. Yes, you may have to put up with difficult people and dirty work until you can find a better job, but keep what you have and do it well. That's survival! Acting on ego or temper usually leads to bad survival situations.

- **Make yourself a valuable survival asset**. You can be worth more than your weight in gold if you have skills and experience. Take any opportunity to get education and experience. Be constantly looking for opportunities to advance your career, but be alert for scams and frauds.

- **Get on the collection side of the equation**. Unless there are exceptional needs, paying interest is the worst way to use money. Save and buy rather than buy and pay. Save money for your first car and then save until you can buy a newer car for cash. Buy instead of rent. If you can buy a rental property at low interest or on contract with the owner, the tenants can pay off the building and all the expense until you can sell it at substantial profit. Not owing money early in life allowed you to save and invest instead. Real estate has value even in a totally collapsed economy. You can provide shelter, and a base for survival business and food production. Investments should never exceed or endanger your home and reserves.

- **Getting out of debt and staying out of debt.** This is the most important survival act anyone can perform. Avoiding wasting funds on bad habits such as the lottery, drugs, cigarettes, and junk goods is a revolutionary form of self-liberation. Knowing the difference between wants that are established by the society and media, and needs that have true value in survival, takes you from victim to survivor.

Risk versus Rewards in Economic Survival

I would be remiss if I didn't admit that a conservative, low-risk survival-oriented financial strategy has a downside. While it increases security through tough times and disasters, it also means living with less and passing up some potentially profitable opportunities and investments. An occasional small loan or debt may be justified for education or for solid tangible goods, but you have to ask yourself, *if this fails, can I survive and recover without loss of my foundation assets*? This process is called risk-benefit analysis.

Conclusions

While prepping may apply to disaster survival true survivalism is a way of approaching every aspect of life. The rules of survival apply to family life, careers, economics, and lifestyles. Your priorities always put life essentials ahead of societal and culturally promoted values. The application of survival principles to personal economic planning greatly improves your chances of surviving and even thriving through any level of economic decline or collapse. Simply put: the better off you are financially during normal times, the better off you can be materially when things get tough.

71   What are the most critical first aid skills for surviving serious medical emergencies?

Once a serious disaster develops, normal medical emergency services may not be available. In addition to traumatic injuries from a disaster situation, there may be medical emergencies (which can be caused by the disaster) that are more apt to result in fatalities due to the lack of available medical care. While the underlying causes of most of these emergencies cannot be addressed by the survivalist or caregiver, they can be effective in disaster situations by buying time and providing an opportunity for recovery for the victim. Knowing what to do for others is a core survivalist responsibility.

Recognition and Treatment of a Heart Attack

A heart attack, also known as myocardial infarction (MI), can occur at any time, but is far more probable when physical and psychological stress are elevated. Those with preexisting heart conditions and the elderly are more at risk. All efforts should be made to reduce stress for these individuals and to be vigilant for any sign of an impending heart attack. Myocardial infarctions (MI) result from obstruction of blood flow to heart tissue. This results in the death of tissue and a cessation of normal heart function. The heart goes into atrial fibrillation, which is a disorganized vibrating instead of beating. No blood is pumped and the brain and other internal organs begin to shut down. If the flow of oxygenated blood is not restored quickly, then death is certain. Effective CPR can sustain life for a while but seldom results in restoring a normal cardiac rhythm and patient recovery. CPR provides a small chance at recovery, and offers a savable patient for the EMS personnel or anyone who uses an AED. The sooner an AED is used, the better the chances of restoring the patient's heart rhythm.

Cardiac Arrest (Myocardial Infarction)

Urgency

Symptoms of a heart attack include crushing chest pains radiating to the back or left arm. The patient may also be sweating, weak, dizzy, or even faint. The afflicted person may verbalize that they think they are going to die. If it might be a heart attack, treat it as if it is one.

Action

Your first priority is to call 911 or send someone to do it. If the person is conscious, ask if they have prescription heart medication to take. Aspirin is a blood thinner and can reduce the severity of a heart attack. If the patient is not allergic to aspirin, having them take two pills may be helpful.

CPR

Most current CPR courses take about four hours, but learning this skill should take only a few minutes. A certificate is nice to have, but provides no additional legal authorization or protection. If you can do what is described below, you can do CPR.

1. Check for responsiveness. Shake and shout, "Are you okay?"
2. Send for help.
3. Open airway and perform a head tilt, chin lift, or jaw thrust (no pulse check).

Figure 1. Opening the airway. Credit: First Aid for Soldiers FM 21-11

4. Look, listen, and feel for breathing for about five seconds.

Figure 2. Look, listen, and feel for breathing. Credit: First Aid for Soldiers FM 21-11.

5.   If the patient is not breathing, then initiate CPR

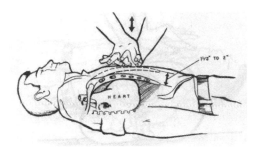

Figure 4. Proper hand position for CPR. Credit: First Aid for
Soldiers FM 21-11.

CPR Instructions

- Start at the nipple line (lower for children).
- Compress the patient's chest 1½ to 2 inches for adults (½ to ¾ inch for children).
- Place hands interlocked, fingers up
- Lock your elbows.
- Place your weight over the sternum, just below the nipple line. Keep your elbows straight and locked. Use your body weight to compress straight down. No bouncing or rocking
- Perform thirty hard and fast compressions straight down.
- Blow two full breaths into the patient's mouth. Tilt the head, then pinch nose.

Figure 5. Proper body position for CPR.
Credit: First Aid for Soldiers FM 21-11

6.   Continue CPR until you are too exhausted, the victim revives, or an AED is used.

For two-person CPR: use same count (thirty compressions, two breaths) alternate between compressions and breathing or take turns doing both.

Note that you should only use one hand for children and just two to three fingers for an infant.

AED

It cannot be said more emphatically. Anyone can and should use an AED immediately and without hesitation on a patient whose heart has stopped. While AED training is desirable, it is not necessary. If you can use a cell phone, then you are capable of using an AED. If one is within reach, just open it, push the button, and follow the instructions.

Note that if the victim starts to cough and regain consciousness, roll them onto their side, so as to prevent aspiration via vomiting that could result in further complications.

Recognition and Treatment of a Stroke

A stroke often results from elevated blood pressure, and elevated blood pressure often results from a psychological and/or physical emergency. This is especially common in the elderly, but can affect anyone subjected to pressure and struggle. Recognition and immediate action are essential to the victim's chances of recovery. Stroke victims who are transported to advanced medical care facilities have a good chance for full recovery and reversal of the effects. When transport and care are delayed beyond one hour, permanent and advancing disabilities are far more probable. If the stroke occurs in a remote location or when care facilities are not functioning, the survivalist's options are severely limited. There are three main causes of strokes, but the signs and symptoms and the required actions of each are the same.

Signs and symptoms of a stroke
- Partial or complete paralysis of one side of the body.
- Diminished levels of consciousness including dizziness, confusion, and coma.
- Difficulties with speaking and vision.
- Difficulty swallowing.
- Altered facial expression.
- Headache without any of the above other signs.
- Convulsions.

Quick diagnosis of a stroke
- Have the victim hold his or her arms out to the side. If one arm drifts downward, that is a sign of a stroke.
- Have the victim smile. A stroke victim will have a facial droop on one side.
- Ask the victim to recite "Mary had a little lamb," or other easy phrases. Speech difficulty will be indicative of a stroke.

Stroke care action
- Keep the victim as calm and comfortable as possible.

- Monitor the airway to prevent choking or blockage.
- If oxygen is available, use it at high flow.
- Continue talking to the victim and monitoring his or her level of consciousness.
- The conscious victim may remain in a seated position, but must not be permitted to stand or walk, as falling is a high probability.
- If it is necessary to transport an unconscious victim on a stretcher, he or she should be placed on the paralyzed side.
- Do not waste time! Get this person to an ER as fast as possible.

Note that a sudden severe headache that is centered at the back of the skull is often caused by an arterial rupture and may be followed by convulsions, paralysis, and loss of consciousness. Such headaches should trigger an immediate transport to the ER.

Recognition and Treatment of Diabetic Emergencies

There are millions of diabetics in America. Under normal circumstances, they manage their condition well through diet and exercise, and carry insulin for managing blood-sugar levels. During an unexpected disaster, a diabetic's blood sugar may be affected, causing it to fluctuate out of range of the manageable parameters. Access to insulin and/or food may be interrupted when it is needed most and insulin shock or diabetic coma may ensue.

Diabetic coma is caused when the victim takes insufficient insulin and/or overeats. It can also be caused by injury, infection, or stress. If not recognized and treated promptly, brain damage can occur. The signs and symptoms are:

- Rapid and deep breathing
- Dehydration indicated by dry, warm skin and sunken eyes
- A rapid and weak pulse
- Low blood pressure
- Impaired consciousness or coma

Insulin shock occurs when too much insulin or too little food results in insufficient sugar to feed the brain. This condition develops slowly, but must be reversed to prevent brain damage. The sign and symptoms of insulin shock are:

- Unusual behavior or combativeness
- Sweating
- Pale moist skin
- Dizziness and headache
- Rapid respirations
- Hunger
- Late-stage seizures and coma

Ask anyone exhibiting these symptoms, "Are you a diabetic?" If they answer yes, then ask "Have you taken your insulin today? Also ask, "Have you eaten today?" Those answers should give a good indication of the problem.

If the victim has not taken their insulin or has overeaten recently, they are probably suffering from a diabetic coma and they can be prompted to take insulin if available.

- If the victim has taken their insulin, but not eaten enough recently, the administration of sweetened beverages or sublingual glucose usually restores normalcy.
- Diagnosis of diabetic coma versus an insulin shock can be difficult, especially in the unconscious patient. If in doubt, providing sweetened drinks if conscious or sublingual sugar or glucose paste if unconscious can do no harm.

Airway Obstructions

While airway obstruction is not necessarily associated with disaster situations, they are a common cause of unnecessary death, and therefore, knowing how to clear an airway obstruction must be included in a survivalist's skill set.

Obstructed Airway/Respiratory Arrest

Urgency

The first act in determining priorities during mass-casualty situations is opening the airway and discerning whether or not the victim is breathing. The longer that the patient has not been breathing, the less likely they are to recover. Within five minutes of respiratory arrest, the heart will stop circulating blood and the brain will begin to suffer irreversible damages. In most cases respiratory arrest is the result of airway obstructions that can be corrected by use of the airway-clearing maneuver or simply repositioning the head. The tongue may also create an obstruction in an unconscious patient.

Recognition:

- If a person is conscious with airway obstruction, then he or she will be unable to speak or cough forcefully. They may give the universal sign of choking by placing a hand at their throat. There is no excuse for a person to die from this.
- A person may be unconscious or semiconscious if he or she displays pale or blue skin coloration. He or she may also be unresponsive or gasping and wheezing.

Action:

If you observe the patient choking before loss of consciousness, initiate the airway-clearing maneuver as shown below.

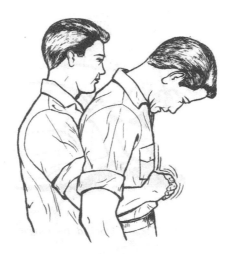

Administering the airway-clearing maneuver to a conscious or semiconscious victim.

Hands clasped just below the rib cage, pull forcefully in and up. Keep at it until either the obstruction is expelled or the patient loses consciousness. You should be braced to lower the patient down gently if this happens. Send for help and start CPR.

If you find an apparently unconscious patient, shake their shoulders and shout "Are you okay?" to awaken them. An unresponsive patient is a medical emergency. Call 911 or have someone do so immediately before initiating any further action. Tilt the head and lift the jaw to open the airway. Look at the chest, listen for breathing, and feel air on your cheek to determine if the person is breathing. Modern protocols eliminate the steps of abdominal thrusts for airway clearing, pulse check, and rescue breathing. If the patient is not breathing with the head tilted as shown in the figure above, then initiate CPR immediately.

72 What kinds of survival and emergency supplies should I keep in my vehicle(s)?

Getting stranded in a storm, or finding that a disaster will prevent you from reaching your home or other emergency supply sources for some time, could put you and those with you in serious danger. Some of the items listed will allow you to restart your vehicle or get it unstuck in snow or mud, while the other items are essential to surviving a few days trapped in a storm or other situation. It is usually not advisable to leave your vehicle when stuck in snow and cold weather. You can run the engine periodically to warm the interior. Be sure the exhaust pipe is clear to prevent being overcome by carbon monoxide.

1. Jumper cables or a charged battery booster
2. Fix-a-Flat
3. A small fire extinguisher
4. Road flares and/or reflectors
5. A small folding shovel
6. A blanket
7. Heavy gloves
8. A flashlight, preferably with an orange flasher attachment
9. Bottled water
10. Energy bars
11. A stocking cap
12. Extra socks
13. Candles and heavy-duty aluminum foil to set on dashboard for light and some heat
14. Matches
15. Heavy-duty towrope
16. Pen and paper to leave notes on the vehicle
17. Pocketknife or multi-tool knife
18. Small first aid kit

73 What are some methods I can use to recognize and avoid accidents, injuries, and personal disasters?

Modern industrial safety techniques can easily be applied to your personal life to reduce the chances of you and your family becoming victims of your own unsafe actions. The fact that over 80 percent of accidents happen to just 20 percent of the population clearly indicates that some people are better at controlling their risks than others. Serious injuries, illnesses, financial losses, or a home fire are devastating and greatly reduce your ability to prepare for or to survive a general disaster. The following are proven techniques used to recognize and prevent damage and injury. They can be used by the survivalist to improve home safety and emergency preparedness as well.

Hazard Recognition

It is very easy to overlook hazardous conditions and unsafe habits as we go about our daily lives. Our parents may have warned us not to seek out trouble, and it is human nature to focus in what we are doing at the current moment. We may not recognize a hazard because we cannot actually see it or because we lack the technical information needed, but the great majority of hazards and unsafe habits are recognizable to anyone with common sense, yet we put off fixing the problem or changing the behavior.

Near-Miss Incidents

In theory, there are three hundred near misses and about thirty small injuries before a serious injury or death occurs from any hazard or unsafe habit. Every near miss incident is a warning and an opportunity to fix the problem or change the habit before it gets you. For example: You almost tripped on that loose carpet on the stairs, or you almost fell of that old rickety ladder. Do you keep going and forget the event, or do you make sure to put correcting these hazards on the top of your to-do list? Never ignore a near-miss incident or something that looks wrong. These are gifts of warning. This also applies to preparedness. Did you almost lose your job? Did an assault or home invasion occur in your community? Did your coworkers get laid off? These are near-misses you need to act on to avoid or survive.

Unsafe Acts vs. Unsafe Conditions

Unsafe conditions such as broken steps or worn electrical cords are dangerous and must be corrected, as the majority (90 percent) of all injuries are the result of unsafe acts of people. A spill on the kitchen floor that is not cleaned up is not an unsafe condition; it is the act of whoever spilled it and did not clean it up. The batteries taken out of the smoke detector was an act. Letting combustibles pile up near the furnace is an act. Unsafe driving is an act. Examine your habits, and the habits of your loved ones, for potential risk-taking.

Unsafe Habits

One of the most common sentences I hear from accident victims is "I've been doing it that way for years." We develop habits based on the immediate rewards we get for our acts. If we complete an action and get any kind of small and immediate reward from it, then we tend to continue doing it. The reward can be saving a few seconds, using less energy, or saving a few dollars. The immediate reward has much more impact than any potential long-term dangers. For example, cigarettes provide an immediate reward (good feeling) and become a habit in spite of the horrible long-term risks. The driver who rolls through a stop sign at deserted intersections and is rewarded by getting to work early will keep doing it until they are hit or hit someone. Safety glasses and gloves are uncomfortable; reading the labels on insecticides takes time. Fire extinguishers cost money you could spend on more immediately enjoyable items. This type of thinking is human nature but can have tragic consequences if not managed. Therefore, it's important to get in the habit of thinking about the long-term results of your habits and correct those that are dangerous to your health and safety

What If Analysis

Most accidents happen when several unsafe conditions and unsafe habits come together. For example, if you are in the habit of wearing flip-flops on the stairs and you never fixed that worn carpeting there, or you are in the habit of walking to your car without looking around and today there is a mugger in the parking lot. It is prudent and proactive to examine your daily actions and your environment (home, work, road, etc.) and ask "what if?" *What if there is a carjacker at the corner? What if a train is coming? What if this gas can leaks? What if my hand slips?* This is called a questioning attitude and it can save your life.

Management of Change

Even in a fairly safe environment, changes can result in disaster. In fact, many of history's greatest disasters were caused by unmanaged changes meeting unsafe acts or conditions. For example, you may be in the habit of backing out of your driveway without looking, but the school schedule has changed today and there are children running for the bus; needless to say, this could end terribly. If you are correcting unsafe acts and conditions, you are much safer, but watch out for changes. Any kind of change in weather, schedules, routes, people, the building, hobbies, or the like can bring new hazards. What was safe before may now have risk. Think and analyze.

Safety Inspections

You seldom see what you are not looking for. You may find it quite amazing what kinds of hazards you find at home once you begin a focused safety inspection. Remember that if a hazard exists, it will result in a problem sooner or later. Safety-related repairs and improvements should always take priority over convenience, budget, and aesthetic considerations.

Root Causes Determination

When you recognize a hazard, even if no injury occurred, ask why it is present. Just fixing the immediate hazard may not be enough. There is probably a deeper cause for the unsafe condition or unsafe act that should be addressed. For example, if you find your child playing with drain cleaner, you get it away from him in time and place it on a high shelf. That takes care of the immediate danger, but why was the drain cleaner available in the first place? The answer may be that you keep lots of chemicals under the sink. But why are chemicals under the sink, at a child's eye level? It's clear that you must search your home and find all kinds of poisons, sharp objects, choking hazards, matches, and on so. that need to be locked up or removed. This can lead you to the root cause of many kinds of problems and provide an opportunity for real improvements.

Remember that most accidents are caused by unsafe acts that you control. Having recognized your unsafe habits, make a list of dos and don'ts. Some key dos and don'ts: don't leave doors unlocked; do turn on the lights before going in; don't stand on chairs; do remove fuses and check for current flow before working on electrical wires; and don't leave loaded firearms out.

74 What are some common items that I can use as improvised survival implements?

- Aluminum foil can be folded or formed into containers to cook food or boil water.
- Clear plastic bottles can be used to hold water and allow solar UV rays to purify it.
- Large plastic trash bags can be fashioned into a rainsuit or protective clothing. They can used be used to gather water.
- Plastic tarps and sheets can be used for shelter or ponchos.
- Napkins can be used as a temporary dust mask or bandage or to filter water.
- Any kind of cloth can be used as dust mask, bandage, or tourniquet.
- A fire extinguisher can be a weapon.
- Saran Wrap can be used as a bandage or eye protection, or to secure a splint.
- Newspaper makes excellent insulation, fire starter, or splinting material.
- A pen or a spray can could be used as a defensive weapon.

These are just a few examples. Nature provides branches, rocks, sand, mud, and other survival items. Towns and cities are filled with metal, wire, cordage, cardboard, plastic, and other materials that could be used in an emergency. All of these materials can be used to create survival tools.

75 What are the most common outdoor, cold-weather-related emergencies?

Outdoor conditions can quickly become hazardous for the unprepared during the colder months. Temperatures and winds can change quickly in autumn and spring. The temperatures in high altitudes can drop drastically even during summer months. The two most common serious medical problems caused by cold temperatures are hypothermia and frostbite. Both can develop into life-threatening and debilitating conditions quickly if not recognized and treated promptly.

Hypothermia (exposure)

Hypothermia is a serious and life-threatening condition. Being inadequately dressed for the cold, or allowing your clothing to get wet from rain, mist, or sweating, can lead to hypothermia, even in temperatures as high as sixty degrees. Physical exhaustion caused by running or survival-related work can increase the danger of hypothermia. This is why energy conservation and staying dry are the first priority in outdoor survival. Many people have died of exposure when caught unprepared for a weather change. You may go out for a few hours on a warm autumn day and be caught in a rainstorm that drops the temperatures to the forties in minutes. As a rule of thumb, always dress for what the weather could be, not for what it is. Always carry survival items that include a rain poncho, dry socks, and a warm cap. Since the survivalist may need to evacuate or operate during cold and/or wet weather, the recognition and treatment of hypothermia can be a critical skill.

The first warning of impending hypothermia is intense and uncontrollable shivering, a sign of the body's last-ditch attempt to get warm. Once shivering stops, the victim becomes sleepy and listless with slurred speech and a stumbling gait. If swift intervention is not initiated, then unconsciousness and death will follow. It must be understood that a person who has ceased shivering and begun to show advanced signs of hypothermia may continue to decline and die, even after being brought into a warm environment, because their internal heat production has shut down. Prevention and early treatment are essential. Treatment of hypothermia includes the removal of cold, wet clothing and the administration of warm sweetened liquids while the victim is still conscious. Warm clothes or heat packs can be placed on the sides of the neck, armpits, and groin.

Avoid rubbing or rapid warming of extremities, which may cause cold blood to rush to the heart, thus inducing fibrillation. Gentle external warming and warm liquids are key. An unconscious or semiconscious victim can be placed into a sleeping bag unclothed with other persons. Hypothermia is a medical emergency! Get the victim to a hospital as fast as possible.

Frostbite

Frostbite can be a disabling and possibly fatal condition. Once your hands or feet become frozen, you will be unable to perform most other survival-related tasks, and so your survival chances are dramatically reduced. Thick gloves and socks should be worn in cold weather, but these may become lost or wet in a survival situation. Keeping two extra pairs of warm socks under your shirt or in your survival kit is highly recommended. Socks can be used as a foot covering, or as mittens when needed. Frostbite usually affects the fingers, toes, nose, and ears first. If nothing is done, the circulation to these extremities is reduced and frostbite ensues. The skin becomes pale, white, and numb to the touch. Continuing exposure results in stiff, leathery, and hard skin as blood circulation is completely stopped. Never rub frostbitten tissue, as this will cause further damage. Thaw the extremity in warm water not exceeding 105 degrees Fahrenheit. The tissues will become red, painful, and swollen. Wrap the thawed extremities in soft bandages. If tissues do not recover sensation, remain numb, and turn black, then the tissue is dead and infection will follow. Prompt medical attention and antibiotics are essential for these cases.

76　What are the most common outdoor, hot-weather-related emergencies?

A survival situation may involve great physical exertions in hot-weather conditions. Additionally, prolonged or indefinite power outages and water shortages could occur as a result of a variety of disasters. Many folks today have become accustomed to air-conditioning and access to fans and cold drinks, and so are highly susceptible to heat exhaustion and heatstroke. Children and the elderly are especially susceptible to heat related problems, and should be observed for the first signs of an issue. These conditions are much better avoided by limiting strenuous activities and exposure to the sun and maintaining a high level of hydration. A prolonged lack of the need to urinate or issuing dark yellow urine indicates inadequate hydration. Don't wait for these signs to start drinking plenty of water. Because prolonged sweating will deplete the body of salt and other electrolytes needed for muscles, including the heart, sports drinks are preferable to water. Therefore, you may want to consider including powdered sports drink in your survival packs as well. Heat exhaustion and heatstroke are the most common emergencies related to hot conditions.

Heat Exhaustion

Heat exhaustion may be regarded as a precursor to heatstroke. The victim will feel weak and dizzy with pale, cool skin and profuse sweating as the body struggles to maintain a safe temperature. Get the victim to a cool, shaded location as fast as possible. If practical, have the victim lie down with feet elevated twelve to eighteen inches as you would for shock. Provide cool, but not cold, drinks. If available, provide electrolyte-enhanced "sports drinks." Keep the victim at rest. Consider calling 911 for children and elderly or chronically ill victims.

Heatstroke

Heatstroke occurs when the body's cooling system has failed. The victim is weak, dizzy, and will have a headache. The most recognizable symptom will be that there is no sweating and the victim will feel hot and dry to the touch. If the victim is not cooled rapidly, then organ damage, brain damage, and death will occur. If EMS is available, call 911 immediately. Cool the victim rapidly by any means available. Place cold packs under the armpits and at the neck and groin to cool the blood. If possible, place the victim in a cold bath or cold shower. Maintain efforts until the victim revives.

　　Those accustomed to hot and humid conditions should be especially cautious in dry, desert-like heat. Evaporation of moisture from the skin is rapid and the comfort can be misleading. Dehydration can occur before you feel thirsty, so drink water frequently.

77   How can I defend my home in a rural area under survival and disaster conditions?

In survival manuals, much attention is given to home defense and survival for urban and suburban areas. But the rural homestead or farm is not immune to raiding and looting by criminal groups and desperate refugees during a truly massive and extended catastrophe. Constant alertness, preparation, and proactive intervention are key elements.

Alertness

- Once it is evident that law and order have broken down and the possibility of assault is evident, the survivalist must establish an around-the-clock watch schedule.
- Long continuous watch shifts are difficult to sustain, and alertness tends to dwindle after three to four hours. Try to set up watch schedules with no more than four hours on and at least twelve hours off. This can be maintained indefinitely without overly fatiguing anyone.
- If at all possible, have two people on each watch to ensure that no one falls asleep. That makes for a total of eight able-bodied lookouts.
- If you do not have enough people for an effective around-the-clock watch, you should hide away from obvious targets such as cabins or tents so that you are not trapped or surrounded.
- Consider having one member pack up and sleep in hiding about fifty to one hundred yards away from the main camp, at a location where he or she can alert or rescue the others from intruders.
- Night-vision equipment is an excellent investment for rural defense at night. Acquiring this gear should be a high priority.
- The sentry's duty is to give warning of the presence of a threat and its nature, direction, and distance as soon as possible. It is preferable that a radio or other silent method is used to alert the group of the threat so that the intruder is not aware of being detected.
- Dogs and alarm devices can greatly enhance warning capability.

Defensive Preparations

- Intruders will probably come from roads and trails from the direction of high-population areas, so be especially observant of these routes and directions.

- Remove mailboxes and signs from roads that may attract intruders.
- If possible, camouflage access roads and driveways with branches and debris.
- Preestablish well-camouflaged defensive positions with trenches, sandbags, and logs.
- Rural defense requires the possession of effective, long-range rifles with high-capacity magazines and a large supply of ammunition.
- Maintain fencing around the close defense perimeter, but do not depend on it alone.
- During times of danger, keep vehicles out of sight from the road, and keep lights off or blanket windows at night so as not to attract attention.
- Plan for various scenarios including single assailants, group assaults, and nonaggressive refugees, and know how to withdraw and evacuate as a last resort.
- Of course, your basic survival preparations should already have stocked enough water, food, and other supplies for a prolonged stay at home.
- One of the most effective preparations you can make is to establish a mutual defense arrangement with neighbors in advance. Such cooperation would confer a huge survival advantage against aggressive looters and gangs in a prolonged catastrophe.

Proactive Intervention

- The group must have preplanned actions for each intrusion situation.
- If it appears that the intruders intend to just pass by without approaching your location, let them do so without exposing your defenses and numbers, but be aware that they may double back or circle around to assault from a different direction or after dark.
- If the approaching group does not appear aggressive, they should be challenged from a concealed and protected location. They should be told to go on their way and that you are armed and will not permit harm to yourself or your family. Do not expose your entire group or weapons. An unknown force is much more likely to discourage aggression and is much better able to fight if necessary.
- Warning shots and threats show weakness, may initiate an unnecessary battle, and may even attract more trouble.
- If the intruders are armed and deploy for an obvious assault, you are justified in executing an ambush before they can besiege your home or camp. A preemptive surprise may be your only chance against a superior number.

78   What kinds of food should a survivalist store at home for long-term emergencies and how much food should they store?

The average home usually has five to ten days' worth of extra groceries that can be used up before you start using your emergency food supplies. Most disasters will resolve within thirty days, or will degenerate into a situation that requires you to either evacuate or prepare for a long siege. If evacuation is more likely, then your thirty-day home stock should be adequate and your focus must be on dehydrated foods in a true, full-sized survival pack. If you think that staying home (shelter in place) is more likely, then start working toward a larger supply of food.

Dehydrated survival foods are useful, but assume that the survivor will have unlimited water available. If storage space is an issue, dehydrated foods are a good choice; however you must then store enough water, fuel, and alternative cooking stoves to reconstitute them. If you have enough room to store nonperishable dry and canned foods, this is a more effective and economical choice. A good compromise would be to start by building up thirty to sixty days' worth of normal, nonperishable groceries and then work on getting another ten months' worth of dehydrated foods. Try to rotate them regularly and replace and use these within a year or two of their expiration. While we can afford to be concerned about additives, salt, sugar, and fat content when food is plentiful, these concerns are insignificant in a disaster situation.

The most common method of assuring that you have food when you need it is stocking up and storing it. In the short term, it is faster, cheaper, and takes less work than other methods. For home survival where weight and space are not a big issue, the best method is too simply stock up on various canned goods and other staples (e.g., sugar, honey, flower, rice, etc.), rotating them into use. Most of these items last at least a few years. Several preparedness supply companies actually provide foods and storage racks for such systems. Where space is limited or where weight is an issue, dehydrated foods are more practical. These are more expensive, but keep much longer and you can carry a lot more food if you need to evacuate. You do need to have a lot of safe water and fuel for heating it to reconstitute these products.

While it is a well-established theory that you can survive three weeks without food, this assumes that you start out well fed, in good health, in a warm environment, and are at rest most of the time. After five to ten days without nourishment, weakness and mental deterioration will impede survival capabilities. It is much better to stretch your rations and eat daily than to depend on going without food for several days.

Two thousand calories per day is the general recommendation for maintaining health. Fifty grams of protein and three hundred grams of carbohydrates are also recommended. These daily requirements are listed on all food packaging, along with the nutritional contents of the product per serving. You can easily calculate how much of each product you need to supply the daily requirements per person for a given number of days. While avoiding fat, calories, sugar, and salt may be prudent dietary choices during normal times, these priorities must be set aside in survival situations. Any food is better than no food. The body's requirements for calories is much higher under the stressful situations that would exist in an emergency. Cold conditions also require higher caloric intake. So the established "minimum daily requirement" may not meet your needs. Try to err on the high side for stored food and water.

In addition to canned goods, dehydrated, and freeze-dried survival foods, there are actually many "off the shelf" grocery store items that are inexpensive, nonperishable, and highly nutritious. The ones shown below are averages of several sources, but in all cases the use of vacuum packaging and dry storage will prolong shelf life.

- **Pasta:** Pasta is high in carbohydrates and easy to use in lots of dishes. Pasta has a shelf life of at least fifteen years. Minimum per person is twenty-five pounds.
- **Rice**: Rice is high in carbohydrates and useful in many dishes. Store only whole-grain rice, as instant rice will not keep well. Minimum per person is twenty-five pounds.
- **Beans**: Pinto beans, black beans, garbanzo beans, red beans, lintels and other types can be stored for twenty to thirty years, are easy to cook, and are a good source of protein. Minimum per person stored is thirty pounds.
- **Grits**: Grits are made from the cornmeal process and are a good source of nutrition. They can be used as cereal, fried, or as a base in many recipes. You can use them to replace part or all of the recommended grain storage.
- **Nuts**: These are usually vacuum packed and store for decades. They are a great source of protein and other nutrients. Minimum per person stored is ten pounds.
- **Peanut Butter**: A forty-ounce jar of peanut butter contains 6,650 calories. That's more than a three day food supply. It only has a shelf life of about three to four years, so you need to rotate it. Minimum per person is three jars.
- **Whole grains:** Whole grains are often sold as survival foods. They do provide good nutrition, but to make baked goods (e.g., bread, etc.), you need a grain mill to grind them into flour. Whole grains keep much longer than flour. Oats can simply be made into oatmeal or in baking. Minimum per person stored is twenty-five pounds.
- **Dried Fruits**: Dried fruits such as dates, raisins, apple slices, banana slices, figs, and apricots can be stored for many years and provide important vitamins to the diet. Minimum per person is ten pounds.

- **Beef and Turkey Jerky**: Jerky or dehydrated meats are an important source of calories and protein to your diet. If you make jerky yourself, be sure to salt it and remove all the fat before drying. Vacuum-packed jerky should keep for at least two years and can be reconstituted in soups or stews, or eaten as is.

- **Powdered Milk:** Powdered milk is a good source of vitamins and other nutrients. Store-bought products should be immediately vacuum packed for the best shelf life, but the vitamins degrade over time. Powdered milk specifically packaged in cans for storage will last up to fifteen years, but should be repackaged in airtight containers once opened. Minimum per person is five pounds.

- **Powdered Eggs:** Powered eggs are nutritious, have a shelf life of about ten years if kept in airtight or vacuum-packed containers. They can be used as scrambled eggs or in a variety of recipes. Minimum per person is five pounds.

- **Canned Vegetables**: Canned vegetables such as spinach, corn, green beans, and carrots are essential to health and keep for four years or longer. Vegetables can be stored for many years, but canned fruits should be rotated every few years as the acid can eat through the cans over time. Minimum per person is fifteen to twenty cans.

- **Canned Meats**: Canned meats such as SPAM, corned beef, or Vienna sausage are very nutritious and store well. You can also stock up on canned tuna and chicken for variety. The recommended shelf life is two to four years, but I have used products that were as much as fifteen years old. Canned anchovies and sardines in oil keep indefinitely. Minimum per person twelve cans.

- **Bouillon and Soup Mixes**: Bouillon cubes and soup mix envelopes take up very little space and provide a way to create tasty soups from what you have stored and what you may be able to gather. Carrying these in your survival pack can make otherwise unappealing foraged foods more palatable.

- **Honey**: Honey is sometimes called the perfect food. Honey keeps indefinitely and can be substituted for sugar in many uses. Minimum per person stored is two to three pounds.

- **Sugar:** Sugar is a nonperishable staple if kept in airtight, dry containers. It can be used in all kinds of recipes. I recommend keeping both white and brown sugar. Minimum per person stored is five pounds.

- **Flour:** Useful in all kinds of cooking and baking. Can last up to 10 years if sealed and dry. Minimum per person is fifty pounds.

- **Coffee and Tea**: Depending on your tastes, these beverages offer comfort, warmth, and stimulation under any condition. These will be high-value trade goods during a long-term disaster. Minimum per person stored is ten pounds or four hundred tea bags.

- **Vinegar**: Vinegar has many uses in cooking and food preservation. Apple cider vinegar is even useful in alternative medicine. You definitely want to have a few gallons.
- **Cooking Oils and Shortening**: A necessary ingredient in baking and frying. Minimum per person is one gallon.
- **Salt**: Used to enhance flavors and for a preservative. It will be in demand during a prolonged emergency. Minimum per person stored is five pounds.
- **Spices**: A good selection of spices can make otherwise bland "survival food" more enjoyable. The selection depends on your taste.

Other Stuff: There are lots of other options and additions. You can add freeze-dried meals to reduce storage space, spaghetti sauce to enhance the pastas, molasses in place of some honey, Bisquick (shelf life of two to three years) baking mix in place of flour. You may want to add a few bags of hard candy for comfort and quick energy. Hard candy lasts a long time if kept dry and cool. Maybe some cans of baked beans or some of your own canned foods.

A number of options for food stocking. Left to right: (1) homemade food stock consisting of pasta, rice, beans, oatmeal, and other storable foods in vacuum packed bags; (2) stack of three ready-made, thirty-day containers of freeze-dried meals; (3) box of six #10 cans of survival foods from a preparedness supply outlet; (4) tote bins full of freeze-dried foods, MREs, and canned goods.

79   What kinds of survival camps would be used by survivalists during evacuations and long-term encampments?

Under most emergency situations, it is best to remain in the shelter provided by your home and use the supplies and equipment there. Once you have elected to take to the road, you are placing yourself and your family at the mercy of the environment and a variety of hazards with the limited supplies you can carry. Unless you have a well-established route to a well-supplied retreat, you should regard taking a hike as the last resort. There are several scenarios that would justify or even necessitate evacuation and relocation under emergency conditions. Your home could be in imminent danger of destruction from floods, fires, or looters. You may run out of supplies. Roving gangs or spreading epidemics could make the area unsafe. Some kind of "police state" action could make moving to the hills preferable to remaining in towns.

So let's look at the various types of camps or bivouacs that one might establish. There are three basic kinds of camps that can be established. There is the "hasty camp" that you put up nightly while on the move or when weather forces you to halt. There is the "survival camp" that an individual or family establishes where they intend to stay for a while to seek shelter, rest, and gather food. There is the base camp where a group of families or an organization sets up a long-term base to provide all life-sustaining supplies and services for an indefinites time. Each of these camps requires shelter, water, food, warmth, sanitation, and security. In many cases camouflage and concealment will be beneficial to survival.

The Hasty Camp

The hasty camp can take many forms, depending on the weather, location, and external hazards. Since such camps are inevitably established in close proximity to routes where desperate people may be moving, concealment and security must take a high priority. The immediate availability of water is not necessary since you should have been gathering water while on the move. Select an area well away from your trail or any other trails or roads. If there is any possibility of a hostile population, you should have a dark cold camp with no fire and no candles or lanterns. Use small mini-lights or red-lens flashlights if you must, but try to have everything set up before dark. If you must use a fire to cook or boil water, do so before dark and minimize smoke. You should locate a site well before dark and scout the surrounding area to be sure that you are truly in a safe spot; this is usually a thicket or natural concealed location. Abandoned buildings or natural shelters can be used only if they are well off the main roads. Remember, if you think it's a good place to go, so will others.

Regardless of how well selected your camp is, you must put security first. Unfortunately there is not much time to fortify a hasty camp. Be sure you establish your escape routes before dark. Use brittle twigs and branches to put up natural looking barriers that will make approaches difficult and noisy.

A hasty abyss of deadfall and branches can slow down intruders and make approaches noisy.

Have your weapon(s) immediately at hand. You should have all of your supplies not used for shelter packed to go. If you have to run, know where you are going next and have your weapon and most of your supplies with you. You should never have any survival supplies you are not immediately using outside of your pack. Of course if you are not alone, take turns on watch through the night.

Minimize your impact on the camp area and cover up or carry out any waste or trash. Signs of a well-supplied camp could make others want to follow your trail. In a hasty camp, you have your water and food from your pack to use. You may be lucky enough to find some edible plants or catch fish or small game, but neither is a priority. The hasty camp is about shelter, warmth, security, and preparing food that you have. While you still need to bury human waste, sanitation is not a serious problem in a short stay.

Note: The above assumes that hostile conditions exist. Under such conditions, any campfire and smoke can be seen for miles and will attract serious trouble. Of course if rescue is needed and/ or concealment is not necessary, a campfire may be desirable. Extreme cold may justify the risk of

With more time sharpened branches can be placed to prevent infiltration or rushing attacks on your camp

a small fire if it is in a pit or well surrounded by logs. Remember that the fire will light up overhead trees and branches like a sign advertising your location.

The Survival Camp

The survival camp is much harder to create than the hasty camp. While it starts out based on what you have brought with you, its success depends on a good location, as well as available water, food, and building supplies. Unless there are pre-positioned caches of food, tools, and other supplies, it will require hunting, foraging, quick thinking, and building skills. You need to spend more time on selection of a site. You may need to try several hasty camps before you are sure that a location is safe for this more permanent campsite. In this case you need to have access to water and be able to hunt, trap, fish, and forage for food in the area. You may also need to forage in nearby towns and abandoned buildings for materials such as wire, plastic, cloth, rope, containers, metal, and other materials. Depending on the situation you may or may not want to interact with other survivors or occupants in the area. Remember that these folks may be desperate and may not welcome your foraging and hunting in the same area. Of course, there are many who may be openly hostile. Your camp should be located well back from any trails, roads, or occupied areas. In this case you probably will need to have fires, and some noise and odors will be unavoidable. But keep fires and smoke to a minimum and do not wear trails to and from your camp. Worn trails, trash, and other signs of foraging will all attract attention. These are particularly troublesome in fall and winter when there is less foliage and tracks in the snow are very hard to conceal. The gathering of firewood and building materials will soon clear the area of deadwood and branches, giving more evidence of your camp. After a few weeks your impact on the area will be hard to conceal. Two solutions to these hazards are:

- Move your camp every few weeks. Doing this gives you fresh foraging and hunting territory while reducing your risk of being raided by hostile groups. You should search out and designate your next campsite as soon as you settle in the current one. You may even want to cache some supplies there and make it your emergency evacuation assembly point.
- If constant moving of the camp is impractical, you can minimize your foraging, hunting, and other activities within a few miles of the camp and go out on foraging and hunting expeditions to remote areas well away from your camp.

Another feature of the survival camp is that it justifies the time and effort to establish basic fortification. You should be able to set up and man a lookout post that will spot intruders well before they can detect the camp. You can use deadwood, branches, ditches, and other material to slow down any form of intrusion long enough to be identified and resisted or for you to evacuate. You should consider having trenches or other bullet-resistant cover available for all camp members. Finally, you must have a plan for evacuation and a plan for camp defense established and practiced.

Sanitation is another issue that becomes critical in a long-term camp. Human waste, cooking waste, and the offal from cleaning fish and game will attract unwanted insects, animals, and disease that will soon render the camp untenable. These wastes must be buried well away from the occupied camp and water supplies. Clear procedures must be in place as soon as camp is established. Since waste disposal and personal hygiene issues will probably be addressed outside of the camp's main defensive perimeter, it will be necessary to have an armed guard accompany anyone visiting these facilities. It is a standard procedure for a hostile intruder to take down a person who is outside the camp and then infiltrate in their clothing as if returning.

80 What are the prospects for survival for the current and next generations?

Many believe that the social, political, and technological developments of the twentieth century shifted societal values from favoring freedom and self-reliance to favoring a culture of compliance and dependency. Urbanization and centralization have created a life-support system that is unstable and fragile. Survivalists and preppers are generally unpopular because they tend to remind people of their own vulnerability. Simply put, our current level of population and civilization is unsustainable. This truth has been recognized by many brilliant thinkers, but denial of this truth is a much stronger political and economic force. The necessary actions to avoid economic collapse, the spread of an epidemic, famines and other catastrophes are often too unpopular and painful to be implemented. How and when a worldwide catastrophe will occur is impossible to predict, but it will happen soon enough. In fact these things are already occurring as increasing natural disasters, political chaos, terrorism, economic decline, and escalating worldwide tensions. Most persons recognize that things are deteriorating, and that the future will likely not be as good as the past. Obsessive entertainment and the addictive use of technology are really opiates to avoid reality and responsibility. The values and skills of self-reliance and personal responsibility have been virtually extinguished over the past fifty years. So we have a mainly helpless and dependent population moving into what may be the most dangerous and challenging times in human history.

Twenty-first-century technology has misled the younger generations into blindly accepting false security while sacrificing their real freedoms and privacy. Human nature is more disposed to avoid recognition of the matrix of dangers and disasters people will experience in the next several decades. Interest in preparedness and self-reliance will grow as reality becomes harder to ignore, but most people will remain in denial until becoming victims of catastrophe. They may survive in a devastated and repressive society, or perish from violence, resource shortages, or diseases.

Survivalists have a moral obligation to attempt to spread survival knowledge and capability to as many members of the younger generations as possible. The foundation of such efforts should be rooted in self-reliance, personal preparedness, and responsibility for one's own survival. These soldiers of survival and their children could make the difference between recovery and the disintegration of humanity.

81 How disastrous would a massive electromagnetic pulse (EMP) be, and what can a survivalist do to prepare?

The true effects of an EMP are subject to considerable debate. A targeted EMP initiated by a hostile power would affect a limited area and recovery could be fairly quick. A larger EMP could be the result of a high-altitude nuclear detonation or a large solar flare. Effects could range from temporary outages and scattered damage to massive destruction of the infrastructure and communications systems. In a worst-case scenario, automotive engines would be rendered inoperable; power generators, city water pumps, and sewage pumps would be destroyed; and radios, computers, and phone systems would be fried. Most of the economic wealth that is actually just numbers in data storage would simply vanish.

Most people tend to focus on protecting their cell phones and computers from such an event. But with cell towers down, there may be no one to call. Your phone is now a paperweight and your computer is just a fancy typewriter at this point. Loss of the internet is the very least of your problems in a massive EMP event. Having no food, water, police, fire, medical, sanitation, electricity, public safety, or access to your bank and credit accounts are your main problems.

The most important electronics in this type of situation are radios and walkie-talkies. After an EMP, the national emergency radio system is the most likely method of communication to recover, so you will want to have at least one AM/FM/MX/GRMS radio protected. Even better, have a multiband or shortwave radio protected. It's also wise to have a laptop computer, along with regularly updated flash drives of your whole hard drive, to permit recovery when and if the internet is replaced.

Most government and major commercial data servers are enclosed on grounded Faraday cages. These are simply metal enclosures that are insulated from the equipment they protect and grounded to catch and ground the incoming electrical energy. You can buy Faraday cages or Faraday boxes online, but they are easy to build yourself. A Faraday cage works by reflecting the incoming field, absorbing incoming energy, and creating opposing fields to protect the contents. Grounding the cage or box has little value to its protective capacity. An effective Faraday box can be made by simply wrapping the outside of a cardboard box in several layers of heavy-duty aluminum foil. In this case, the foil reflects and conducts the energy and the cardboard insulates the devices inside from the foil. A steel ammunition box lined with rubber or foam makes an excellent Faraday box, while providing protection from other sources of damage. Grounding of a Faraday box or cage is not necessary, but will absorb the energy instead of reflecting it.

Antistatic bags can be used to protect portable radios, walkie-talkies, and cell phones in pockets and survival packs. They also protect your phone data from being copied by nearby hackers. These bags should be durable and should be rated at a MIL-PRF-8170 or MIL-PRF-131 protection level

82 What items should I carry in an outdoor survival kit?

Survival kits are intended to keep you alive, help you to get back home, and facilitate rescue in outdoor emergency situations. They are not complete survival or evacuation packs, but should be carried even if you intend to just spend the day hiking, fishing, or hunting. You can be injured, lost, ill, or get caught in an unexpected weather event. These supplies would be carried in a multi-compartmented backpack or light daypack. You may want to trim it (pick and choose items) for your own needs, but do not overlook shelter, warmth, water, and signaling capabilities.

List:

1. 1 quart (minimum) water
2. 1 bottle of water-purification tablets and/or water-filtration straw
3. 1 miniature survival manual or survival cards
4. 1 miniature compass
5. 1 signal whistle
6. 2 flares and/or orange smoke bombs
7. 1 multi-tool or Swiss Army knife
8. 1 durable Space Emergency Blanket or disposable emergency blanket
9. 1 plastic rain poncho
10. 1 stainless steel Sierra Cup or canteen cup (to heat water, etc.)
11. 1 can of Sterno or 6 to 8 heat tablets
12. 1 magnesium fire starter
13. 1 small LED flashlight
14. 2 tea candles
15. 1 pen and 6 index cards to write notes
16. 1 12" x 24" sheet of folded HD aluminum foil (mirror, heat reflector, etc.)
17. 2 vacuum-packed energy bars and/or candy, jerky, etc.
18. 1 N95 dust/mist mask (dust, cold air, etc.)
19. 1 small first aid kit with assorted bandages, pain relievers, antiseptics, etc. in a plastic bag
20. Map of the area you are traveling

Optional:

1. 1 wool stocking cap
2. 1 pair of heavy socks
3. 1 weapon (e.g., pepper spray, .22-caliber pistol, etc.)

Inspect Your Emergency Supplies Regularly!

There is nothing worse than reaching for your emergency equipment when you really need it and finding that critical equipment and supplies are not usable. Batteries leak and decay, food goes stale and loses nutrition, and plastic, cloth, and rubber can weaken. Dampness and mold can get in. Inspect your emergency supplies at least every six months. Replace and rotate in fresh items as needed. Update and upgrade your equipment.

83 How important is it to have survival items immediately on hand when an emergency develops?

It's what you have with you that counts in an emergency. What you have in your pockets or a small survival kit is far more important than what you may have at home if you are caught somewhere else when disaster occurs. The items in your pockets and maybe a survival kit will be all you can depend on if you are lost in the wilds or caught in a blizzard. Most people spend more than half their time on the road or at a job. If you are one of those persons, then you must have items with you to help you get through immediate hazards and reach home. You also have to consider the possibility that you will not be able to get back to your home and your main supplies. Whistles, dust respirators, flashlights, survival blankets, compact food and energy items, extra prescription medications, self-defense devices, small knives, bandanas to make bandages and tourniquets, and fire-starting devices are just a few items that are good to have.

84   Why is having bleach on hand important in survival situations?

Household bleach is a powerful disinfectant containing about 6 percent chlorine. In water, it will be important for maintaining health when water supplies, sanitation services, and medical help may be unavailable. Here are some uses.

Decontamination

Make a 10 percent solution in water to disinfect biologically contaminated clothing and equipment. This solution can be sprayed in a mist from an aerosol bottle or from a garden sprayer to decontaminate larger area.

Waste Disposal

A 10 percent or stronger solution can be added to bags or pails of human waste prior to sanitary disposal.

Water Purification

Tap water is usually pure as is. Well water may or may not contain some biological contaminants. Containers may also be contaminated. To be safe, rinse out the containers you are going to store water in with a 10 percent bleach solution before filling. Add eight to ten drops of bleach per gallon to any potential contaminated water, mix and let stand for fifteen minutes before use. For one-quart canteens and water bottles, add two to four drops of bleach, shake, and be sure that the cap and lip of the container are wetted. Then seal and wait fifteen minutes before use

Wound Cleansing

For preparation of Dakin's solution used to flush deep wounds as below:

1. Boil 4 cups of clean water for fifteen minutes.
2. Add ½ tsp of baking soda and let cool.
3. Add 3 ounces of bleach.
4. Store in sealed container protected from light.

85   What are some other methods of purifying water?

Access to clean, safe water is the foundation of survival capability. Whether it's a massive disaster or a wilderness survival emergency, being able to access and purify water will be your most critical need. In addition to storing water at home and including some clean water in survival kits and packs, the survivalist must be able to gather and purify water from various sources. Roof water gathered in rain barrels, rain water, condensation, melted snow, puddles, groundwater, streams, and ponds may have to be collected, filtered, and decontaminated prior to use. Outdoor lakes, streams, and ponds will almost always be contaminated. During major disasters, municipal water supplies may be contaminated as well. Rainwater gathered in clean containers should be safe unless a nuclear or chemical incident is involved. Roof water will pick up animal feces and other contaminants.

Boiling

Boiling is generally the best method of purification and is preferable to using bleach or iodine. Bringing water to a rolling boil for one full minute is sufficient to purify water. Boiled water often tastes flat. Shaking or pouring back and forth can restore natural taste.

Bleach and Chlorine

If access to fuel for boiling is limited, then bleach, chlorine tablets, or iodine tablets must be used.

Filtration

Turbid or cloudy water can be filtered through cloth or coffee filters before boiling or adding bleach.

Iodine

Iodine is an alternative to using bleach to purify water. It does make a less desirable taste and can be harmful if overused, but is effective. It can be purchased in tablets or you can use basic, medical tincture of iodine at two drops per quart of water. For cloudy and highly polluted water, use up to ten drops per quart.

Sunlight UV Exposure

Sunlight can be used to kill most waterborne biological contaminants. The method involves simply exposing the water to direct sunlight and letting the ultraviolet rays disinfect the water. UV-A light devices are sold for this purpose. In a survival situation, you can just use the free sunlight and some clean, clear plastic bottles to do the same in an emergency. Six hours of exposure to direct sunlight by this method will kill the following bacteria: *Escherichia coli*, *Shigella flexneri*, salmonella, *Yersinia enteroclitica*, *Campylobacter jejuni*, and *Vibrio cholerae*. It will also work well against rotavirus and giardia. This method will also kill the Cryptosporidium parasite as well, but at least ten hours of exposure to full sunlight is required in order for that to work. The water source can be a pond, puddle, or roof water. This rain barrel contains relatively clean-looking water, but bird and animal droppings and decaying plant matter in the gutters have probably contaminated it with biological hazards. Water may contain various dirt and particulates that need to be filtered out before pouring into a small pint or quart, clear plastic bottles no larger than two liters. Glass bottles filter out most of the UV-A rays and larger bottles will not let the UV-A rays reach all of the water so they cannot be used. The six-hour exposure time assumes that there is direct and full sunlight. Under cloudy conditions, it may take up to two days to ensure effective purification. The bottle is laid out horizontally in the sunlight. The use of aluminum foil or other reflective backing is not necessary, but it will increase the effectiveness of the UV-A exposure.

This clear plastic bottle placed in the sun for six hours can remove biological contamination from water. The addition of the aluminum foil can increase the effectiveness of this method.

Commercial Filter

Commercial water-filtration and purification devices are available for home emergency use and should be one of the first purchases in a home preparedness program. Small filtration units, canteens, and straws are made for outdoor use and must be included in every survival kit and pack.

86   How can I determine someone's medical condition without medical instruments?

While having a stethoscope, sphygmomanometer (blood pressure monitor), thermometer, and other devices is handy, we all have diagnostic tools in the form of our senses of sight, smell, hearing, and touch. Here are some examples:

- Pinch the skin on the back of the patient's hand. It should recover quickly. If it remains tented for more than a second, the patient is probably dehydrated.
- Pinch a fingertip. The color of the nailbed should promptly return to pink. If it remains pale or bluish, there is poor circulation and impending shock.
- Feel for a radial pulse at the wrist. If you feel one there, the patient's systolic blood pressure is at least 90 mm Hg. If there is no radial pulse, then feel for a pulse at the side of the neck. If a pulse can be felt there, then the patient has a systolic blood pressure of at least 60 mm Hg. No carotid pulse indicates the need for immediate CPR.
- Use your fingers to palpate the radial pulse at the wrist. This should be from 60 to 80 beats per minute for adults and faster for children. Pulse rates that are higher or lower indicate medical issues. Lack of a radial pulse is a sign of serious shock or heart failure.
- Respiration rates for adults should be from twelve to twenty breaths per minute and can be counted by observing the chest rise and fall. Breathing rates in excess of twenty-four or below twelve breaths a minute usually indicate serious medical issues.
- Establishing the victim's level of consciousness is the easiest and most important diagnostic action anyone can take. There are four levels of consciousness. These are: Alert, Verbal, Painful, and Unconscious, or AVPU.
- Asking a patient if they can state their name, the day of the week, and their location can determine their level of consciousness. If they can provide the correct answers they are termed as being alert. If they cannot answer, but do respond in some way to your question, then they are responsive to verbal stimulus. If they do not respond to speech, you can pinch the patient's arm. If they react to this, they are reactive to painful stimulation. If they do not react, then they are truly unconscious; this is a very bad sign. Continuously talking to a trauma victim is important. Their level of consciousness may decline rapidly as shock or head injuries progress.

- If a victim is found to be alert, immediately ask about how they were injured, what medications and medical issues they have, who to contact, and what they may be allergic to. If consciousness declines, this information will be important to responding medical personnel.
- You can determine if a limb is deformed, discolored, or swollen by observation. If in doubt, compare its appearance to the opposite uninjured limb. If they do not match, it is probably fractured or sprained, and should be splinted.
- You can determine if a patient has a fever by placing the back of the hand on their forehead, then pausing and comparing it to how your forehead feels.
- Use a flashlight to determine if a patient's pupils react normally to light. Shine a light in one and then the other. Pupils should contract quickly. Failure to contract may indicate use of drugs, head injury, or poisoning. Pupils that remain wide usually indicates deep unconsciousness or death. Pupils that react differently from each other indicate a serious head injury.
- Skin color is an obvious indicator of health. Pale skin indicates poor circulation. Pale or bluish (cyanotic) skin color is a sign of insufficient oxygenation from shock, respiratory problems, or heart attack. Reddish skin color is seen in heatstroke victims. Bright red skin color is seen in cases of carbon monoxide exposure.

Using just your senses and these guides will permit you to determine the nature of an injury or illness and indicate a course of action.

87   Can superglue be used to close wounds?

The short answer is yes. While surgical glue is available, normal commercial superglue can be used to close straight, shallow lacerations. It is not recommended for deep cuts, jagged tears, or lacerations on joints. Wounds must be disinfected and free of debris before gluing. Be alert for signs of infection. Add superglue and some butterfly bandages to your first aid kit for closing wounds.

88 What can I do to survive a major epidemic?

An international pandemic is both the most feared and most probable cataclysm facing civilization. Most experts agree that it is not a matter of "if" but "when" a worldwide epidemic of a serious disease will occur. Such an event would be as devastating to civilized societies and the world economy as a nuclear war.

In addition to the accidental, incidental, or deliberate initiation of a pandemic, a pandemic could be a secondary effect of a primary disaster. A financial collapse would cause civil disorder that could result in the interruption of sanitation systems, medical services, water purification, and food production and delivery. All of these occurrences would open the door to communicable diseases.

Additionally, a nuclear war could result in radiation sickness that compromises the immune system and exhibits many of the symptoms of communicable diseases to begin with. A large-scale natural disaster, an electromagnetic pulse (EMP), or a cyberattack on the power grid could also trigger a domino effect that would lead to an epidemic.

Effects of Infectious Diseases and Biological Agents

The chart below includes all of the essential information about the most likely epidemic sources for your reference. Note that radiation sickness is included to fill the last two columns. While it is not a communicable disease, this does provide a useful basis for comparison of effects, and radiation exposure reduces one's immune system.

Disease / Agent	Typhus	Typhoid Fever	Encephalitis	Brucellosis
Infective	High	Moderate	High	High
Transmittable	None	Moderate	None	None
Incubation Period	6 to 15 days	7 to 12 days	5 to 15 days	7 to 60 days
Duration of Illness	14 to 60 days	14 to 60 days	7 to 60 days	14 to 60 days
Mortality Rate *	10 to 40 percent	10 percent	10 to 80 percent	2 to 10 percent
Vaccine Available	Yes	Yes	No	No
Antibiotic Effectiveness **	Yes	?	No	?
Typical Symptoms	Headache Chills High fever Muscle pain Swollen lymph nodes Skin rash Stupor	Headache Weakness Sweating Muscle pain Dry cough Abdominal pain Diarrhea or constipation Rash Swollen abdomen Delirium	Headache Fever Muscle and joint aches Fatigue Confusion and delirium Paralysis Double vision Hearing and speech difficulty Unconsciousness	Headache Fever Chills Sweating Weakness Muscle and back pain

Disease / Agent	Pneumonic Plague	Septicemic Plague	Bubonic Plague	Cholera
Infective	High	High	High	High
Transmittable	High	High	High	High
Incubation Period	2 to 5 days	2 to 5 days	2 to 5 days	2 to 5 days
Duration of Illness	7 to 30 days	7 to 30 days	7 to 30 days	10 to 60 days
Mortality Rate *	100 percent	100 percent	100 percent	5 to 75 percent
Vaccine Available	?	?	?	No
Antibiotic Effectiveness **	Yes	Yes	Yes	?
Typical Symptoms	Fever Headache Weakness Chest pain Difficulty breathing Cough Pneumonia Bloody mucus	Fever Chills Abdominal pain Weakness Bleeding into skin and other organs Skin turns blue or black at toes, fingers other parts of body	Fever Headache Weakness Painful and swollen lymph nodes	Diarrhea Dehydration Blue, dry skin Stomach cramps Muscle cramps Vomiting Weakness Low blood pressure

Disease / Agent	Smallpox	Anthrax	Yellow Fever	Hemorrhagic Fever
Infective	High	Moderate	Low	Yes
Transmittable	High	None	High	High
Incubation Period	7 to 16 days	1 to 5 days	1 to 5 days	2 to 3 days
Duration of Illness	12 to 24 days	3 to 5 days	7 to 30 days	20 to 60 days
Mortality Rate	5 to 60 percent	100 percent	5 to 40 percent	90 percent
Vaccine Available	Yes	Yes	Yes	No
Antibiotic Effectiveness	No	Yes	?	?
Typical Symptoms	Fever Headaches Severe fatigue Severe back pain Vomiting Red lesions starting on face and hands and spreading to trunk. Lesions turn to pitted weeping blister	Raised itchy bumps Swollen sore lymph nods Nausea and vomiting Fever Headaches Bloody diarrhea Abdominal pain	Acute Phase Fever Nausea Light sensitivity Dizziness Red eyes, face, tongue Chest pain Shortness of breath Fever Shock Toxic Phase Yellow skin Vomiting blood Bleeding from nose and mouth Brain dysfunction Liver and Kidney damage	Headaches Capillary bleeding Fever Skin swelling and bleeding Bloody diarrhea Purple skin spots Low blood pressure Vomiting with blood Muscle and joint pain Shock

Disease / Agent	Influenza	Dysentery	Radiation Sickness (Mild)	Radiation Sickness (Severe)
Infective	Yes	Moderate	No	No
Transmittable	High	High	No	No
Incubation Period	2 to 3 days	2 to 3 days	On contact	On contact
Duration of Illness	7 to 15 days	10 to 50 days	7 to 30 days	6 to 12 months
Mortality Rate *	5 percent	15 percent	0 to 20 percent	50 to 100 percent
Vaccine Available	Yes	No	No	No
Antibiotic Effectiveness **	No	?	?	?
Typical Symptoms	High fever Runny nose Vomiting Sore throat Cough Muscle pain Headache Diarrhea Fatigue Dehydration	Fever Diarrhea Dehydration Stomach cramps Muscle aches Rectal pain Vomiting Shock Delirium	**Symptoms appear in only 10 to 50 percent of those exposed within twenty-four hours** Vomiting Nausea Fatigue	**Symptoms appear in more than 50 percent of those exposed on the day of exposure** Vomiting Nausea Fatigue Hair loss dehydration Diarrhea Shock

*Mortality rates are highly dependent on the age and general health of the victims, as well as on prompt available care.

**The effectiveness of antibiotics depends on the victim's condition and on how soon that medicine is administered. In some cases the antibiotics may not directly affect the disease, but may treat secondary infections and thereby improve the recovery rate.

Surviving a Contagious Disease Epidemic

Although not always listed specifically, almost all communicable diseases can cause some combination of nausea, vomiting, loss of appetite, sweating, and diarrhea. These conditions lead directly to severe dehydration that in turn results in organ failure and death if not treated. Maintaining good oral hydration and electrolyte balance in the early stages of these diseases is critical. Once the patient can no longer tolerate oral fluids and/or is unconscious, oral fluids must be avoided and only IV and rectal (fluid enemas) are feasible. Maintaining hydration and the use of antibiotics where effective can greatly reduce mortality rates for most of these diseases.

The single most effective defense against being infected is the ability to restrict or eliminate all contact with the population and sources of contamination as soon as possible. Once symptoms are detected and the word of an epidemic is spreading, you must be able to instantly isolate yourself and your family, and continue to remain isolated until the epidemic has burned itself out. Being able to stay safe in your home for four to eight weeks with enough food, water, medical supplies, fire extinguishers, defensive arms, and

The use of latex gloves, hydration solutions, N95 respirators, bleach solutions, and available antibiotics shown above could provide a significant advantage in surviving a large-scale epidemic.

lighting and heating capacity is the only sure way to avoid becoming a victim of deadly pathogens. The places where you are most prone to exposure are public transportation hubs, grocery stores, hospitals, and disaster aid centers. If other potentially infected persons attempt to enter your home, you are justified in turning them away and using force if necessary to protect your own life and the lives of your family.

In a worst-case situation where you are forced to evacuate your home or are unable to get to your home, you will need to have survival packs and skills that allow you to survive for an extended time without aid or contact with others. Water filtration, respiratory protection, safe food, and defensive arms will be especially important to survival in the open.

Anything and anyone coming into contact with you during an epidemic should be considered dangerous. Wearing N95 respirators when you are away from home or while caring for afflicted family members is essential. All water (regardless of sources) should be boiled for five minutes or treated with bleach at a quarter teaspoon per gallon. Wear latex gloves when handling any potentially contaminated items and use a spray of 10 percent bleach/water solution to decontaminate surfaces, canned goods, and any other potentially contaminated items from outside.

89 There is so much to prepare for and so many different kinds of emergencies; where do I start?

Remember the old Chinese proverb: "The best time to plant a tree plum tree is twenty years ago; the second best time is today." The same is true of survival preparedness and education.

True survivalists are seldom at a zero preparedness state. Furthermore, increasingly frequent and violent disasters produces new survivalists every day. The sudden realization that you are vulnerable to life-threatening events and have neither the skills nor the equipment to care for yourself and those you care most about can be alarming. The scope of the preparedness challenge may be overwhelming and even lead to paralysis of action. Any action is better than no action and even the smallest preparedness steps are far better than nothing at all.

Put away five to ten gallons of water for each family member. Start allocating canned goods to be kept for emergencies. Determine to add a week's worth of nonperishable food (e.g., canned, pasta, beans, rice) to your survival stocks every month or two. Buy more candles and a good flashlight. Don't forget a fire extinguisher and a battery-powered AM/FM/WB radio. Buy or create evacuation packs for all family members. That's pretty simple stuff, a task which anyone can complete without spending a lot of cash. Doing just these things gives you a good base in an emergency and starts you on the road to greater self-reliance. If you are already a full-fledged survivalist, this is how you can advise and help your neighbors to get started.

90 When can a survivalist use deadly force?

Some images of survivalists propose that they are trigger-happy individuals, anxious for a shoot-out. This is the opposite of good survival thinking. Getting into a situation where deadly force of any kind is involved should be avoided whenever possible. Retreating, rerouting, taking cover, and being aware of threats is far safer than any armed or physical combat situation. Even trained combat shooters get killed sometimes. Survivalists do not go looking for trouble, but they are always ready when trouble cannot be avoided. In such cases, the use of a firearm or other device to disable or kill an assailment can be justified and necessary.

You are justified in shooting an assailant when an armed or physically superior individual is moving toward you and are within twenty feet of you and do not stop. This rule is based on the fact that a charging assailant closer than twenty feet can reach you with a fist, knife, or blunt weapon and do serious harm before you can pull the trigger or before your shot can stop them.

You are justified in shooting an assailant whenever they attempt to employ a firearm in order to do you or others bodily harm. You are not obliged to wait until they point the weapon at you or anyone else, and you are certainly not obliged to let them shoot first. You will need to prove that they had hostile intentions and you had reason to fear for your life. If they have not drawn their weapon, you may elect to warn them that if they reach for their weapon you will fire.

Assailants do not have to be armed to justify the use of deadly force. They just have to be obviously capable and having intentions of physically harming you. A 240-pound, twenty-two-year-old assailant threatening a seventy-year-old man or a 120-pound woman justifies the use of deadly force. Multiple assailants that outnumber the potential victims usually would justify deadly force.

In most states, you are justified in using deadly force on any intruder that enters your home regardless of whether they are armed or not. Under normal circumstance it is better to call the police and take up a position to defend yourself and your family than it is to go looking for a confrontation. However, if they come after you, then your justification is clear.

You are usually not justified to use deadly force in defense of property alone. You cannot just shoot someone who is stealing your car. If you confront a thief on your property and put yourself between them and the property or if they chose to assault you instead of running away, then you can use deadly force. But remember that initiating a deadly force confrontation is always dangerous and legal justification may be difficult.

The use of deadly force and the killing or wounding of another person, no matter how justified, is a traumatic experience for most individuals. Even when morally justified and obviously necessary, it can cause emotional distress. Regardless of the circumstances there is going to be an investigation. You will be interrogated and you may even be arrested. Don't move anything, don't say anything, and cooperate with the police, but get a lawyer. Even the most obvious self-defense cases can have complications.

91 Should a survivalist be trained in hand-to-hand combat?

Most survival situations are more likely to require non-combat-related skills such as first aid, water purification, food acquisition, escape techniques, or shelter building than hand-to-hand combat. Many survivalists will lack the physical capability to be proficient at this kind of combat; but all survivalists should have some level of armed-combat capability as their first option.

Immediate, effective actions are essential to hand-to-hand combat. Such reflexes can only be achieved when constant training has implanted each move into muscle memory. While reading a book about combat techniques or watching demonstrations is better than nothing, only professional training and physical conditioning will provide one with real capabilities. Such training takes time and dedication. If you do elect to take self-defense training, be sure to use a reputable and professional provider.

Basic self-defense training is often offered by local police departments and other agencies. This usually focuses on breaking holds and escaping from various criminal assaults. This kind of training is recommended for women of all ages, but is limited to crime prevention, not survival combat.

A true survivalist avoids physical combat except in defense of life and freedom and only if no other option is available. As with armed combat, the stakes are kill or die so survival combat training should focused on delivering blows that immediately disable or kill the aggressor. Martial arts forms that emphasize throws, holds, and pins are of limited value in true mortal combat. Fist-fighting and wrestling skills that work in competition are not enough when no rules apply.

In these situations, armed always beats being unarmed. Don't hesitate to use a firearm, knife, club or improvised weapon (spray can, rock, stick, thrown sand in eyes), if assaulted.

If you are forced into a situation where you are cornered, grabbed, or forced into a physical-contact fight and you have no immediate weapon, there is always some part of your body that is free to strike the assailment and there is always a critical part of the assailment's body that is open for you to hit hard.

Your weapons:

- Your head is hard. You can smash a nose, knock out teeth, and hit other areas to telling effect.
- Your elbows can strike forward and back at the head, face, abdomen, and groin.
- Forearms are hard bones that can swing to block and strike hard.

- Wrists are better than fists against many targets.
- Knees are powerful and tough. They can be used against the groin, head, abdomen, or other available target.
- Feet can kick forward and back as well as stomp.
- Hands can grab, pull, push, and gouge.
- Palms can strike at ears and chins.
- Fists can be used like hammers or to punch.
- Teeth can bite ears, fingers, and other tissues.

Your enemy's target points:

- Ears can be bitten. A hard palm strike to one or both ears can rupture the eardrums and disorient the assailant.
- Eyes are vulnerable to finger pokes, thumb gouging, and elbow strikes.
- The nose can be struck by the head, elbow, or fist. An upward drive below the nose can be lethal.
- The jaw and teeth can be broken by a head-butt, elbow, or fist.
- A hard blow to the throat can crush the trachea and prevent breathing temporarily or even permanently.
- Hard blows with the fist, elbow, knee, or head to the center of the abdomen below the rib cage will usually disable an assailant.
- The kidneys on each side of the abdomen are vulnerable to hard kicks, knee strikes, and punches.
- Any strike to the groin will disable a male assailant.
- Fingers can be bitten, smashed, and bent until they dislocate
- Kicks and strikes to the knee joint or the elbow joint in the opposite direction that it normally bends will disable that extremity and usually the assailant as well.
- Shins and arches can be kicked.

Consider your body as a collection of weapons and your enemy's body as a collection of targets. The one who uses the best weapons against the most vulnerable targets most effectively will win. Hesitation and slow responses will usually result in being seriously injured or killed. Since mortal combat is the only kind of survival combat, you cannot leave a temporarily or partially disabled assailant or assailants behind to attack you or others again. Under normal circumstances they must be disarmed and restrained until the police can take custody, but under extreme survival situations further actions may be necessary to prevent future assaults.

92 How can I survive emergencies in the outdoors?

Most survivalists engage in some kind of outdoor activities such as hiking, fishing, camping, or hunting. In some cases, survivalists engage in high-risk activities such as whitewater rafting, caving, rock climbing, or cross-country skiing. These are excellent survival-skill-building activities, but they can generate serious survival emergencies in themselves if proper safety precautions are not taken. Here are some basic outdoor safety rules that should always be followed.

1. Always tell someone where you are going, what your intended route is, and when you plan to return. Failing to do so is probably the number-one cause of people dying in the outdoors.

2. If possible, always travel with one or more companions. If one of you is injured, the other can provide aid or go for help. The preferable minimum number for any high risk or off-trail activities is three capable adults. In an emergency, one can provide help for the victim while the third goes for help, or two can carry the victim.

3. Know your limitations. You are not an expert in everything. Listen to those who are more experienced. When you are in a new region or environment, pay attention to locals. A swamp survivalist is not a desert survivalist and a "country boy" may not survive in the city, and vice versa.

4. Don't be afraid to speak up. If a route looks dangerous or the weather is turning, or if for any reason you think caution or turning back is advisable, then say so. Ego and pride should never be allowed to put you or others in danger.

5. Use extra caution when using knives, axes, and other devices that can cause injuries. Even a minor injury can be fatal when help is not immediately available.

6. Watch where you step. You can easily twist an ankle, break a leg, or sustain a serious fall. In some regions, poisonous snakes may be a hazard as well. Being disabled in the outdoors is far more hazardous than at home. Carrying a walking stick is an excellent idea.

7. Always, always carry a survival kit with some form of protection from wind and rain such as a rain poncho, survival blanket, or tarp. The kit should also include flares, a whistle, a signal mirror, energy bars, water flashlight, waterproof matches, and first aid items. You should always have a knife of some kind when in the outdoors as well.

93 With the availability of modern GPS devices, why does a survivalist need to know basic map and compass usage?

While GPS systems are certainly effective and fairly reliable, a true survivalist should always be ready to navigate without the aid of GPS. Even a very basic compass can be useful in finding your way in the outdoors. Dependence on GPS is not a good survival practice. The survivalist must still know basic compass usage and have good map-reading skills. A compass is of little help if you suddenly realize that you are lost, unless you have some idea of which way that you need to go to return. Unless there are good visible landmarks, it may be difficult to orient your map, find your location, and determine your route, unless you have used the map throughout the trip. Normal walking always leads us in a curved path, causing us to circle, even when we think we are going straight. Once lost, it is essential to have a way of determining and maintaining a direct route to safety.

In all but the most remote locations, just maintaining a straight line of travel will take you to a road, river, trail, railroad or other route to safety. Establish a compass bearing that you intend to maintain as a route, then use the compass sight to establish a target such as a prominent tree, hilltop, or rock formation. Proceed to that point and then sight on another landmark on that same bearing and repeat the procedure. If you have followed a compass bearing to your destination, you can then simply add or subtract 180 degrees to that bearing to get the return route. For example, if your bearing on the way from your vehicle to a cabin was 330 degrees, then the return bearing to follow would be 150 degrees. Moving through wooded and rough terrain along a bearing will usually result in some deviations, so you may not get back to the exact spot where you started, but should get close enough to see the destination or be at a point along a road, trail, or river to guide you to it. If the distance to the baseline (road, trail etc.) is

This compass is sighted on a tree at about 80 degrees (slightly north of straight East).

considerable, you may want to set a return bearing a few degrees to the left or right of the exact 180-degree return course so that you know which way to go when you reach it.

Even if you have no compass, you can establish the direction that you think will be most likely to get you to a road, trail, town, or other desirable location and then take a sighting on three lined-up landmarks and then go to the middle one and establish the next further landmark that aligns with the other two and repeat the process to keep moving in a relatively straight course.

94   How can I determine direction when I do not have GPS or a compass?

Determining direction without the benefit of a compass can be difficult, time consuming, and unreliable. Even the cheapest compass is better than having to use these methods, but you should know them as last resort. But watch out for old wives' tales. The idea that moss always grows on the north side of a tree is generally false, especially in thick forests and damp areas. Moss is more apt to grow on the north side of trees that are in the open in dry climates. Here are a few common techniques you can rely on for determining directions.

Finding the direction using your analog watch

1. Hold the watch flat in your hand or palm.
2. Rotate the watch until the hour hand points in the direction of the sun.
3. Between 6 a.m. and 6 p.m. (standard time) a line dividing the distance between the hour hand and twelve will point true south.
4. Disregards the position of the minute hand.

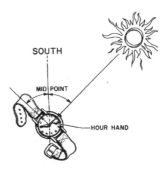

Stick and shadow method of determining direction

Credit: Air Force Regulation 64-4 Vol. 1.

This method is only usable in sunny weather and when you have time to wait for the shadows to move.

1. Drive a stick into the center of a flat open area of ground.
2. Drive a stick at the very tip of the shadow cast by the first stick.
3. Swing a circle around to an equal distance and angle opposite the second stick. Place a third stick at that point.
4. Wait until the shadow moves around to the last stick.
5. Draw a line from the center stick through a point halfway between the other two sticks.
6. This line will point due north.

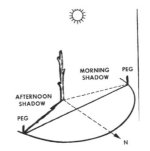

Credit: Air Force Regulation 64-4 Vol. 1.

Finding north by the stars

In the Northern Hemisphere, the Big Dipper is one of the most identifiable constellations. A line through the outer edge of the dipper will point to the North Star and indicate north.

95 What is a key consideration in survival preparedness and emergency action?

The key is to happen to it before it happens to you. This is a survivalist's life mantra. Of course, things will still happen to you, but constantly moving ahead of survival issues (and life issues) reduces the probability of many personal and local survival problems. Obviously, disaster preparedness is a key part of happening to future events, but maintaining your health and building personal economic stability, as well as involvement in community preparedness, crime prevention, and safety measures are all important parts of proactive survival actions. There is a lot more to survival than just having a pack and a plan.

96   How can I survive an active-shooter situation?

An "active shooter" is someone who initiates a shooting and either remains at the scene or in motion, while shooting multiple rounds at multiple victims. Active shooters target crowded locations such as stores, theaters, airports, and public buildings where every round fired may potentially hit one or more victims. If caught in this type of situation, you can be sure that the killing will continue until the police engage the shooter or the shooter has killed everyone in sight. Even the police have admitted that civilians caught in such situations should take certain actions rather than stay calm or try to reason with the terrorists. Below are steps and actions that you can take to survive such an event.

Being Prepared for a Potential Active Shooter

- **Be observant and alert!** In any crowd, you must observe for suspicious behavior. Are people wearing unnecessarily baggy or long clothing? Do some people have suspicious bulges in their clothing or are they carrying odd long packages? Are some people wearing backpacks or leaving backpacks or bags behind? Are some people moving around suspiciously and looking about as if getting ready to take some action? If your sixth sense is telling you to get out or get down, then do it!
- **Make an escape plan.** In a restaurant, shopping mall, theater, or other public building, make sure to constantly be aware of the location of all exits. Exits can be fire doors, windows, over railings, or anything that gets you out. Consider routes to all the exits that offer the most bulletproof cover. If true escape is not safe, then seek any room with a solid door that can be locked and barricaded with heavy furniture.
- **Identify potential bulletproof cover.** While you may hide behind furniture, car bodies, or plaster walls, these will usually not stop bullets. They provide only concealment. Bulletproof cover is offered by brick walls, cement walls, heavy appliances, engine blocks, and other very solid objects. Constantly identify these as places to go if escape is not immediately available.

What to Do When the First Shots are Fired

- **Act immediately!** If you have accepted the possibility of an active-shooter situation and taken the steps above, you can move from denial to action while other hesitate and become victims.

- **Take cover.** If you are already in the shooter's vision or if there is no covered escape route that will not expose you to the shooter, this may be your only option. Get behind the strongest, thickest object possible immediately. Stay low or lie flat. If you are wounded or among those who are wounded, lie down and play dead. Shooters will instinctively shoot anyone they see who is moving.

- **Escape.** If the shooter(s) has their back to you, or you are out of their immediate vision, you have a chance to escape or at least reach good cover before they turn around. Remember that there may be more than one shooter. If you go through a door, get to the right or left of the door immediately and keep moving toward any cover, since the shooter may shoot through the door or follow you out the door. If you choose to run, leave your belongings behind and keep your hands visible and fingers spread. Remember that you will be running toward police who do not know you from the shooters. Do not stop to ask the officers for information. Avoid pointing and screaming. Others outside the building may be unaware of the situation inside and could be about to enter. Tell them that there is an active shooter and to get away from the building.

- **Hide and barricade**. If you cannot exit the building safely, your next best option is to get into a securable room. Turn off the lights. Be sure everyone's cell phone is on silent. Block the door with anything available and get out of sight. Quietly call the police and tell them where you are.

- **Engage.** Police agencies have now recognized that civilians may need to take action on their own before law enforcement arrives to save themselves and others. If you cannot escape or find cover and the shooter continues to shoot, your best chance is to distract, delay, or disable the shooter. Discharging a fire extinguisher, throwing a heavy object; tackling, clubbing, or stabbing are all justified in this situation. If you have a firearm, use it! Yes, shoot them in the back if necessary. Shoot for the head as they often have bulletproof vests. If possible, shoot from a low position so your bullets go upward and avoid hitting bystanders. Don't hesitate and don't try to get them to surrender. They will just shoot you. CAUTION: Remember that the police will consider anyone they find holding a gun as the enemy! Once the shooter(s) are down do not pick up their weapon(s), and put your weapon down and your hands up and wait for the police.

- **Communicate.** If not in immediate danger, use your cell phone to call for help. Provide the police with any information that you can, such as the description and number of shooters, location of the shooters, and the type of weapons being used. If you are barricaded or behind cover, provide your exact location and your own description. The police will be getting a lot of calls, so you may get put on hold or even get disconnected. If nothing else, pull the fire alarm to warn others and distract the shooter.

- **Recovery.** If you are lucky enough to have survived such a violent event you are not safe yet, since police are going to be very jumpy upon entry. Shooters have been known to hide among victims, and then escape or open fire at the police. The police will consider everyone present to be a potential threat until they are searched, interviewed, and cleared. Follow police instructions carefully. Raise your hands and spread your fingers immediately. Keep your hands visible at all times. Do not reach for your cell phone or any other object. Avoid making any quick movements toward the officers. If you are carrying a firearm (open or concealed) be sure to immediately tell the police while keeping your hands up.

- **Help others**. If safe to do so, direct others to escape or to shelter. If you have any medical training try to help the wounded until the medics arrive. Stop severe bleeding by immediately applying direct pressure over the wound and/ or applying a tourniquet above the wound. Treating for shock may be an important lifesaving action.

Recognition of a Potential Active Shooter

In most cases, active-shooter situations could have been prevented if others had recognized and reported the shooter's actions and mental state in advance. The next active shooter could be a family member, fellow employee, or neighbor. If you know or encounter someone with one or more of the following traits, contact authorities, employers, and psychological support organizations immediately. Do not confront or argue with such individuals.

- Obsession with extremist and violent political or religious ideas combined with interest in and access to firearms or explosives.
- Increased anger at others such as employers, family, or religious groups.
- Talk of revenge or getting even.
- Increased mood swings, absenteeism at work, drug and alcohol use, and depression.
- Paranoia, hostility, and withdrawal.
- Obsessive interest in violence, firearms, and explosives.

97 What do I need to do to survive a worldwide economic collapse?

The world's economic system is so interconnected that any number of situations could trigger a total collapse of the system. War, a massive electromagnetic pulse, a large-scale cyberattack or any combination of natural and man-made disasters can easily trigger a financial disaster. Even if there is no traumatic collapse, the world economy is likely heading toward a poorer and impoverished general condition. Any economic collapse (slow or fast) would trigger a number of other survival challenges. Civil disorder, revolution, martial law, epidemics, and even war would probably be initiated. The failure of food supplies, police, and municipal services might even be a result of a failed economy.

Obviously the value of stocks, bonds, and cash will decline or evaporate completely. Since it is impossible to predict how soon a collapse will occur, it would not be wise to abandon solid investments and savings, but these should not be your only economic holdings. Shifting enough of your wealth to hard assets that could provide for your needs through a prolonged situation is a wise precaution. You must be able to live and make a living even if all of your investments and savings were gone and you are permanently unemployed. Avoid any dependence on Social Security, pensions, annuities, or disability benefits as these can be lost as well. Can you still have shelter, food, water, and other essential needs after those income sources are depleted? Do you have trade goods and skills to barter for what you need? Do you have the means to recover and rebuild a personal economic foundation in a post-collapse society? Your overall disaster preparedness and self-reliance capacities should be helpful, but in a chaotic economy and governmental collapse, you will need a far deeper survival system.

Real estate is a collapse-proof investment. Buildings provide shelter, a base for post-collapse business, and storage space for survival supplies. Land (even a backyard) can be used to produce food, gather water, and even camp on. Real estate can be rented or bartered when nothing else can. In a collapsed economy, land is the new gold, but it must be owned, not mortgaged. Mortgaged and rented property will be repossessed quickly by banks and the state because of its value.

Nonperishable trade goods including survival gear, storable foods, fuel, batteries, tools, firearms, ammunition, toilet paper, medications, water-filtration products, blankets, coffee, razors, clothing, shoes, soap, toothpaste, and cleaning products will be high-value trade goods. Garden seeds and gardening tools will come in demand as well. Some people will trade a lot for alcoholic beverages and cigarettes despite their low survival value.

The best trade and barter item that takes up no room is your skills and capabilities. The proverbial "handyman" will be more valuable than any lawyer or banker after a collapse. Medical technicians, nurses, auto mechanics, gunsmith, skilled fisherman and hunters, and those who know how to sew, can, garden, forage, and fix things will be on top of the social and economic ladder. Those with the ability to transport goods will also be in demand. Being able to bring in fuel, farm products, and other critical goods in exchange for bartered goods and services will be survival traders. If fuel runs out, bicycles, boats, and even horses could of great value in moving goods.

Arguably, the most important resource in surviving a general financial collapse will be your survival network. Your family, friends, and neighbors will form your survival economy. Building up skills, supplies, and plans with the people around you will be the key to success.

Surviving a long-term and widespread failure of the economy will be the ultimate test of determination and survival skills. Whether civilization recovers as a happy and free society or withers into a depressed and oppressed remnant will depend on how well survivalists mange the challenges.

98 How should a survivalist interact with the police?

The media often portrays survivalists as the enemies of the police. People who are involved in criminal activities or are confrontational with police are not survivalists. Survivalists are not involved in criminal activities, so your interactions (if any) will involve minor issues such as traffic stops or mistakes. The list below provides some helpful tips on what to do to avoid being pulled over, and what to do if you are pulled over.

- Since the media often gives the wrong impression about survivalists and gun owners, avoid having "Don't Tread on Me," pro-NRA, or other bumper stickers on your vehicle as this may automatically up the level of tension.
- If you are armed or have a firearm in the vehicle, tell the officer immediately what it is and where it is. Whatever you do, don't reach for it!
- If you are not in a safe location to pull over, slow down, turn on your emergency flashers, and drive slowly to the nearest shoulder or driveway.
- If pulled over, stop your vehicle in safe spot, lower the driver's-side window. Turn off the ignition and place both hands on the steering wheel.
- Follow the officer's instructions slowly and carefully.
- Answer questions and provide your driver's license, vehicle registration, and, if applicable, your carry permit.
- When interacting with police, it is important to understand the "ladder of authority" rule. The officer will always act to assert a level of of authority slightly above that of the citizen. If the officer starts by using polite tones and respectful terms and you respond with abusive language, the officer will then become forceful. If you escalate to any kind of threats, then the officer must prepare to use force. Any aggressive action on your part requires the officer's use of corresponding force and probably a call for backup and an arrest. Just be cool and polite.
- You could be pulled over by several police vehicles with full lights and siren and they get out with guns drawn. They may be responding to a violent crime committed by someone matching your description or driving a similar vehicle. Stop immediately. Do not get out of your vehicle. Keep your hands in sight. Obey all instructions. This is a very dangerous situation that happens often in urban areas.
- The police do not have the right to search your vehicle without probable cause or a warrant. The loophole is that if they casually say "you don't mind if we

check your trunk" and you say "okay" you just gave up your rights. If you say "no," they may become a bit hostile but they are not likely to go for a warrant without evidence. Of course, if you're sure you only have a spare tire in there, it's up to you.

- Understand that an officer cannot let a potentially dangerous or armed suspect just run away. Someone who has just committed a violent assault, has a weapon, or has threatened to harm others cannot be left to endanger the community. The officer that abandons a pursuit or lets someone run off is held responsible for that person's next crime. This is called "failure of duty." The officer is not obligated to tackle or wrestle with armed or physically superior suspects. Disabling or using deadly force is usually justified. Driving away or running away (guilty or not guilty) seldom ends well.

- If the police think that you may be a suspect or person of interest and start asking you questions related to a crime, ask them, "Am I under arrest or am I free to go?" If they were just fishing they have to let you go, but if they have "probable cause" they may arrest you. Stop talking and get a lawyer.

While survivalists by nature are independent and averse to authority, we recognize the value and necessity of police officers. Most police officers are respectful of citizens' rights. Many survivalists are also police officers.

99   How can a survivalist survive in a gang-dominated neighborhood?

Many urban areas are controlled by gangs, who in turn may be soldiers of drug cartels. Most small-town and even rural areas have a growing gang presence within their populations. There are more than fifty gangs with over 68,000 members in Chicago alone. Nationwide gang membership outnumbers the US Army and National Guard. These organizations drain hundreds of millions of dollars from the economy while killing thousands of Americans. Since these gang members are sometimes unwitting employees of uber-wealthy and powerful drug cartels, the gangs can easily arm their street soldiers with weapons, regardless of what prohibitions are imposed on the citizens. Gangs have also infiltrated the military and have the knowledge to use highly potent weaponry if general disorder breaks out. Once law and order breaks down, these gangs will ravage their own communities and spread terror far into adjoining regions. Nascent gangs in smaller towns and rural areas will become aggressive and will be an added challenge to surviving most disasters.

Surviving in a Gang-Controlled Area

If you are unfortunate enough to live in a gang-controlled community, then being a survivalist is a daily challenge rather than just a future possibility. The fact is that the police only control the spot they stand on while they are there, but at all other times the streets, alleys, stores, and homes belong to the gangs. Those who do not do drugs are often considered with suspicion or are treated as outcasts. Residents are frequently unable to disavow gang members and criminals within their families. Talking to the police or reporting criminal activity is an invitation to being injured or even killed. Having a job, money, or nice possessions is often derided and victimized. And perhaps most troubling of all, children are constantly tempted and intimidated by gangs, drugs and viciousness.

You are already living in a disaster zone, and preparedness for additional disasters is extremely challenging. Survival in such communities is a special skill. Compromising and recognition of gangs may be necessary as long as you minimize your actual involvement. Keeping as low a profile as possible is critical. Appear passive and peaceful, but do not become an easy target. You must keep your children away from drugs and gang membership at all costs.

Participate and support any community efforts to end violence and drugs. Avoid direct "anti-gang" confrontations. Gang retaliations can involve violence against you and your family members. Regardless of the laws or what others tell you, you must be armed. Since burglaries are a common gang activity, you should keep the fact that you own a gun or guns confidential. It is especially important that you keep firearms away from children and adolescents. If they don't know you have them, they will not tell others or be under peer pressure to get hold of them.

If you can escape a gang-controlled area, then do so, but be aware that gangs have a long reach and often follow families to new locations. You will have to detach yourself by abandoning all friendships, affiliations, and even family members who are still involved with gangs. If law and order break down, law-abiding citizens must have a plan to evacuate if possible or fight for survival in place. Families, religious organizations, and other organizations should plan for such situations in advance.

Preventing Gangs from Taking Control

If you live in a suburb, town, or rural area, do not assume that you are safe. Only awareness and preventive action can ensure that you will not find yourself in the grip of gangs. There is no disaster that will be more devastating than allowing gangs to take over your community. Complacency, procrastination, and denial of gang infiltration will breed crime, violence, decay, and destruction in your community.

An increase in graffiti, petty crime, and drug usage in your community are the leading indicators of gang invasion. Immediate removal of graffiti, as well as the active persecution of shoplifting, drug possession, and other crimes must be insisted upon. Community support and involvement is essential. All schools should have DARE antidrug programs and active community crime watch programs that call police at the slightest suspicion; these programs will discourage criminals. Building codes and strict requirements for property maintenance will prevent the development of gang hangouts and drug houses.

Get involved in your community. Insist on strict law enforcement. Support your police and all anti-crime programs. Your safety, property values, future, and loved ones all depend on it. Once in control, these gangs are well-armed, organized, and ruthless. Don't wait until you have to battle them in your streets.

Survival Challenges Near to Gang-Controlled Areas

As economic conditions worsen, gang-promoted crime tends to spread farther out from urban areas. Street crimes, home invasions, and assaults target the less-prepared residents who have more valuables. Carjacking and robberies are common in gang-controlled areas and nonresidents are more attractive targets. Shopping areas and parking lots become hunting grounds for all kinds of criminals. During a true survival situation, these dangers multiply significantly. Being aware, prepared, and armed is a necessary responsibility for a survivalist in such areas. The ability to stay off the streets and defend your home and family by all necessary means is especially important when looting and lawlessness breaks out in such areas.

Gangs must be considered as terrorists and serious survival threats even during normal times, and must be taken into account in any disaster planning. Serious efforts to eradicate this problem remain politically unacceptable. The existence of gangs and their activities will continue to degrade our society until some situation generates a massive confrontation or until they become the dominant force in our society, as they have in many South American countries. This should be prevented at all costs, as local, regional and federal governments in gang-controlled nations are coerced and bribed into cooperating with them, leaving citizens with no hope.

100 If I am on a very tight budget, how can I prepare for survival situations?

If you are already struggling to get by, it can be challenging to cope with the possibility of a disaster situation. The survival market is full of costly supplies and equipment that many people just cannot afford. The survival rule of BTN applies to those on a budget. "BTN" means that having something is "better than nothing." While having significant funds for preparedness is certainly desirable, being short on cash is no excuse for not being able to improve your survival chances. Set a budget and set aside or spend that amount every month for survival-related items or supplies. Here are some ways to build your survival capacity on a tight budget:

- The most important survival supply you can have is water. Do not waste money on bottled water. Clean out large beverage containers with bleach water and then fill them with tap water. Seal them well. Water does not spoil, so this costs you nothing.
- Food is the next high priority for survival. Grocery stores often have cans with dents or torn labels on sale. Products such as pasta, dried bean, rice, and oats that are "expired," are often still good for years, if kept sealed. Check out local food pantries for free storable food items to build up your supplies.
- Thrift stores often have used camping items, sleeping bags, and clothing.
- Yard sales are a great source of camping supplies, stoves, lanterns, and other survival supplies.
- Dollar stores have candles, batteries, lamp oil, and other items at low prices.
- Military surplus stores and catalogs are a source for high-quality knives, tents, sleeping bags, stoves, packs, clothing, and even survival foods. Military gear is as good as or better than sporting goods items and is usually much cheaper.
- Flea markets are a good place to find all kinds of survival gear and a great way to develop contacts and develop bartering skills for an alternative economy.
- While brand-new firearms purchased from reputable dealers are best, you are better off having a good used weapon than none at all. Gun shops and gun shows often have a good variety of reasonably priced handguns and rifles. Try to stick with established brands (e.g., Colt, Smith & Wesson, H&K, etc.) and have someone who knows how to evaluate a firearm help you make a wise selection. You do not want an excessively worn or defective weapon when

your life depends on it. Reloaded ammunition from a reliable dealer is usually cheaper than new, name-brand ammo.

- Explore eBay and other internet sources but be aware that these sites are rampant with scammers and all of your purchases will be recorded by various agencies.

Even if you have adequate funds, there is no point in wasting money on overpriced brands when you can use the saved funds for other supplies. Good budgeting and wise spending are key survival skills.

101   How can I build up a survival library?

Every survivalist will have differing needs for survival knowledge. No one can remember everything they need to know to survive in every situation, so it is essential that a survivalist assemble a library of reference and instructional books as part of an overall preparedness program. While websites, search engines, and online videos are useful tools, they are not a substitute for well-written and illustrated volumes. Storing survival knowledge on electronic devices or depending on access to the internet in a disaster contradicts basic survival reasoning.

The choice of survival reading should be based on what is anticipated and the most probable challenges. Someone living in an urban area would need to have books on self-defense, crime survival, home preparedness, and basic disaster situations, but would not need to know much about wilderness survival, fire building, or animal trapping. Someone who lives in more rural areas or spends a lot of time in the outdoors (e.g., camping, fishing, hiking) may need more traditional books that cover outdoor survival skills. A basic first aid manual is a good place to start. There are many books on surviving natural disasters such as tornadoes, hurricanes, floods, and earthquakes that would apply to almost everyone. Military "survival" manuals are usually slanted toward outdoor and escape-and-evasion skills, but some also cover nuclear, chemical and biological survival. Once you have the basic survival information for getting through the most likely situations with water, food, shelter, and other essentials, you can start buying books that enhance your longer-term needs. Advanced medical skills, foraging, gardening, bartering, food preservation, and general self-reliant living is your "phase two" library. Do not overlook books that address the psychological and philosophical aspects of survival.

Building up a good variety of books about outdoor and home emergency survival can be essential. You cannot be dependent on the internet for information once a disaster situation is in progress.

Will and mental conditioning are as important as supplies and skills. Reading stories of how others survived disasters or being lost throughout history can be entertaining, inspirational, and educational.

102 Should trade and barter be part of a survivalist's skill set?

Our modern society has become so accustomed to price-and-pay acquisitions that the paradigms of trade and barter have been lost to most of the population. Short-term disasters and emergencies seldom require such skills, but a general financial collapse or long-term disaster would certainly generate such opportunities, in triggering what is called survival wealth. Survival wealth means that you have everything you need, and also a lot of what others may need or want after a disaster. As essential supplies run out and emergency aid agencies fail to provide for needs, those who have both stocked up sufficiently and put aside extra supplies of trade goods to build their survival economic system, survive better and recover faster. Those who did not prepare will be willing to bargain for essential goods, but many will also be ready to use violent means to take what you have. If you are bartering out in the open, you likely will attract attention. The would-be survival trader must put a heavy emphasis on security and armed defense.

Some of the goods available on the barter market are likely to have been stolen or looted, and the dealers are likely to be armed and prepared to take what you have without any trade. Be aware of this and know who you are dealing with. It is best to have armed companions and deal in a safe location.

If you have adequate funds to build up a barter stock and an adequate and secure place to store them, here are a few suggested items.

- water-purification tablets and filters
- Oil lamps, lamp oil, and candles
- Rechargeable and non-rechargeable batteries
- Battery-powered radios
- Flashlights
- Coffee
- Sugar
- Flower
- Vinegar
- Salt
- Spices
- Vegetable seeds
- Prescription drugs and painkillers
- Matches and lighter
- Soap and detergents
- Toothpaste

- Plastic sheeting and tarps
- Alcoholic beverages
- First aid supplies
- Sanitary napkins
- Disposable razors
- Alcohol and disinfectants
- Toilet paper
- Tobacco products
- Duct tape, wire, paracord, rope,
- Sewing supplies
- Ammunition in common calibers such as .38, .45, .40, .22, 9mm, .308, 5.56 NATO, 7.62 Russian, etc.
- Fuel

Other items will depend on your location and anticipated needs. Recreational items such as children's toys, playing cards, and paperback books will gain value as the situation lengthens.

103   Is basic home safety a necessary part of survival preparedness?

Being prepared for a major disaster will do little good if you or your family experience a serious injury or personal disaster because of poor safety practices at home. Over 15,000 people die each year in the United States as a result of home accidents. The great majority of these deaths are preventable. Conducting a home safety inspection monthly can significantly reduce the chances of you becoming one of those statistics. Focused inspections are much more effective in actually identifying hazards. The list below is by no means a complete list of potential hazards, but can help identify the most common hazards found in the home. Think "what if" and assume a "worst case" situation as you go through each room. Safety and survival are inseparable practices.

Tripping and Falling Hazards
- Are there loose carpets or throw rugs, exposed extension cords, items on the stairs, or worn stair treads that could cause a fall?
- Are railings on stairs loose or broken?
- Are damaged ladders and step stools still in use?
- Do the tub and shower have grab bars installed?
- Are your sidewalks free of cracks and holes?

Fire Hazards
- Are there working smoke and carbon monoxide detectors in the basement, hallway, and each bedroom?
- Does your family have a fire evacuation plan that everyone knows and has practiced?
- Do you have fire extinguishers in the workshop, garage, and kitchen?
- Are flammables stored outside the house or in fire-safe metal cabinets away from ignition sources such as furnaces, stoves, and hot water heaters?
- Is your fireplace inspected and does it have a good screen to catch sparks?
- Is your furnace professionally inspected annually?
- Are there exposed or frayed wires or plugs?
- Are all appliances grounded with three-pronged plugs?
- Are paper towels, curtains, packages, and aerosol cans a safe distance from stove tops and other sources of ignition?
- Are matches, lighters, and other fire starters kept away from children?

General Emergencies

- Do you have a phone and flashlight next to every bed?
- Do you have a fully stocked first aid kit?
- Are firearms and ammunition stored securely and kept out of reach of children?

Chemicals and Medications

- Are all medications stored out of reach of children?
- Are all acids, corrosives, poisons, and flammable household cleaners kept in locked cabinets out of the reach of children?

104　Is there any way to reduce my stress levels and calm my nerves during a survival emergency?

When something really bad happens, we get a surge of adrenaline that can work for, and then against, us. Once we have escaped the immediate danger, we need to calm our nerves so we can perform the next survival actions. Controlled breathing can help reduce shaking, lower blood pressure, and adjust carbon dioxide levels in the blood. This technique is used by police and military going into combat situations.

1. Inhale slowly for four seconds.
2. Hold that inhalation for four seconds.
3. Exhale slowly for four seconds.
4. Wait four seconds before inhaling again.
5. Repeat until you feel calm and in control.

105 Is being armed necessary for a survivalist?

The combat-related aspects of survival are often overemphasized by non-survivalists and provide a misleading image to the public; however, being appropriately armed must be a part of any realistic survival preparation. As with all aspects of survival preparedness, selection of equipment must be based on anticipated needs.

For home protection against intruders, one should select a reliable handgun. If you feel the need for legal concealed carry, there are many small automatic pistols available and plenty of safe, concealable holsters. Once you acknowledge that a civil unrest or chaotic evacuation situation is possible, you must increase your armament. A shotgun may be effective as a defensive weapon in urban evacuations. A medium-caliber, high-capacity rifle with multiple magazines may be necessary for defending an assault on your home or reacting to threats on the road. Larger-caliber, high-capacity handguns are usually carried as well in these situations. It is best to stick with common military weapons that are durable and reliable, and that use commonly available ammunition. The survivalist should take every opportunity to practice the use of the survival weapon and become familiar with disassembly, cleaning, and how to clear a malfunction.

The AR-15 style rifle is lightweight and durable. It uses 5.56 NATO ammunition, which is common and plentiful. The rails permit the installation of tactical sights, lasers, and telescopic sights. The AK-47 clone below is a bit heavier and a bit less accurate than the AR, but is extremely reliable even without maintenance. The 7.62 mm .39 ammunition is also commonly available.

Automatic pistols come in all sizes. Left to right: full-size 9mm, medium-frame 40-caliber, compact 9mm, and subcompact 380 caliber. The full-size weapon has a seventeen-round magazine down to twelve rounds, eight rounds, and just six rounds for the subcompact.

Revolvers are easy to use and reliable, have a limited number of shots and are slow to reload. The small .38-caliber revolver on the left is good for home protection and concealed carry, but not the best for serious combat. The large .357 Magnum at the top actually holds eight rounds instead of the usual six.

106   If I do not have access to prescription pain relievers, what are my alternatives?

The overuse of opioids and other potent pain relievers is highly dangerous. While keeping old, unused prescription drugs is generally unsafe, most medications can be effective long after their listed expiration dates and should not be discarded if a serious shortage of medical needs is anticipated. Most over-the-counter pain relievers can be used a few pills beyond their recommended dosages for a short time, if necessary. Avoid combining different kinds of pain medications. One exception is that two acetaminophen and three ibuprofen tablets can be taken together safely, providing pain relief comparable to codeine. It might be wise to stock both in your supplies.

107   How can I survive a nuclear event?

While massive nuclear war still remains a possibility, more confined nuclear events and conflicts have become far more probable event. The effects of an actual nuclear blast include massive burns and trauma from blast pressure and flying debris. A person close enough to experience these blast effects and survive will have been exposed to significant and potentially fatal doses of radiation. Radioactive fallout that blows downwind from a detonation or leak can travel for hundreds of miles, regardless of the source. The most probable sources of public exposure to radiation are described below:

- Single or multiple nuclear power plant meltdowns, such as Fukushima and Chernobyl. Such events could result from cyberattacks, earthquakes, or other major disruptions. The safety systems and backup systems at these plants are designed to cope with limited and short-term disruptions. However, there is no such thing as fail-proof. Such events could result in regional contamination in major population areas.
- Terrorist initiation of a limited nuclear detonation, dirty bombs, or the covert spreading of radioactive material in public places. Such events would limit exposure to a limited number of people in a limited area.
- Limited nuclear wars overseas are potential scenarios where a few or even dozens of nuclear weapons could be detonated. Fallout would travel westward to the United States. During the 1960s nuclear testing by the USSR in Siberia, and by France, Great Britain, and the United States in the Pacific was a regular occurrence. Radiation sickness did not affect Americans, but cancer and other illness rates did increase. Limiting any exposure, particularly in the first weeks and months after such an event, would be prudent.

Radioactivity Exposure and Its Effects

The table below provides the estimated effects of radiation exposure. Note that even without the benefit of knowing the dosage in roentgens (a unit of gamma radiation), how soon the symptoms appear, and how many people in the same area are affected, is a good indication of developing disability and fatality rates. Be aware that disability and death rates may vary widely depending on the health and age of the exposed personnel. Lower exposures of fifty to 120 roentgens might be anticipated from distant events such as overseas nuclear exchanges or nuclear power plant accidents. Being close to or downwind of a nuclear detonation or power plant meltdown could result in exposures from one hundred to three hundred roentgens, depending on distance and how long you spent in the contaminated area. Higher exposures would be limited to those directly in or near to a nuclear detonation. Any exposure can increase your potential for cancer and a host of other medical issues in the future. It is particularly important to protect children and adolescents from any exposure, as it is more likely to cause chronic illnesses later on.

Expected Effects of Short-Term Gamma Radiation Exposure

Acute Dose (Roentgens)	Anticipated Effects of Radiation Exposure
0 to 50	No obvious symptoms. Possible minor blood changes
60 to 120	Vomiting and nausea will affect about 5 to 10 percent of exposed personnel within twenty-four hours of exposure. Some fatigue may occur, but no disability or deaths anticipated.
130 to 170	Vomiting and nausea will affect about 25 percent of exposed personnel within about one day. This may be followed with other symptoms of radiation sickness, but no deaths can be anticipated.
180 to 220	Vomiting and nausea will affect about 50 percent of exposed personnel within about twenty-four hours. This will be followed with other symptoms of radiation sickness, but no deaths can be anticipated.
270 to 330	Vomiting and nausea will affect nearly all of exposed personnel during the first twenty-four hours. This will be followed with other symptoms of radiation sickness, prolonged recovery time and a 20 percent mortality rate within two to six weeks can be anticipated.
400–500	Vomiting and nausea will affect all exposed personnel within the twenty-four hours after exposure. Severe symptoms of radiation sickness will last months and 50 percent of exposed personnel will die.
550 to 750	Vomiting and nausea will affect all exposed personnel within four hours after exposure. Severe symptoms of radiation sickness. Few survivors and prolonged recovery time for those who survive.
750 to 1,000	Vomiting and nausea will affect all exposed personnel within a few hours of exposure. Few or no survivors from radiation sickness
5,000	All exposed personnel incapacitated almost immediately, with 100 percent **fatalities** within one week.

Rule of Thumb for Estimation of Total Dosage Accumulated

D= Dosage in Roentgens
I= Intensity of Roentgens per hour
T= Time of exposure in hours
D= I x T

For example: If the dosage rate is found to be 70 roentgens per hour and you have been exposed for three hours, then it is 70 x 3 = 210 roentgens accumulated dosage

Nuclear detonations or accidents will result in the production of radioactive fallout. Fallout is simply radioactive dust that is thrown upward by the blast. Since the heavier particles fall, first they start falling downwind closest and soonest after the blast. This makes these particle the most dangerous. The finer dust will fall further downwind over days and weeks following the initial blast. All radioactive fallout is subject to decay in radiation, so it is most dangerous within the first hours and days after it is created, but continues to radiate at a declining rate for years.

In the event of a dirty bomb or the covert spreading of radioactive materials by terrorists, radiation levels may vary widely and exposure areas will be limited to a few buildings or a few blocks. Those who may have aspirated radioactive particulates or unknowingly spent extended time in contaminated areas may develop varying levels of radiation sickness.

Understanding Radiation

Fallout debris can range from sand-like particles that fall close to the source of a nuclear event to very fine dust that travels hundreds of miles from the source. There are three sources of radiation exposure from fallout.

1. Alpha particles cannot penetrate unbroken skin, but if ingested or inhaled, they can reach unprotected internal organs can have serious effects.
2. Beta particles can cause beta burns if left on the unprotected skin and can cause more serious damage if ingested or inhaled. Both alpha and beta exposure hazards can be reduced by washing or dusting off particulates and wearing an effective dust mask.
3. Gamma rays are like X-rays in that they can penetrate most materials with ease. These rays pass through the body, damaging cells and vital organs. The more intense the gamma radiation is and the longer the time of exposure, the more severe the damage is. In addition to keeping particulates out and off of

your body, you must get out of the contaminated area as quickly as possible and thoroughly decontaminate yourself once out of the area. All clothing and equipment exposed to fallout must be abandoned or decontaminated. Clothing probably will be difficult to clean of all fallout.

Fallout shelters use massive amounts of soil, concrete, and other materials to reduce the amount of gamma radiation from outside that penetrates into the shelter. Additionally, filtering of air reduces the amount of radioactive material that enters the shelter. The more time you spend in such a shelter or even within a massive building or basement, the less your accumulated exposure will be. However, if the area of contamination is limited, such as downwind of a nuclear power plant, prompt evacuation and decontamination would be far more effective than remaining in the contaminated area in any kind of shelter.

Signs and Symptoms of Radiation Sickness

Radiation sickness results from the damage that gamma rays cause to the cells and organs of the body. How soon the signs and symptoms appear and how severe they are is a good indication of exposure rates and potential mortality. Initial symptoms include nausea, irritability, vomiting, diarrhea, and general fatigue. These symptoms may disappear after a few days, but reappear within one to two weeks with more serious symptoms of hair loss, hemorrhaging, and bleeding under the skin. Compromised immune systems will result in fever, infections, and disability. Vomiting, diarrhea and internal hemorrhaging result in severe dehydration. The sooner that these symptoms appear after exposure the lower the survival rate will be. Radiation sickness is not contagious. Exposed but decontaminated victims cannot "infect" family members or caregivers.

What to do if you are or think you are being exposed to radioactive fallout

- Get out of the contaminated area as fast as you can to reduce total exposure rates.
- Immediately put on a dust mask or improvise a respirator from dampened cloth to keep particles out of the body.
- Dust off any contamination on your clothing.
- If possible, wear ponchos, raincoats, plastic bags, or other waterproof and dust-proof clothing. Be sure to have your head covered to keep particles out of your hair.
- Once out of the contaminated area, carefully remove contaminated outer garments. Dust and wash skin, hair, and feet as thoroughly as possible. Remove the dust mask last. Leave contaminated clothing and material well away from shelter.

- Decontaminate any food cans, utensils, and equipment before use.
- If available, take potassium iodide pills or liquid per dosage instructions.

Treating Radiation Poisoning

In addition to preventive use of potassium iodine tablets, there are other measures you can take to improve your survival chances and shorten recovery time.

- Maintain hydration with vitamin- and electrolyte-fortified water. When and if oral hydration cannot be tolerated, the use of intravenous fluids or fluid enemas may be necessary.
- Strong iron supplements should be given to combat severe anemia and weakness.
- Antibiotics should be given at the first signs of fever or infection as the immune system may not be able to fend off even minor illnesses or infections.
- Burns and wounds must be treated with special care to avoid any kind of contamination.
- Since internal bleeding often occurs in radiation poisoning, aspirin should be avoided.
- Milk of magnesia or Pepto-Bismol may be used to reduce diarrhea and vomiting.

Radioactive Decay and the Rule of Sevens

Although heavily radiated areas can be unsafe for decades, most contaminated areas will become safer and safer as time passes. This is because of radioactive decay. Simply put: radioactivity declines by a factor of ten for every sevenfold increase in time after the initial event. This is known as the Rule of Sevens. So after seven hours, the residual fission radioactivity declines 90 percent, to one tenth its level of one hour. After forty-nine hours, the level drops again by 90 percent. So now it's just 1 percent of the lethal dosage it was after one hour. After fourteen days, it drops a further 90 percent, and so on. After fourteen weeks, the rate drops even faster.

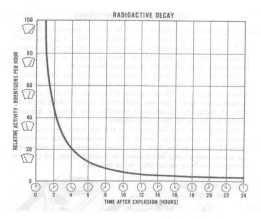

The chart figure at right illustrates a typical fallout footprint. The size of the fallout area footprint depends on the size and altitude of the initial dust plume and the strength and direction of the wind. If you

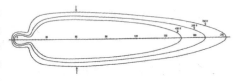

know what happened and where, you can make a pretty good guess as to what direction to evacuate toward. Lowering levels indicate the best way to go, but if you are moving downwind your exposure time will still be higher than if you move at right angles to the wind's direction.

Radiation Detection Instruments

There are a lot of reasonably priced older dosimeters and survey meters available. Uncalibrated radiation detectors sell for about $20, while used calibrated survey meters sell for about $80 and new ones sell for about $150. There are also more modern nuclear radiation detectors and monitors on the market. These range in price from $180 to $300.

Regardless of calibration, any detected exposure levels ranges or area radiation above normal is cause for concern.

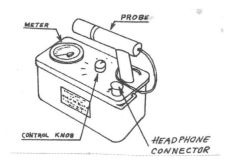

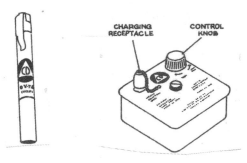

Surplus civil defense survey meters such as the CV-700, 751, or 720 can be purchased at reasonable costs. Some are calibrated and others are not, but calibration services are also available. These CD V-742 pocket dosimeters and CD-V750 chargers are also still available. These are used to register personal exposure rather than area radiation.

Dosimeters are intended to be worn in the pocket and checked frequently to determine how much radiation the wearer has been exposed to. They come with a charger and instructions. A charger and two dosimeters retail for about $40.

Additionally, potassium iodide is a specific blocker of thyroid radio-iodine uptake. Taking potassium iodide effectively prevents the thyroid gland from being saturated with harmful radio-iodide from fallout contamination that can lead to cancer. Fourteen 130 mg. potassium iodide pills retail for about $20.

108 What kind of pack should I use for my evacuation and survival packs?

The selection of a pack depends on your budget and the situations you anticipate using it in.

A basic evacuation pack is intended for short-term endurance, and so carries limited contents. This is basically a day pack. It still should be reasonably durable and comfortable to carry. A pack in a teardrop shape with well-padded shoulder straps, which can hold fifteen to twenty pounds, is sufficient.

A true survival pack must be a larger, high-quality, multi-pocketed backpack with, wide comfortable shoulder straps and preferably a waist belt to distribute the load. There are plenty of good military and commercially designed bags meeting these specifications. Be sure there are attachments and/or pouches on the front straps for you to place items such as a compass, weapon, knife, etc. that you may need in a hurry. The pack should also include plenty of outside pouches for small items and tie-downs to secure sleeping bags and ponchos. The size of the pack should match your carrying capacity and survival needs. Avoid bulky outdoor packs with frames as they are designed for trail hiking, not survival and escape situations. Smaller waist or butt-bags are good for a field survival kit or backup survival, kit to keep in your vehicle. Although military-style packs are well designed for survival, they tend to attract attention that you may want to avoid. There are a lot of non-camouflage packs and even luggage that comes with shoulder straps that may work for you. These usually come in dark and subdued colors as well.

A variety of survival and evacuation packs. The small survival kit hanging on the tree would be okay for short-term emergencies. The tan pack below could be a bugout bag or evacuation bag. The larger, camouflaged bag in the center would be a full survival pack. On the right is an inconspicuous carry-on bag used as a small survival pack and a small, green day pack that could be an inconspicuous evacuation kit.

109   What should a survivalist do if lost or stranded in the outdoors?

Being lost in the woods is the classic survival situation. Many people die each year from exposure, dehydration, and other causes related to having become lost in various outdoor environments. Such problems are not confined to amateurs. Even experienced survivalists can get in trouble when they become complacent or overconfident. Most of these problems can be avoided by letting others know where you are going, what your route will be, and when you should be returning. Using a map and compass to maintain constant knowledge of where you are is far easier than finding your location once you realize you're lost. A survivalist could be forced to flee into an unfamiliar area or take an off-trail route for various reasons. The unprepared can be caught in a sudden rainstorm or blizzard. You could be injured or disabled and not be able to get back to civilization or your camp.

A true survivalist is never lost. You may not be able to identify your location on the planet and others may not know where you are, but you are right there and you own that place and situation.

Take charge, evaluate your situation, resources, and capabilities, and make decisions.

In most normal "lost" situations, it is recommended that you stay in place and wait for rescue.

This assumes that rescuers will know that you are missing and they will know where to look for you.

Thrashing around and exhausting yourself is definitely not a good plan. If you are sure that rescue is not likely, make a plan and take a route that maximizes your chances of reaching help.

Because humans have a dominant direction, you will always walk in a circle unless you can move toward an easily visible landmark or follow a terrain feature to maintain a straight line. If no landmark is visible, you can maintain a straight line of travel by lining up three trees or other landmarks in a row. Walk to the second tree and then line up the trees behind with another tree. If you can follow a straight line long enough, you will usually intersect a road, trail, railroad track, or stream that you can follow to civilization. Creeks run into streams, and streams run into rivers. Follow flowing water when possible. Try climbing a tree or hill to spot landmarks that you can move toward. Following the slope of the land downhill usually leads to roads, streams, and towns. If you camp until dark, you may be able to see light from houses or towns or headlights moving on distant roads that were not visible during daylight hours. Towns and highways also cast a glow on the clouds that may indicate a promising direction to go toward. Take bearings and head in that direction after dawn. Night travel is hazardous and should be avoided.

Regardless of your intentions to stay put or walk out, you must not permit yourself to become exhausted, dehydrated, wet, or cold. If it is raining, snowing, or you are caught with inadequate clothing, shelter and warmth are your first priorities. You may have to wait out a rainstorm or blizzard and conserve your strength before trying to travel. In such cases shelter building and that survival kit will be lifesavers.

110   How can I signal for help if lost, stranded, or injured in the outdoors?

Attracting attention is the first priority. In many cases just the sight of smoke, the sound of a whistle, a red flag, or gunshots will cause investigation by someone. Three dots, three dashes, and another three dots is Morse code for SOS. Three well-separated fires, three smoke sources, three timed whistle blasts, three gunshots, three fires, three smoke columns, or three flashlight blinks will be recognized by most as a distress call. A large "SOS" laid out with clothing or branches, or dug into the sand can be used to attract rescue aircraft.

The man is sighting through the hole on the military signal mirror found in his survival kit. Any reflective object can be used in an emergency.

111 What is the single most important survival tool a survivalist can have?

There is no single item that defines, establishes, and sustains an individual's survival, self-reliance, and freedom more than the knife. The knife and, its predecessor the spear, was in use long, long before the arrow, sling, or firearm. Flint blades predate almost any other man-made device. In fact, the identifier "Saxon" in the term Anglo-Saxon comes from the name of the long, heavy-bladed knife called the *seax*, which was often carried by the Anglo-Saxons. Carrying the *seax* was the mark of a free man. Slaves, of course, were prohibited from carrying arms.

Today, virtually everyone uses some kind of knife in their daily lives. The possession of a knife imparts a huge survival and self-defense advantage to anyone. If you have nothing else with you, a knife gives you a chance to survive. Not carrying a knife of some kind is essentially surrendering your survival potential to luck and the whims of nature and man. The prepared person will carry a pocketknife or a pouch knife throughout the day. He or she may keep a larger survival knife or hunting knife in their vehicle or other accessible location.

Further, there should be a well selected set of blades for outdoor activities stashed in a survival pack. One may carry a heavy four- to six-inch blade length belt knife for heavy work. A small thin-bladed pocketknife for fine work and maybe a Swiss Army–type knife or multi-tool with a variety of blades and gadgets as well. Some multi-tools even have LED flashlights and fire starters included. Some "survival knives" come with a match compartment in the handle and a compass in the butt. These are good for backup caches or extra knives, but most are weakened by the hollow handle and may break during heavy survival use. (The exception will be covered later in this chapter.) You may want to consider one of the military bayonet/knives that work with the sheath to cut wire. Going cross-country in most areas will mean crossing a lot of wire. The M9 and M10, as well as the AK-47 bayonets, all have wire cutters. Small sharpening stones are often included in a pouch right on the sheath. This is a highly recommended feature. A blade that goes dull or breaks when you need it most is no bargain, but there are overpriced knives where you are simply paying for style or a brand name. Ultimately you have to select your knife set based on as much quality as you can afford. Survival and self-reliance knives can be classified as pocketknives, pouch knives, sheath knives, and combat knives. The following are some recommended selections from several knife experts.

Pocketknives are single- or several-bladed knives that fit into a pocket comfortably and unobtrusively. For our purposes, we can narrow down the description further to imply that a pocketknife is a single or double-bladed knife of no more than three-inch blade length. You want this knife to be thin and light so you can carry it comfortably at all times, but you also strong and sharp. You may want a double-bladed knife so you can have both a larger and a smaller blade. In addition to your primary carry knife, it's a good idea to have cheaper, small knives in every jacket pocket, or even a small one on your key chain so you always have something as a backup.

Multi-tool devices are handy. They include pliers, wire cutters, and other devices that can have important survival applications. These are usually too bulky for the pocket, but come with a belt pouch. Many of the devices require that you open them in order to access the knife blade inside. The knife in this configuration is too hard to access and clumsy to wield. Get one that has the knife blade accessible without opening the plyers, or carry a separate knife.

Pouch knives are those that are carried in a belt pouch or may be kept in other places, but are too large for comfortable pocket carrying. This includes large folders, Swiss Army knives and multi-tools. If your normal apparel is work clothes or blue jeans, you may be able to wear a belt pouch without attracting any negative attention. This provides the opportunity to carry larger and more versatile knives.

Sheath knives are larger, carried blades ranging from the short-bladed USAF Survival Knife, to the US Marine KA-BAR, to machetes of lengths of twelve inches or greater. The actual military surplus USAF Survival Knife and US Marine KA-BAR are good values. Oversized knives are generally not needed. So-called survival knives that have hollow handles for storing matches and survival items are generally cheap and apt to break in hard use, but can be used in backup kits or as "better than nothing" options.

Other Blades: In most cases a good pocketknife, sheath knife and multi-tool is a

Left to right: A small low-cost, two-bladed pocket knife. Basic lock-blade pocket knife and high-end knife with seat-belt cutting notch, safety-lock, and belt clip.

Multi-tool device and Swiss Army knife. Both have a variety of devices and blades. Newer versions of the multi-tool have blades that open and lock from the outside like a regular pocket knife making them much more effective.

Top: Air Force survival knife; bottom: K-Bar style survival knife. Both knives are ideal for survival situations where strength and durability are critical.

complete blade set for a survival situation, but in the backwoods and forests heavier cutting instruments may be helpful. Hatchets and small axes can be attached to the survival pack for use in constructing shelters and cutting firewood. Short machetes are useful both for clearing brush and small trees, and for building shelter. Get a machete with a good sawblade on the back. The saw can be helpful in many survival tasks. There are also combination axe, shovel, and saw tools that may fit your needs.

Top: a medium-length machete with a sawblade on the back; Bottom: a "Recon-Tool combination axe, shovel, and saw. Both are good tools for extended survival situations.

Combat knives are specially designed for fighting and so are not ideal for other survival uses. Combat knives range from small, concealable three-inch blades and throwing knives to boot knives and "commando" knives. While knife fights are possible, they are not probable.

Leaving knives out is an invitation for trouble. They can be lost, stolen, damaged, picked up by children, or even used against you. Keep them in their sheath or pouch and in a safe location when not in use. Clean and lightly oil multiblade knives so they open freely when you need them. Knives are not intended for prying or hammering. Keep your knives sharp and clean. Learn how to properly sharpen all of your knives.

A classic Sykes-Fairbairn style combat knife. It is designed for combat and so is not the best choice for a survival blade.

Your choice of a knife will depend on both your anticipated uses and your worst-case emergency needs. No one knife will be the best for every situation. You should have at least one high-quality pocketknife, pouch knife, and sheath knife, and carry all three if possible when in a potential survival threat situation. Carry more than one knife if possible. Cheaper knives that are stashed in various locations (e.g., vehicle, office, pack, etc.) will be far better than nothing if you are unable to access your primary blade.

112   How can I survive a disaster if I live in an apartment or condominium?

People living in an apartment or condominium are at a huge disadvantage compared to those living in a separated house or duplex. An apartment resident's survival chances are dependent on the actions or inactions of the other residents. Once a fire starts or looters are given access to one apartment, all hope of survival is lost. These risks are amplified if the survivalist resides on an upper floor and/or in an urban area. Unprepared residents are liabilities at best and will likely be a source of danger to the survivalist. The more tenants there are, the greater the hazard. The wise survivalist should seek the lower floor of a small apartment building with only six to eight other apartments. Most apartments usually do not have enough room for storing large quantities of water, food, and other supplies. Municipal water, sewers, heat, and gas are more likely to fail and alternatives are much harder to provide in an apartment dwelling.

Certainly short-term utility interruptions, storms, or other "normal" emergencies can be coped with by having a few gallons of water, several days' worth of food, candles, flashlights, and other supplies on hand, but more severe or extended situations will usually make sheltering in place untenable. Once other tenants and neighbors become desperate and civil disorder breaks out, you may be trapped and overwhelmed. The capacity to evacuate with or without a vehicle must be a priority for apartment-dwelling survivalists. Evacuation has considerable risks, but it likely to be necessary when a true, long-term, large-area disaster develops. Since you are more likely to need to fight off looters and even fight your way out of the building and out of the area, the apartment survivalist should give more attention to weapons. In addition to a handgun for personal home and street protection, a short shotgun with self-defense or buckshot loads may be necessary. You will also need to stock and carry more ammunition. If you are stuck anywhere above the second floor you must have an alternative way to get down. Escape ladders and even strong knotted ropes should be part of your supplies.

The previous Mossberg 500, twelve-gauge "camper" model came with a pistol grip (no stock). This was easily replaced with an Advanced Technology folding stock and a five-round shell holder. This could be a good choice for the apartment-dwelling survivalist that may need to deal with multiple assailants and threats.

If you must consider sheltering in place, it may be worth the effort to gradually introduce your fellow tenants to preparedness and defense without letting on that you are ahead of them.

113 Is camping an important activity for a survivalist to engage in?

The classic image of a survivalist is of someone out in the woods by a campfire or in a tent. In truth, the majority of survival scenarios do not relate to camping situations, and many survivalist are focused on surviving assaults, fires, long-term self-reliance, or other non-camping-related issues. Camping may not be practical or affordable for every survivalist. However, camping and acquiring camping skills and equipment can certainly enhance survival capacity in many ways.

Backpacking and primitive, out-of-the-pack camping is a healthy hobby and a huge benefit for those for whom long-term evacuation from civilization may be necessary. A few backcountry hikes and camps test both your capabilities and equipment, and is highly recommended for those who can do it.

Domestic camping at a campground or state, or national park is valuable to any survivalist individual, family, or group as it provides an opportunity to build unity and teamwork while actually using self-reliance skills and equipment. Many essential survival items are also camping items. Camp stoves, tents*, camp heaters, sleeping bags, water filters, packs, axes, and dehydrated foods are necessary items for home survival as well. Camping also requires one to have sturdy boots and outdoor apparel that will be important in many survival situations. Fire building, navigation, camp cooking, tracking and other outdoor skills have survival application as well. Taking up hunting, fishing, and edible plant foraging can enhance your camping and survival skills greatly.

The ability to camp in winter and other cold-weather conditions should be the goal of the camping survivalist. If you truly believe that you may have to camp out or even camp at home in an emergency, you must consider that such a situation can occur at any time of the year and last for an extended time. Tents, sleeping bags, clothing, and other gear that are sufficient for mild weather may be completely inadequate for rain, snow, or freezing cold. Camping in these conditions is the only sure way to find out.

The camping experience builds confidence and a true sense of self-reliance beyond just reading and buying equipment. An experienced and well-equipped camper will be far ahead of the non-camper in many emergency situations.

---

*Tents may be erected inside a home to conserve warmth in cold weather when electricity and fuel are interrupted.

114 How can I control my fear in an emergency and control my fears of future events?

Fear and anxiety are unavoidable elements in any survival situation, and therefore both deserve special attention when managing our mental state. One definition of fear is that it is a psychological and biological reaction to real or perceived threats to life. Of course, we all fear bodily injury and death, but we may also have fear for other people or fear for the loss of property or freedoms. Fear can manifest itself in many ways. The knot in the stomach, the inability to concentrate, the urge to run, headaches, loss of sleep, nausea, and loss of fine motor skills are some manifestations of fear. Fear is normal and must be expected and accepted. Fear can save you or doom you depending on how you manage it. Sometimes fear is an indicator of what you should avoid. At other times, the thing you fear is the very thing you must do to survive. If the object of fear didn't matter it would not be feared, therefore it requires action and management by you. Fear should stop you from taking unnecessary and foolish risks. Fear should not misdirect you into harm's way. Fear should not be allowed to get between you and an objective of worthy value.

Fear begins with our physical and psychological environment. Each person has his or her own list of potential threats. The nature of these threats depends on many factors including the immediate situation, age, knowledge, health, financial situation, past experiences, vocation, lifestyle, and location among other factors. You may be expected to fear the smoke coming in under your bedroom door or of losing your job, but regardless of the understood expectation, you are still afraid. This is where the threat or no-threat response comes into play in order to determine an appropriate response. There are three states of threat response: ignorance, awareness, and preparedness.

Ignorance may be deliberate or accidental. There are those who simply avoid any source of enlightenment. These persons may be lazy or just avoid any kind of challenging information. This is an example of being deliberately ignorant. On the other side of the coin, accidental ignorance can happen to even the most educated and responsible person. Let's face it; no one can anticipate everything that could happen. That "bolt out of the blue" can catch anyone off guard. Ignorance may be bliss, but it can also be fatal. In this case, there is no fear here only because there is no awareness.

Awareness of that which is to be feared is an essential survival skill and instinct. At this stage, the main source of fear is the recognition of threats for which we are inadequately prepared. This is true fear and it comes in two varieties. There is "chronic fear" of bad things that are anticipated in the coming weeks, months, or years. Examples include fear of economic collapse, fear of declining health, fear of being a crime victim, fear of an epidemic, or fear of a terrorist attack. Symptoms of chronic fear include loss of sleep, inability to concentrate, anger, depression, use of drugs or alcohol, poor decision-making, headaches, and loss of appetite. Chronic fear must be recognized and corrected before it leads to even more real and immediate threats to your life and freedom.

Acute fear is an immediate threat to your existence or freedom such as some smoke coming under your door, a gun aimed at your head, freezing in the wilderness, or being on a sinking boat. Symptoms of acute fear include nausea, shaking, loose bowels, psychological paralysis (freezing), and loss of fine motor skills, tunnel vision, and fight-or-flight reactions. The boosted adrenaline and other fear-generated physiological reactions can help save you if controlled. Here you have to act fast but also act right. Even the best trained have been known to panic, but training and mental conditioning are your best defense.

Preparedness is the state where a fear has been recognized, managed, or neutralized in advance. Preparedness requires that the psychological, physical, and material requirements of threat response have been addressed. The psychological aspects are addressed through training and mental conditioning. Building self-confidence in the required abilities, having faith, developing a personal mission, and having a plan are effective ways to psychologically prepare for fear-generating situations. How one addresses the physical aspects of a hazard will depend on age, sex, physical condition, and overall health; but regardless of these factors, there are steps that can be taken to improve physical preparedness. A healthy lifestyle including weight control, regular exercise, and medical checkups is always a good idea. Stocking medications and having devices that compensate for any physical limitations is important. You must ask yourself, *if disaster happens, do I have the strength and endurance to survive*? If the answer is no, then improve your condition, plan ways to compensate for your problems, or do what you can to avoid that situation. Material preparedness is simply having the necessary items to avoid, neutralize, or survive a hazard. Survival kits and home preparedness are addressed in other chapters and need not be covered here. It should be said be said that the possession of survival items can compensate for some physical limitations and impart some level of psychological comfort but the physical items alone can give false confidence.

Both acute and chronic fear can be divided into three categories. These are fear of the unknown, fear of pain (physical and mental), and fear of one's own inadequacies. While these can never be completely removed from our minds, they can be anticipated, managed, and reduced.

Fear of the Unknown

In the movies, it's always the monster you don't see that is the scariest. Fear of the dark, fear of the future, and fear of other people are all forms of this fear. Fear of going someplace or doing something for the first time is one of the most widely experienced examples of fear of the unknown. In its chronic manifestation, it is a source of constant worry that wears us down and holds us back. In its acute form, it is better known as fear of the unexpected. It is the unexpected situation that jumps up and forces us to make fast choices without knowing much about the situation. For example, you wake up to the sound of the smoke alarm and you don't know what caused it. Fear initially seizes you. You may suddenly realize that you do not know where you are, and panic can make you do things that make your situation much worse. While it is easy to say, "Expect the unexpected," it is by definition impossible to do. However, there are things you can do to reduce the potential dangers of fear and panic generated by the unknown and unexpected. While some events are truly unpredictable, others are unexpected because we just don't want to think about them. These can be substantially reduced by a processes known as what-if analysis. As the name implies, what-if analysis is the process of mentally considering what the result would be if an undesirable and hazardous situation occurred and mentally dealing with that result in advance. *What if I am bitten by a snake out here? What if that guy approaching me intends to assault me? What if I can't get home in this blizzard? What if that smoke is from a big fire?* You can use this process as soon as you recognize a potential hazard. You do not have to wait until you smell the smoke or hear the snakes rattle. A fear of something unknown can also be reduced by deliberately going at that fear through education and experience. Learn more about the things you fear and if possible gain experience with them in a safe manner. Planning is an especially effective way to reduce chronic fear.

Convert the fear of an undesirable event into a plan to cope with it. Instead of focusing on *what if I lose my job?*, focus on the plan. If you lose your job, then you will cut spending. Instead of thinking, *Those people are going to kill me*, think *I can avoid or counter them if they do attack*. By applying what-if analysis to potential acute fears and planning for things you chronically fear, these fears can be greatly reduced. Doing these things does not make you paranoid. Anticipation and mental preparation for potential challenges reduce anxiety and contribute to a calmer and more confident psyche.

Fear of Pain

Most people find pain to be unpleasant. Used here, pain implies physical pain from injuries and illnesses, the more subtle pain of heat, cold, hunger, and thirst, and the psychological pain we may experience from shock and grief at losses. For example, we may put off going to the dentist when we know we should, or we may delay putting a pet down. It is normal to avoid pain and in most cases it is wise, but fear of pain can work against our best interests, as it does in those two aforementioned examples.

How you react to pain is a result of your experiences and culture. But no matter who you are or where you come from, be assured that the pain will come. Knowing this, you can plan for the pain by treating the injury, seeking shelter, or taking pain relievers before it hits you. Here again, planning and preparation can reduce fear. Knowing first aid, carrying medicine, or having experienced cold and hunger can greatly reduce the fear of pain. You must not let pain break your will. As long as it hurts, you are alive, and as long as you are alive you have a chance to beat it. In some cases you may even have to do things that cause you physical or psychological pain to assure your survival.

Fear of Personal Inadequacy

Most people will acknowledge that they have some inadequacies. We all have mental and physical limitations that make us fear situations. We all fear the social implications of admitting that we don't know something or that we can't do something. We fear the real hazards of being unable to shoot straight, climb a cliff, stop severe bleeding, or know the way out of the woods. We are afraid of not knowing what to do, of not doing the right thing, or of not being able to do the right thing. We fear our own shame and the disapproval of others. This fear most often manifests itself in a failure to act. We see a danger, but we don't want to say or do anything that would make us look silly. You may not take a class or try a new skill because you fear failure. Those things you fear are often the exact things that will provide the greatest rewards and best chances for future survival. There are two things you can do that will help to deal with this fear. First, you must accept that inadequacies are normal and that everyone has them. But success and survival depend on not letting such fears stop you. Outright failure is better than not trying. The second method of fear reduction is to define and adopt a life mission of continuous self-improvement in order to reduce your inadequacies and prove to yourself how good you can be.

Fear is a very powerful force that can doom those who should survive and save those who might otherwise perish. It allows the weak to subdue the mighty, and the few to intimidate the many. It is why small forces can send whole armies into retreat and why whole populations can be enslaved by a brutal few. Being able to manage and overcome fear is vital to staying alive and staying free. Courage is not being unafraid. Courage is being afraid and doing the right thing anyway.

115 What causes the most deaths from severe injuries and illnesses?

Hypovolemic shock plays a major part in the death of victims of severe external or internal bleeding, large-area burns, and many communicable diseases. Loss of blood due to a severed artery will quickly (in seconds) drain the body of necessary fluids. Burns result in sustained fluid loss. Many illnesses cause hemorrhage, diarrhea, vomiting, and sweating while inhibiting oral fluid intake. Fluid losses lower blood pressure and affect organ functions. Recognition of the potential for shock and the signs and symptoms of shock are critical survival and lifesaving skills. Shock is certain to result from serious bleeding, but may also result from unseen internal bleeding and from other kinds of injuries. The first signs of shock are evident when the victim becomes agitated, restless, and anxious. They will exhibit cold wet skin, profuse sweating, pale skin, and extreme thirst, eventually progressing to dull eyes or dilated pupils, nausea and vomiting, and shallow, labored breathing. If not treated immediately, unconsciousness and then death will follow. If available, call 911 immediately. Quickly stop severe bleeding if present. Place the victim in the prone position and elevate the feet twelve to eighteen inches above the ground. Use a blanket to keep the victim warm. But avoid exposure to excessive heat. Calm and reassure the victim. Splint fractures and bandage injuries as needed. Do not give liquids, as this may only produce vomiting and further complications. You may moisten the victim's lips.

116 If help is not available, what can I do to prevent dehydration in injured or ill victims?

Dehydration is one of the primary causes of death, as it is a result of shock, heatstroke, radiation sickness, and many communicable diseases. If emergency treatment is not immediately available and the patient is fully conscious, oral hydration can be sustained using the following solution: Eight teaspoons of sugar and one teaspoon of salt to one liter of water. Provide small four-ounce drinks every hour.

Caution: giving water or other liquids to an unconscious, semiconscious, or seriously injured patient may cause them to vomit and aspirate, eventually causing pneumonia. Generally these patients can be rehydrated by intravenous methods at the ER.

117 What kinds of weapons should a survivalist have in a true survival pack?

A true survival pack must provide supplies and devices for all contingencies. This includes methods of hunting and self-protection. While the survivalist may carry a rifle, shotgun, and/or handgun *with* the pack, there are some weapons that should be kept in the pack itself. These provide backup and alternative weapons.

Compact Survival Bows and Arrows

Large, complex bows are too large for practical survival applications, but the smaller take-down, compact, ultra-compact, and survival bows offer an alternative to (not a replacement for) firearms. The advantages of these weapons are:

1. They are silent and thus will not attract unwanted attention. This advantage may also permit a second shot at game or fowl
2. They use retrievable, reusable ammunition and you can even make arrows in an emergency.
3. The skill acquired using a bow and arrow could help you to make an improvised bow and arrow under extreme conditions. Practicing with a bow and arrows costs much less than with a firearm.
4. They are versatile and can be used for hunting both small and medium game, as well as fishing, line throwing, and other techniques
5. Survival bows take up very little room and are relatively inexpensive.

Carrying a survival bow and some arrows in your pack or vehicle gives you some important options in a survival situation. For this reason, consider placing one in your survival kit.

Typical survival bow and four arrows. Note that the arrows break down for compact carry as well. This forty-five-pound pull bow can be assembled in less than one minute.

Survival Slingshots

While not as deadly as bow and arrow, slingshots definitely have a place in the survival pack. The advantages of slingshots include:

1. They are silent and do not attract attention. You can usually get multiple shots at small game without disturbing them until you get a hit.
2. Practice is virtually free, and practice makes perfect. I remember making shots with my slingshots that I would have a hard time doing with a firearm.
3. Slingshots are cheap, light, and take up very little space in the pack.
4. Modern survival slingshots are powerful and can achieve velocities of 450 feet per second, and effective ranges of 250 yards or farther.
5. While slingshot projectiles lack the penetration of arrows or bullets, they are effective against small game and can be lethal to humans if hit in the head.
6. Slingshots are cheap. You can purchase a fairly powerful slingshot for about twenty dollars or even make your own. Some models have optional arrows, sights, and ammunition stored in the handle.

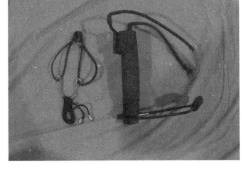

Two extremes. The very small and cheap slingshot on the left is very compact but has limited power compared to the much larger device on the right. That one has greater range and power at the expense of taking up more room in your pack. Wrist-rocket-style slingshots that permit greater power and accuracy are recommended for survival kits.

There is really no reason not to include a slingshot in your survival pack. Include some 000 buckshot or small ball bearings, as conveniently sized rocks are not always handy.

Compact Survival Rifles

A commercial version of the Air Force AR-7 survival rifle can be purchased at most gun stores. They come as-is, with a rather bulky floating stock, but weigh a mere 2.25 pounds. The stock takes up too much valuable room in the pack, but can easily be replaced with an after-market, folding stock with handgrip. Extra eight-round and twenty-round magazines are also available. Designed for survival, this rifle is reliable and tough. With the stock folded it takes up very little room, adds only a few pounds, and provides a reliable firearm for small game and minimal self-defense. A few hundred rounds of .22-caliber, long-rifle ammunition takes up just a few inches of space in the pack

You can add any or all of these devices to your pack without sacrificing much room and adding only a little total weight.

AR-7 with barrel removed and stock collapsed is only fifteen inches long and takes up very little room in the pack. The barrel can be attached in a few seconds.

118 How can I assess and determine my highest risk factors?

There are three steps to improving your ability to survive emergencies and become more self-reliant. The first step is to determine the true threats to your life, liberty, and property. Once this is done successfully you can move on to the second and third steps of planning and preparation, respectively. Hazard analysis is critical. The key factors in determining what events are the most dangerous to you and your family are probability and severity. These factors may be mitigated by intended or unintended preparedness factors already in place. You can calculate the degree of hazard posed by a specified event, based on how likely it is to happen to you, plus how much harm it will do to you, minus how much protection and preparedness you already have. For example, long-term loss of utilities (water, heat, electricity) may be likely and have dire effects but you may have a fireplace, swimming pool, a generator, or other tools that would greatly reduce this hazard. Of course, this is just a guiding concept, not a rigid mathematical formula. The table below illustrates this method by assigning a numerical value of 1 (unlikely) to 5 (certain), as the probability and severity increases. The hazards you would rate at 9 or 10 would require the highest priority in your preparedness and planning program. Those with a rating of 7 or 8 will need attention but you may be able to put off actions to address hazards rated at 6 or below. Keep in mind that as you plan and prepare for the high-priority hazards you will probably reduce the probability and severity of the other similar hazards.

Probability > Severity v	Certain To Happen In The Near Future 5	High Probability To Happen In The Near Future 4	Reasonably Likely To Happen Some Time 3	Potentially Could Happen Some Time 2	Possible But Unlikely To Happen 1
Catastrophic Results: loss of life 5	10	9	8	7	6
Very Serious Results: death, injury, property damages 4	9	8	7	6	5
Serious Results: Serious injuries, property damage 3	8	7		5	4

Moderate Results: Minor Injuries, and Property damages 2	7	6	5	4	3
Minor Results: small injuries, inconvenience, etc. 1	6	5	4	3	2

Using the method above you can produce your own survival preparedness matrix, as illustrated below. We list the potential hazards along the left side and then assign a probability and a severity value. Next we subtract a factor for any mitigating risk reduction or preparedness actions already in place. For example: cleaning out the attic and garage could reduce the home fire probability, two incomes can reduce the severity of job loss, or a shelter could reduce the effects of a tornado. The chart above illustrates this method, but the reader may choose to simply assign priorities based on potential effects and probabilities with this concept in mind.

Hazard: potentially harmful to your life, liberty and property	Probability: How likely is it this will happen to or affect you?	Severity: How severe are the consequences to you?	Mitigating Factors: Subtract preparedness that already exists	Hazard Rating	Planning and Preparedness Priority
Home Fire	3	5	-2	6	2
Epidemic	3	5	0	8	1
Job Loss	4	3	0	7	1
Nuclear War	1	5	0	6	2
Street Crime	4	4	-2	6	2
Civil Unrest	2	3	-2	3	5
Tornadoes	1	4	0	5	4
Earthquake	1	3	0	4	3
Flood	3	4	-1	6	2
Economic Collapse	3	4	-2	4	3

In the above example assume that smoke alarms, fire extinguishers, and good housekeeping have reduced the probability of a house fire; that security systems and weapons have reduced the crime and riot factors; and that pumps and sandbags are ready for a flood. Of course your list of hazards will be different than the ones used in the example above. Some factors that will create your personal hazards include.

Your health and physical condition: Chronic ailments, smoking, weight, etc. can drastically affect your survival options.	**Your job and hobbies:** Working in high-risk jobs or partaking in dangerous pastimes can create hazards if you do not follow procedures and wear necessary protection.
Your financial situation: Often overlooked. You can't buy emergency supplies without funds.	**Your travel means and routes:** More diving through dangerous urban areas or backcountry roads increases risk.
Your lifestyle and habits: Hanging around bars and clubs, risky associations, time in crowds where diseases spread, etc.	**Your selection of friends and associates:** If your associates are involved in risky activities, it's time to get away from them.
Your family: Your family's strength and support can greatly increase everyone's chances to survive and thrive in hard times. Weak and untrustworthy members can bring everyone to ruin.	**Your community:** Is your community divided and/or controlled by gangs and drugs? Are your neighbors unwilling to be responsible and prepared?
Your knowledge: Your general education will increase your financial strength so you can build your survival capacity. Your survival skills broaden your options and self-confidence.	**Your climate:** Obviously the weather in your area can affect your survival chances greatly but every area has its own set of hazards. There are no safe areas.
Your home: Here many people die of fires, carbon monoxide, falls and other totally preventable causes. A safe and secure home should be your first priority.	**Your location:** Is your location prone to earthquakes or floods? Are you downwind of chemical plants? Would your area attract looters?

You have at least some control of most of the above factors. You can change your habits, increase your knowledge, move to another location, and change your friends. You definitely should remove fire hazards from your home and install smoke and carbon monoxide detectors. It is impossible to find a totally safe area, a completely safe job, or a risk-free lifestyle. You can, and should, however, consider the risks to your life, health, liberty, and property versus the benefits. For example: a good-paying job as a police officer may be worth the benefits if you determine to follow all risk-reduction procedures. Smoking or letting combustibles accumulate in your basement are risks with no benefits at all. Assuming that you have recognized your main risks and taken steps to avoid or reduce them where practical, you now have to prepare to survive and thrive through risk-laden challenges.

Survival Planning

Survival planning means thinking through the chronology of the hazard event and having an effective action ready to minimize the event's impact on your safety, liberty, and property. Reading the stories of those who have survived similar situations can be very helpful. Doing a walk-through or what-if analysis of the potential event can also be helpful. Your plan should assume that nothing is "normal": phones will not work, roads will be closed, family members will not be home, etc. etc. The plans should be simple and easy for everyone to understand. You might have a house fire escape plan, a crime intruder plan, a power outage plan, and a long-term survival plan.

Survival Preparedness

Survival Preparedness means gathering the equipment and acquiring the skills needed to survive the anticipated emergency. Depending on the anticipated hazard, this could mean a fire extinguisher and a first aid kit, or it could mean serious survival training and a fully stocked shelter.

If the key to effective medical action is diagnosis, then the key to an effective plan to survive and thrive in today's world of hazards is analysis. Having the right stuff when you need it and where you need it depends on accurate analysis of your hazards and vulnerabilities.

119   How can I survive a wildfire or forest fire?

Wildfires are becoming more and more common throughout the United States as a result of droughts and longer dry seasons. In past decades, most destructive wildfires occurred in the West and Southwest during the late summer and early autumn months. Additionally, in recent years the development and population of heavily forested regions have grown dramatically. We now have hundreds of thousands of people inhabiting dry forests and grasslands. Now climate shifts have created massive fuel shortages, while the presence of more people has increased the sources of ignition and the danger to life and property. Climate shifts have also resulted in higher winds and more frequent lightning, resulting in fast-developing firestorms that can overrun communities before effective warnings and evacuations can be initiated. Prolonged droughts have resulted in all-year fire seasons throughout the western states. Even more troubling, grass fires and forest fires have recently devastated southern and eastern regions that were previously considered immune to these hazards.

Since it is not possible for the individual to prevent a wildfire that originates outside of their property, the only choice is to prevent the fire from reaching you and your home. If a wildfire has fuel and your home is on its path, then there is little chance of preventing ignition of the structure: at that point your only option is to evacuate.

Creating a Defensive Space

The only effective way to prevent a wildfire from reaching your home is to remove the fuel path and create a defensive space where the fire has nothing to burn. In the case of grasslands, dry grass and shrubs must be cut and removed before the dry season arrives. In the case of forests, you may need to cut down and remove trees from thirty to as far as two hundred feet away, depending on the slope. If your home is located on a slope you will need to clear brush and trees much farther on the downhill side. Unless you own the land for five hundred or more feet in all directions from your home, it will be necessary to get your neighbors to clear their defensive spaces as well. A defensive space will not guarantee that embers will not come down on your roof. During a wildfire all fire departments will be fully employed and your power may go out as well. Even if you have municipal water, the pressure may be too low to help put out embers and sparks. A pool or pond connected to a gasoline- or battery-powered pump should establish an inner defense. Backpack water-pump sprayers and shovels may also be helpful in extinguishing embers and hot-spot fires. The following charts and tables will be helpful in creating an effective defensive space.

The Three Rs of Creating Defensive Space

REMOVAL	Completely remove the entire plant. Cut down trees, dig up shrubs, and plow under grasses.
REDUCTION	Thorough pruning of trees and bushes, regular mowing of grass, and removal of all cut wood and mowed grass.
REPLACEMENT	Substitute less-flammable vegetation such as flowers or low growing vegetables

Defensible Space Recommendations

Steepness of terrain → Vegetation Type ↓	Home on flat or gently sloping ground	Home on moderate 20 percent to 40 percent slope	Home on steep slope of more than 40 percent
Grasses and widely scattered shrubbery	**30 feet**	**100 feet**	**100 feet**
Shrubbery and small trees	**100 feet**	**200 feet**	**200 feet**
Forested areas	**30 feet**	**100 feet**	**200 feet**

Recommended Practice for Types of Dead Vegetation

Type of Fuel	Recommended Practice
Standing dead trees	Remove these within the defensive space.
Down dead trees	Remove if recently fallen, If embedded in the ground, cut off exposed branches.
Dead shrubbery	Remove these within the defensive space
Dried grass and wildflowers, etc.	Once they are dried out, cut down and remove from defensive space.
Dead needles, leaves and branches, and twigs on the ground	Clear all leaves, branches, and twigs. If pine needles are dry, remove until you reach damp decaying layer. Do not remove decomposing material.
Firewood and other combustible debris	Keep firewood, grass clippings, and combustible debris at least thirty feet uphill from the house.
Unused and decaying structures	Old sheds, barns, and other structures within the defensible space offer a bridge for the fire. These must be removed.

Ladder fuels can elevate a small grass fire into a crown fire if not removed. A bush below a small tree that is then next to a tall tree can escalate the danger significantly. Remove shrubs and bushes from below trees to at least three times the distance from the lowest tree branch to the ground.

Evacuation

Regardless of how well you have established your defensive space and fire-suppression systems, a wildfire may overwhelm you. You must always

Dry grass and dead trees provide an easy path to the home in the background for fire.

have an evacuation plan and not hesitate to evacuate. Wildfires (any fires) move incredibly fast and in unpredictable ways. If you can see the flames and smell the smoke, that fire could be on you within the hour or less. A brush fire with eight-foot-high flames will travel at about five miles per hour without a wind and consume three thousand acres per hour. A shrub and brush fire with flames averaging ten to twenty feet will move at six to eight miles per hour, consuming up to five thousand acres per hour. High crown fires with flames one hundred feet or higher can race through forests and jump roads and rivers at up to three-hundred yards per minute. If ash begins to fall in your location, the fire may be only minutes behind. Delaying is not an option. Don't be complacent or procrastinate!

Have a wildfire escape plan ahead of time. If possible move children, pets, elderly people, and valuables to a safe location outside the fire zone as soon as wildfire is detected in the area and before evacuation is mandatory.

Pets and children pose special problems for evacuation. Plan on how you are going to get them to safety quickly as a fire roars toward your home. Determine what you are going to take if you need to evacuate and have those items in packs, bins, or loaded in your vehicle well in advance. Fire-resistant safes are rated to protect the contents for a limited time and temperature. Read the labels before you buy one. You can have ammunition cans in holes ready to fill and cover if needed. Have a wildfire survival kit (see below) for every family member.

Surviving a Wildfire

A wildfire may start so close to you or move so fast that you may be overtaken at home or on the road. If you can see flames and smell smoke you need to move quickly away from that direction. It is always best to move upwind and downhill from the fire. If you can hear crackling and feel heat it may be too late to escape. You cannot outrun a fire at this point. Look for lakes or ponds to submerge in or seek ditches, bridges, culverts, caves and overhangs that may offer some protection. If nothing else is available, find a large green grassy area or low spot and lie down. Even digging a small indentation in the soil will help. Remove all synthetic clothing that may melt to your skin. Cover your head and face with wet non-synthetic cloth to avoid breathing in hot air and soot. If you have enough water, moisten your clothing. Lie flat and the fire may pass over you. Stay calm and wait until the fire passes. Remember that the ground may be still be hot and embers may be hot enough to ignite your clothing and burn your skin. Move carefully downhill and upwind of the fire through burned-out areas to reach safety.

Wildfire Survival Kits

Wildfire survival kits are not like FEMA evacuation packs or bugout bags. If you survive and escape the fire, you will reach help fairly quickly. You don't need food and a lot of gear for prolonged survival. Your equipment needs to be focused totally on surviving and escaping the fire.

- You should have at least six N95 dust/mist respirators to keep soot, smoke, and heated air out of your lungs.
- You need to have a pair of good safety googles to protect your eyes from sparks and debris.

- You need to have a good pair of long-sleeved work gloves to move hot embers and debris.
- Have a wide-brimmed "boonie" hat to keep sparks and embers off your head and neck.
- A powerful flashlight can penetrate smoke and help rescuers find you.
- One or two quarts of water to wet clothing and douse sparks.
- A good camp shovel may come in handy if you have to dig in or clear a path.
- You will need plenty of water to wet down your clothing, hat, and masks, and put out sparks on your clothing and skin.
- If you feel you are likely to be trapped and have to dig in and let the fire pass over you, you may want to invest in a fire blanket. These are flame-resistant and heat-resistant covers that you can put over yourself as you lie flat in a low, clear area or a trench you have dug. You can find these at FireSafetySource. com. One of these weighs just five pounds, comes in a pouch, and costs less than one hundred dollars.
- Of course you will want to have copies of all of your identification, insurance, medical, and financial documents.

In this case, a lot of food and additional survival gear is just going to slow you down.

Wildfire Safety Tips

- If you see a wildfire and have not heard a warning or evacuation order, call 911. Do not assume that it has been called in.
- Be sure you are included in any email or call alert system in your town or county.
- If you do get an order to evacuate, do it immediately, but let others know where you are going and then contact them when you have safely arrived.
- Keep your vehicle fully fueled and in good condition. Have your emergency supplies and a change of clothes in the vehicle.
- After a wildfire, only return when authorities say that it is safe to do so.
- After a fire has passed, maintain a fire watch and inspect for smoke, sparks, and embers throughout the house, attic, and roof.
- Discard any food that has been exposed to heat and smoke.
- Be sure to photograph all damages for insurance purposes before cleaning up and removing debris.
- If you or anyone with you is burned, cool the burn with cool water and cover with a sterile bandage. Go to an emergency room or aid station for treatment.
- If you inhale smoke and/or hot air, you may suffer respiratory disorders later. Go to a hospital and report this exposure.

120   Should a survivalist be good at identifying and using edible wild plants?

Any survival skill is good to have, but for most situations, wild edible plants will not be a significant food source. One should also be aware that going from a normal diet to one based in edible wild plants can cause significant intestinal distress. At best you may be able to supplement your rations with a few wild edibles. Most urban and suburban survivalists are unlikely to be lost in the forests and dependent on foraging. Some easily identifiable edibles—dandelions, plantains, and purslane are common even in the city lots. Wild raspberries and strawberries are easily identifiable. There are books and even cards that can help identify edible and poisonous plants. Since poisoning is the last thing you need in a survival situation, it is best to avoid trying to eat any wild plants. In the gravest extreme when food supplies are exhausted and rescue or escape is improbable, you can use the following method to determine if a plant is edible.

1. Smell the plant to detect strong or acidic odors. Obviously if it smells unappetizing, it probably will not be suitable.
2. Break the plant into its parts (root, stem, leaf, and flower) and test each part separately. Some plants have highly poisonous parts while other parts are quite edible. If part of a plant proves to be edible that does not imply that it is safe to eat other parts. Each part that you plan to eat must be tested individually.
3. Place the plant part you will be orally testing on the inside of your elbow or wrist for about fifteen minutes. If a rash or irritation develops, the plant should be rejected as a food source. If no irritation develops, then continue.
4. Consume nothing but clean, safe water for eight hours prior to oral testing.
5. Touch the plant part to your mouth and see if there is a burning sensation.
6. If after fifteen minutes there is no reaction to your lips, place the plant part on your tongue for fifteen minutes.
7. If no adverse reaction, chew thoroughly and hold in you mouth, but do not swallow.
8. If there is still no burning or irritation after fifteen minutes, swallow the food.
9. Wait eight hours. If no ill effects, prepare about one-half cup and consume that. If there are no ill effects after eight more hours, you can include this plant in your diet.

This is a time-consuming test to establish each edible plant, but a handy thing to know for a survivalist who anticipates extended wilderness isolation.

121 Should a survivalist be skilled at knife fighting?

While survivalists usually carry some kind of knife whenever possible and are bound to include a serious blade in their survival kits and bags, combat knives are rarely considered. Of course any knife can be used as a weapon, but survival knives are designed as a tool first and weapon second. The most probable scenarios for a survivalist are (1) being confronted by an unarmed assailant, in which case a knife of any type settles the issue; or (2) being confronted by a knife-wielding assailant when the survivalist then uses a firearm to deal with the threat. The old adage "never bring a knife to a gun fight" certainly applies here. Knife fighting is best avoided. Even the best knife fighters usually get cut. Often there are no winners, as both combatants may be seriously injured or one or both bleed to death. Use a knife against a knife only if you have no better weapon and cannot retreat or escape the attack. The only rule in a knife fight is to survive. If such a confrontation is unavoidable, here are a few tips.

A typical commando-style knife.

- An assailant will often focus on your blade, leaving himself open to disabling kicks and strikes.
- If you can access anything to use as a shield, do so.
- Wrap a coat or other material around your arm to absorb and deflect stabs.
- Throw things to distract the knife-wielding assailment. Even throwing small objects or liquids will force reflexive distraction.
- Bright light, dirt, sand, and aerosol sprays can be used to blind the assailment.
- An amateur knife fighter may thrust or slash wildly, offering a chance to move in and grab their knife arm, twisting it and smashing the back elbow joint to dislocate it, while smashing your forearm and elbow against their face and your knee to their groin.
- In the absence of a firearm, the best defense is to use both of your feet to run like hell if you can.

If you elect to carry a fighting knife you can choose the Sykes-Fairbairn two-sided stiletto that was favored by World War II commandos or the curved karambit used in Far Eastern combat principles. Such combat knives are not effective for most other survival uses.

122 Should survivalists use and depend on advanced technology?

Survivalists should make maximum use of currently operating technologies to gather information and build networks, but should not establish such systems as permanent or essential systems. Here are some guidelines and cautions for using modern technology as survival tools.

- Non-networked, freestanding self-reliance technologies such as solar power, wind power, and hydroponics should be embraced and combined with older technology to build sustainable self-reliance systems, but dependence on interconnected, internet-dependent, or externally controlled systems should be avoided.
- Technologies that permit other entities to monitor your communications, purchases, habits, movements, and even listen to your conversations are counter to basic survival philosophy and practices.
- Dependency on or addiction to cell phones, social media, and artificial intelligence devices effectively negate any pretense of survival capability.
- Use good internet security. Avoid opening unidentified emails. Avoid online banking, change passwords frequently, do not put information on social media, and do not respond to online surveys. Buy at stores with cash when possible to avoid having your purchases and habits tracked and your banking information available to the world.
- Real, active training and group building is the only reliable way to survive and remain independent in the future.
- Useful survival information may be gathered from the internet, but depending on that source in an emergency is foolish. Hard copies are still the only reliable storage method.

Regard technology as a tool to be used, but not depended upon. Use the tools, but do not let the tools use you.

123 Should survivalists organize or join survival groups and prepper clubs, or should they remain isolated?

Many survivalists prefer to keep their concerns and preparedness efforts confidential. The bad press given to survivalists makes it difficult for many to admit to being a survivalist or to discuss survival-related subjects with others. The modern survivalist may be surprised to find how many closet survivalists are among his or her neighbors and associates. Survivalists are no longer part of a small subculture. We are an important part of a responsible and important movement.

Beyond surviving immediate, short-term future emergencies, the survivalist is going to need to work with others for sustained survival and recovery. No one person can stay alert and on guard twenty-four hours a day; no one person can provide medical aid for him- or herself and others simultaneously; no one person can have the skills, knowledge, and physical capacity to do everything needed in any sustained disaster. You will need a prepared family, team, organization, community, or network. A group may adopt some or all of these survival-related missions.

124   What kinds of missions can a survival group have to retain a positive focus?

Most groups of any kind fail without a clearly established mission. The following four suggested mission statements for a survival group provide a guide to help you and your group or family create a coherent mission statement. Having this sorted out creates a path to security and independence for the group and its members and also establishes responsible goals for community support.

Member Emergency and Preparedness Support

Support members and their families in achieving the capability to survive and recover from common short-term natural and man-made disasters without the support or interference of outside agencies. To this end, provide training, information, equipment, and supplies in affordable and practical programs.

Member Liberation through Self-Reliance

Support members and their families in achieving increased self-reliance and independence from centralized or failing sources of essential needs such as food, water, energy, protection, and medical aid. Work to create a semi-independent lifestyle and economic network that reduces risks, regulation, taxes, and waste, while improving life security and quality.

Strength through Networking and Mutual Support

Recruit and develop new members, while developing networks with other organizations with compatible and like-minded goals. These networked communities of self-reliance will be able to exchange instructors, share resources, combine operations and purchases, and engage in trade and barter for critical supplies and skills in an emergency.

Community Service and Education

Advocate and educate for preparedness and self-reliance through community-based programs including educational seminars, speakers, and fairs. Support government and private community preparedness and emergency response programs wherever practical.

Additionally, to build a successful survival group, stay focused on your mission and set goals and schedules based on that mission. Broaden your leadership base to include as many others as possible. Other helpful tasks include:

- Welcome new members and give them something to be involved in. Attrition is inevitable. People move away, change jobs, or become ill. If you are not constantly bringing in new members your group will evaporate over time.
- Constant and constructive activities are essential. These include meetings, field trips, training, community outreach, and classes. Review of plans, show-and-tell, and disaster drills can all be ways to sustain interest. Don't overlook non-survival-related activities such as picnics or holiday parties.
- Focus on the quality and compatibility of your group, not the size. Three or four devoted and loyal members is better than dozens of inactive and unreliable ones. A group much larger than fifty persons probably needs to divide and network.
- Setting limited goals can leave your group dead. You are never ready enough or self-reliant enough. There can be no point at which you are done preparing.

125 What are the dos and don'ts for a new or existing survival organization?

The great majority of so-called prepper or survival groups wither or self-destruct within three to four years. In most cases the cause is related to what they did wrong, or that they failed to do that needed to be done.

Here are some of the things that long-standing, dynamic survival groups regularly do.

- Have an established and positive mission.
- Have a vision of where you want to be one, five, or ten years into the future, regardless of events and conditions.
- Develop a solid core group of leaders and instructors.
- Be ready to work with other like-minded organizations such as fraternal, business, religious, or community groups. In fact, a survival group or emergency preparedness group can form as a subgroup or committee within such existing organizations. Military families do this now.
- Be good neighbors. Get out there when people need help. Support local charity and aid events. Share your knowledge and skills. Even sponsor preparedness or outdoor survival class and fairs.

Here are some of the major errors that have caused survival groups to dissolve.

- Permitting mission creep or diversion. Make sure to stay on point. Getting involved in political activities, religious issues, or other activities outside of survival and self-reliance usually leads to internal problems, misunderstanding, and disillusionment. You can support any and all kinds of groups as their survival consultants and supporters, but not let them divert time and resources from your mission.
- Getting hung up on the "apocalypse of the month." Getting ready for a certain doomsday event leads to a dead end when it fails to happen. True survivalism is about getting ready for anything and achieving increasing levels of preparedness and self-reliance no matter what happens or when.
- Becoming internalized and paranoid. Fifty percent of your activities should be concerned with gathering more members and establishing your level of responsibility. The other 50 percent should be internal activities for the benefit and security of members. This balance assures sustainable growth

- Compromising on membership. No matter what skills or resources they may offer, you must reject and avoid association with those with violent, criminal, or extremist views and ideas.
- Getting discouraged. You will probably have failed activities. You may not get the support you need. Success and the opportunities to succeed only come to those who are out there getting involved and trying. That may be the most important survival attribute of a leader.

Note: No one ever achieved anything from inside a bunker. Those who are underground are dead or at least irrelevant. That's not much of a survival mission.

126 What kinds of military-style training and tactics would be of value in survival situations?

While a survivalist is not a soldier and a survival group is not a military or paramilitary unit, there are several tactical skills and capabilities that survivalists should learn and practice. In today's world, civilians are often the main target of terrorists, gangs, and foreign or domestic paramilitary forces. Any large-scale collapse and civil disorder would result in situations where combat capabilities and military tactics would be essential for survival. It is important to understand that for military organizations the objective of taking a hill, building, or town takes priority over personal or group survival; but for a survival family or group, survival *is* the primary objective. In most cases, the tactics explained in this chapter should be used defensively or to facilitate safety and security. Exceptions where aggressive tactics might be applied would be for rescue situations.

The individual survivalist who has not served in the military will have more difficulty dealing with combat situations. Most military tactics assume that the participants are healthy, relatively young, and well trained. Most survivalist families will have mixed capabilities and cannot afford any casualties. For these reasons, survivalists should avoid military-like combat situations whenever possible. However, when plunged into a life-or-death scenario, any level of training and tactical capability will confer a great advantage. Most assaults, ambushes, and raids will be initiated by untrained gangs and groups that will be dealt with effectively by the application of basic military movements. Even if you are assaulted by some kind of organized paramilitary group, your knowledge and training will confer a greater chance for survival and escape. While it is not practical to fully explain all of the necessary techniques and tactics in a few pages, what follows are the basic principles. The survivalist should study military texts and take advantage of any opportunities to experience practical training.

Weapons-Use Skills

Tactical usage of firearms goes well beyond the basic self-defense use of a handgun that is necessary for normal civilian crime-resistance applications. The survivalist who anticipates a potential military-like combat situation must become proficient in the use of high-capacity tactical rifles. Most current tactical rifles are based on either the US Military AR-15 or Russian Kalashnikov AK-47 designs. These are classified as assault rifles, but are highly effective in self-defense and survival, as well as hunting for game. The AR-15s and similar designs are reliable and accurate, but require more care than AKs. AK-47s are not as accurate as the AR-15s, but are extremely reliable and can function without maintenance and cleaning for extended periods. The ARs use 5.56mm ammunition that is

232

plentiful and therefore may be available in survival conditions. The AK-47s uses 7.62 mm Russian ammunition that is available during normal times, but might become scarce in the future. In any case, the survivalist should have no fewer than two thousand rounds of ammunition and six spare thirty-round magazines on hand along with spare parts and cleaning kits. If you anticipate combat in urban areas or within buildings, short carbine or folding-stock versions may be worth consideration. Reflex sights might also be a useful addition. Although combat rifles have an effective range of 400 meters or farther, the defensive use will probably be at much closer ranges. The survivalist should be proficient at hitting man-sized targets at about 100 yards before developing longer-range capabilities. If possible, fire at least 200 rounds from your primary survival rifle quarterly. Fire more often if practical. Then practice disassembly and cleaning. You should also practice rapid magazine changes, as well as firing from kneeling, standing, and prone positions and from behind cover. These options are usually available at combat ranges and training facilities.

Typical commercial version of the military AR-15. This one has a folding stock and a reflex sight mounted on the accessory rail.

A commercially made version of the Russian AK-47. This one has a folding stock in place of the more common widen stock.

All survivalists should understand the difference between cover and concealment. Concealment simply means that you are in a place where the enemy cannot see you. This may prevent your being shot at or at least reduce your chances of being hit, but it will not stop a bullet if the enemy does decide to fire in that direction. Use cover that is a truly bulletproof or at least bullet-resistant location, such as behind the engine block of a vehicle, a brick wall, a large tree, or a trench. Armor-piercing rifle ammunition can penetrate auto bodies, several inches of hardwood, cement blocks, and appliances. Cover only lasts until the enemy maneuvers around it, so it is a temporary refuge to buy time for escape or counteraction.

Route selection while on the move is a critical military skill. Under hostile conditions, you cannot just walk down the road and expect to survive. The obvious and easy path is usually going to lead you to destruction. Use your binoculars to view your route in advance. Consider where you might be ambushed or trapped. If you cannot avoid these places, have a plan to scout them and clear them rather than just walk into them. The routes for daytime movement and nighttime movement are usually different. In the daytime you do not want to be out in the open or silhouetted for an enemy hiding in the woods or rocks. You will want to stick to those areas where you are best concealed and can find cover immediately. Stumbling at night through heavy foliage and rough terrain may be more risky than using flat terrain, but you must avoid being silhouetted. Stay low. Use low ground and stay quiet. Moving down gravel roads is particularly risky at night, as the crunch of feet is easily heard. Avoid moving on any kind of road. Stick to the shoulders, where movement is better concealed and cover is closer at hand.

A survivalist should be able to move safely under fire. Shuffling along, marching or casual walking are not good enough under threat conditions.

Movement under combat conditions is always risky. The advantage always lies with the potential ambusher or sniper. If possible, avoid moving through any potentially hostile area. Stay put or take a longer and safer route if possible. If you must move about, do so in a combat-ready condition.

Whether you are moving in daylight or at night, discipline is essential. Talking in normal tones is prohibited, and whispering should only used for essential communications. Everyone's gear must be secured so it does not squeak, rattle, or clang. Have everyone jump up and down before starting out to detect and secure any noise sources. Any shiny or glowing objects should also be covered. If extreme stealth is needed, rags or heavy socks can be placed over shoes. Only muted or camouflage colors can be worn. This includes shoes and socks. White flashlights should never be used at night. Red-lensed flashlights, preferably covered under ponchos or coats, can be used to consult maps if absolutely necessary. Needless to say, cell phones are strictly prohibited.

Bunching up and lack of attention are invitations to assault. Even if there are just two or three people, they must maintain a distance from each other in a staggered formation, so that they cannot be taken or shot all together. The distance depends on the terrain and the visibility. At minimum, each member should maintain a distance of at least four to six feet from others in all directions. This distance can be a bit farther in open terrain, but may need to be closer on dark nights. Members should always be in position to support and protect each other in a staged formation that permits firing in multiple directions without endangering fellow members.

In every group, one person must stop, squat, slowly turn around, and listen every few minutes. A group must have clearly assigned directions of responsibility such as front and right flank, left flank and rear, etc., to assure 360-degree coverage. Larger groups should send out a point man and have a designated rear guard. Additionally, a flank security person or team may be needed in some kinds of terrain. The point man's task is extremely fatiguing as it requires constant vigilance in all directions. This task should be rotated frequently. Normally, the point man should be just in view of the lead person in the group. The rear guard usually stays closer to the group, but must stop periodically and turn around to watch for enemies. The people at the rear of the group should always be checking to be sure the rear guard is still there and safe. In a single-file column, every other person should keep guard on the alternating sides, with the front person watching ahead and the rear person regularly checking behind. In a double column, the right row covers the right side and the left row covers the left side. Frequent rest stops are necessary, but are not a time for conversation or bunching up. Select a well-concealed spot off roads and paths for these stops. Put out 360-degree security. If a small group stops, they should all face outward while resting.

Crossing Lanes

Crossing roads, railroad tracks, and other open lanes is particularly hazardous under hostile conditions. Anyone looking down that lane has a clear field of vision and fire. Cross at a narrow point or a sharp bend where your action is least visible.

There are two schools of thought about crossing. You can send one scout across to secure the opposite side and in advance. This may only alert the enemy that more are coming. The other tactic is to all rush across at once before the enemy can react. Both methods have advantages and risks. You do not want to wander across or loiter. If you know the crossing will be opposed and cannot find another route, you can use fire and maneuver by having half the group fire to pin down the enemy, while the other crosses and then fires to cover the second group's crossing; this is an exercise a survival group should practice. If you have smoke bombs, these can be of great help in such crossings.

Diversion and Misdirection

Diversions and misdirection are key military skills. Smoke or fireworks can be used to draw attention away from you while you escape or maneuver. A false campsite can attract looters and raiders while your real site remains hidden. Dummy defenses and bunkers can draw fire away from your true location. False trails can be laid away from your true route.

Counter-Ambush Techniques

The ambush is the most deadly situation a group can find itself in. The best way to avoid being a victim is to avoid movement, especially at night. The advantage always lies with the ambusher who chooses the place and time and remains hidden.

Since it is most likely that survivalists will not be encountering well-trained and heavily equipped ambushers, basic ambush avoidance and counter ambush methods should be effective.

An ambush may simply be a group of shooters hiding along the side of the road or in buildings where they have good concealment. A more sophisticated ambush would involve a roadblock or debris to stop the group in the kill zone. Sharp turns in a road or down a path can permit ambushers to fire down the length of your group as well as from a flank. These are the locations that a survivalist on the move must be especially aware of. The point man should be constantly alert for signs of activity, noises, and shadows, and signal the group to halt if anything looks or feels suspicious. Since the group may already be in or near a kill zone, it may need to back out and consider ways to avoid or eliminate the threat. There are several counter-ambush tactics that are effective depending on the situation. The survival group should be well trained in each counter-ambush drill.

If the group has not entered the kill zone, the best action is to back out while maintaining good order, and fire if necessary. You can then opt to go around the ambush, or flank them and flush them out of the position.

If the group is well into a kill zone and under fire, you may be able to fire on the ambushing location while quickly running out of the danger zone or crawling to safety.

If quick escape is not an option, then your only other choice is to charge the ambush site with all the firepower you can bring in hope of overrunning or dispersing the ambushers. The one thing you do not want to do is remain in the kill zone and engage in a firefight. The leader must call the counter ambush and the team must execute it immediately. Regardless of training, being caught in an ambush almost always results in casualties. If the ambushers are well trained and/or numerically superior, you may expect very serious losses.

When any kind of counter-ambush drill is executed, your group is going to be dispersed. This is particularly true in heavy forests and at night. Having preestablished rally points and passwords will be critical in reestablishing the group and avoiding additional losses.

Basic Military Maneuvers

Fire and maneuver is the most basic military drill and should be understood by any group that anticipates a combat situation. The British call this tactic "bonding over watch." Simply put, one person or team shoots at the enemy while the other moves to a better position. In an offensive situation, the fire team pins the enemy with fire while the maneuver team moves closer. Then they change tasks so that the maneuver team becomes the fire team, while the fire team maneuvers even closer until the objective is taken or flanked. In withdrawal, the same alternating persons or teams execute the maneuver until they are out of range or into a safe position. While fire and maneuver can be used to facilitate an assault or withdrawal, flanking to the right or left should always be preferred if possible. Frontal assault or a running retreat is generally costly and often disastrous. Survivalists that truly anticipate combat situation should be trained in execution of fire and maneuver.

Field fortifications are a necessary skill for survival. Failure to dig in has doomed many complacent units in the past. Trenches, foxholes, and improvised bunkers provide the defender with a great advantage against even a superior force. When time is short or the ground is hard (rocky or frozen) scraping even a shallow spot with some dirt, rocks, and debris in front is far better than lying in the open. A pile of dirt in front of a trench or foxhole may give away your location, so try to camouflage them with leaves and debris.

In general, foxholes should hold no more than two people, but be close enough together for mutual support. Trenches should zigzag or curve. While barbed wire may not be available, interlaced tree limbs and sharpened stakes can be used to slow down assaulters. Fortifications of any kind should be located so there is a clear field of view in front of them. Rocks, low ground, or close trees and brush would permit an enemy to get close without risk. Clear grass shrubs and other obstruction out to at least fifty yards. Lay plain wire to trip and slow approach. Empty cans with stones inside can be attached to these obstacles to make noise at night. Below are a few simple types of field fortifications that could be used to protect a survival camp or other position. A day practicing, digging, and using these kinds of fortifications would be time well spent.

Urban combat is to be avoided whenever possible. The cost and risk of this kind of combat far exceeds the value. Extensive training is necessary to have any level of proficiency, and even the best military units take heavy losses in urban environments. For a survivalist, home defense and a fighting escape are the only urban combat necessities. The same principles of stealth, camouflage, diversion, fire and maneuver, and counter-ambush apply, but are all more complicated. Multistory buildings add a third dimension to threats. Hiding places are everywhere for you and for the potential enemy. Route selection must take into account how you are exposed, where you can use concealment, where you can find cover, and where threats may lurk. Open streets are almost always the worst routes. Moving house to house, yard to yard, or alley to alley is much slower but often safer.

Defending your home against a few unorganized criminals is achievable with good weapons, combat skills, and constant vigilance, but defense against organized assault will be extremely difficult. The military would simply flatten the adjoining houses, and cut down the trees to clear field of fire for automatic weapons. You do not have these options. Adjoining houses may be occupied by shooters or set on fire to drive you out. Walls and fences will provide cover and concealment for shooters to get closer. While older, brick homes are basically bulletproof, frame houses and brick veneer homes can be riddled by rifle fire. Once a group of more than two or three has decided to besiege your home, you are in serious trouble unless you have organized a block or community defense team. You should have evacuated already or have an escape plan to execute before you are trapped. There is one other option. Instead of waiting for the attackers to get to your home, you can go out and help your neighbors by ambushing or outflanking the shooters before they get to you. Be careful, though; it's a calculated risk.

Physical Security

A single survivalist cannot remain at full alertness for twenty-four hours a day. The entire family or group must be capable of completing sentry duty at home or in a camp. Ideally, sentries should be on duty just one or two hours, but no more than four hours per shift, and working in twos if possible. They may be assigned to just look out from fixed positions or walk a perimeter or both. If a perimeter patrol is established, it should be done at irregular intervals and routes. A clearly understood procedure for challenging intruders must be established and include a consistent challenge phrase and password. These should be changed daily. Sentries are never, ever stationed or permitted to sit around campfires or in lighted areas, and they should avoid using flashlights as this will give away their location while ruining their night vision. The sentries must be armed and have a method of alerting the other members if a threat is imminent. The family or group should be ready and have an assault response plan in place. If personnel are available, patrols can be sent out to detect signs of activity in adjoining areas. Obstacles, barricades, and warning devices can be used to inhibit surprise entry into a building or camp. Since firebombs are often used by looters and criminals, all combustibles should be moved away from windows and wire screening can be nailed over windows to deflect such devices. Most importantly, multiple large fire extinguishers should be available.

Note: Keep in mind that in an age of infrared and night-vision equipment and drones, well-equipped and authorized military and police forces have much greater advantages than any unofficial force in the field, and under extreme circumstance they could consider any noncompliant group (no matter how peaceful) to be hostile.

127   Should survivalists relocate to rural or wilderness areas?

While rural and wilderness areas have survival advantages in many disaster scenarios, they also include their own hazards and disadvantages. Remote locations are not immune to wildfires, floods, storms, earthquakes, and other natural disasters. Violent crime is not limited to urban and suburban areas and access to help is usually less available. Fire, police, and medical response times are much longer. Power outages can be more extended and access to supplies may be more difficult. Such locations are definitely less vulnerable, but not immune to civil disorder, looting, grid failure, and epidemics. The priorities and needs for survival are essentially the same for the rural survivalist, but the emphasis on long-term, shelter-in-place survival is greater. The capacity and readiness to evacuate must still be maintained, even in remote locations. The vast majority of survivalists live in urban, suburban, or small-town locations because they have jobs, family, and educational responsibilities that outweigh other concerns. The higher risks of these locations requires a higher level of awareness and preparedness. Ultimately, it's not where you are, but who you are that determines your survivability.

128   How should a survivalist budget and spend for survival gear and supplies?

Unless you have unlimited funds, it is important to establish a budget that constantly improves your survival and self-reliance capabilities without seriously degrading your everyday life.

- Don't waste money on survival stuff that is just ordinary gear packaged as survival items. Survival water is just water. Survival kits are just collections of things you could put together yourself, and survival foods are usually just pasta, rice, and other ordinary grocery store items.
- Don't buy overpriced survival items just because of the brand name or advertising. Price does not always equate to higher quality. Elite clothing brands, custom knives, and high-end firearms are not functionally better than established quality items at lower prices. The money spent for show is better spent on other practical supplies.
- Don't be cheap on critical survival and self-reliance items such as sleeping bags, packs, knives, flashlights, firearms, binoculars, and packs. There are plenty of good-quality items at sporting goods stores.
- Military surplus knives, packs, tents, and other items offer high quality at lower prices and are an excellent value for the budget-minded survivalist. A good rule of thumb for survival items is that the best values lie just below the most expensive, but never at the cheapest levels.
- If you have a limited budget and you are just starting to develop your survival system, you may have to compromise on quality at first in order to cover all of your needs. It would make little sense to spend all your funds on a survival knife and a pack and not have any kind of stove, water filter, firearm, or first aid kit. Once you have a complete set of survival items, you can start upgrading. You can replace your used firearm with a new, high-quality one. You can buy a better pack with stronger materials and better design, etc. Remember that any survival item is better than nothing. Once you start upgrading your equipment, your original items become your backup.

129 Should survivalists use social media and the internet to improve survival capacity and build survival networks?

The internet is the ultimate double-edged sword for the survivalist. Social media provides the most effective way to promote survival education events, gatherings, and network building. However, it also opens all of your interests and activities to organizations, agencies, and individuals who regard survival and self-reliance with suspicion and even hostility.

- Never share your personal emergency plans or equipment acquisitions on social media. Showing pictures of yourself at a gun range or showing off your latest firearm purchase is the height of poor personal security. It's not even wise to discuss specific plans or equipment in emails.
- While it may be beneficial to promote survival meetups or educational events on the internet, specific emergency plans and group activities should be strictly hard-copy and face-to-face communications.
- Consider the development of preestablished code phrases and code words to be used on social media and other internet systems to communicate survival-critical information.
- The smart survivalist and survival group should develop and use alternative communications systems such as CB, SW, GMRS, and other methods.

No survival group or survival plan should depend on the internet. It would be the height of foolishness for survivalists to depend on the security and reliability of the very systems that a disaster would render dangerous or even nonexistent.

130 How can a survivalist prepare to survive an extended famine?

While storing food for emergencies is an essential part of survival planning, and being able to produce some food items is a step toward self-reliance, a famine is seldom considered as a disaster scenario. America's climate and vast areas of fertile lands make famine seem unlikely, but there are some scenarios where food shortages could be severe and sustained.

- The food processing and distribution systems are so complex and vulnerable that a cyberattack or other technical disruption could prevent effective delivery of food from remote fields to high-density population centers.
- Any disruption of fuel supplies would severely affect harvesting, processing, and delivery of most foodstuffs. Petroleum is used to power all farming machinery, create most fertilizers and insecticides, and process and preserve many foods. The world supply of this commodity will exhausted before the end of this century and will continue to be more and more costly. Without large-scale farming, the current population levels cannot be sustained.
- Any disruption of available labor such as an epidemic or general civil disorder would stop all food processing and transportation.
- Terrorists could randomly poison foods, making all vegetables and fruits potentially unsafe, or they could initiate biological or chemical attacks on crops and livestock.
- Extremely cold weather conditions caused by volcanic activity, solar variations or other situations could devastate crops on a worldwide basis.

In many situations there will be initial looting and even food riots in urban and suburban areas, but depending on the nature and extent of the disaster, food shortages could extend into a general famine. If such conditions were to develop in late autumn or early winter, it would take up to ten months for new crops to be grown and harvested.

Food can be used to control and coerce populations. Food is power. An oppressive or paranoid government could elect to take control of the food supplies and use selective rationing to intimidate and starve opposition elements.

In reality, famine is already a major issue in many parts of the world. No population is immune to a potential famine.

The effects of a food shortage of any kind would be immediate civil disorder and panic. Once all the stores and warehouses have been looted, people would resort to stealing from each other. Gardens would be quickly stripped. Those who could fish, hunt, or forage would do well for a while until all of the game, fish, and edible plants were exhausted. The elderly, the ill, and the young would the first ones to perish. Criminals and gangs would prey on anyone carrying food home and would raid any residents who appeared to have food. In the early stages of a famine, urban residents would travel to farms to trade or raid for food, but farmers would quickly stop trading while organizing armed defenses against looters. The government would establish rationing and no doubt a "black market" for food products would develop.

Famines usually burn out in a year or two as the hungry population diminishes and as food supplies and systems adjust. Those who had stored some food in advance, are good at foraging and living off the land, and are well equipped to defend themselves and stay healthy, usually survive. Food is freedom, and food is power, so the survivalist that has access to and control of significant food supplies will survive and triumph during and after a famine.

131 What can I do to prevent or survive a carjacking?

Modern vehicles are becoming more difficult to steal from the street, so carjackings are an increasing probability in populated areas. During a disaster, criminals and even desperate unprepared survivors may resort to force in order to obtain a vehicle. The following recommendations apply to crime prevention under normal conditions.

Park your vehicle in a well-lit area. When coming out to the street, look around for suspicious people loitering nearby. If concerned, go back inside and get others to accompany you. Do not go directly toward your vehicle or activate the unlock button until you are just ready to jump in. This keeps potential assailants from intercepting you. Try to observe under and around your vehicle and adjoining ones as you approach. Windowless vans with sliding doors close to your driver's side are particularly suspicious. Lock your door immediately upon entry. Always drive with your doors locked! Do not under any circumstances stop for someone other than police flagging you down on the street. This is a common technique to make Good Samaritans into victims.

Be very vigilant at stoplights at uninhabited intersection. If someone points a gun at you while sitting at a stoplight you have three options.

1. Drive through the intersection.
2. Say okay and slide out the passenger side and run, leaving them with a running car.
3. Turn off the vehicle, get out, and throw the keys one way while running the other way.

Whichever you do, do it fast. Never ever let them get into the vehicle with you still inside or make you get back into the vehicle.

Carjackers and "snatch and run" thieves will approach from your blind spot while you sit at a traffic light or in a parking lot. Adding a convex mirror to your side mirrors can help you spot them as they approach close to the side of your vehicle. A mirror or two in your trunk lid will help you spot attackers close in on you while you are loading or unloading groceries.

The convex mirror gives a better view of the vehicle's close side.

Under disaster conditions where you may be trying to escape or evacuating with your family and your survival supplies through lawless areas, the display of weapons, the use of deadly force and running through those who attempt to stop you would be justified and necessary. Your vehicle is essential to survival under such circumstances. You cannot afford to be stopped, assaulted or put out into a civil disorder environment.

132   What can a survivalist do to prepare for a utility outage?

You do not have to live off the grid to be a survivalist, but you do have to be able to live off the grid when necessary. The majority of natural and man-made disasters result in some interruption of the grid, which provides life essentials such as electricity, water, and fuel. A truly massive disaster could involve temporary or even indefinite interruptions of electrical power, water, sewage systems, heating fuel, gasoline, food deliveries, garbage pickup, fire departments, medical facilities, and police protection. The general public has become completely dependent on centralized and networked sources for virtually every need and has little or no capacity to cope with their interruption for more than a few days.

- Natural gas–powered generators have become more popular and are an excellent investment if affordable. Gasoline-powered portable generators are a must, but can only be effective while gasoline is available. There are many disaster scenarios where gasoline and even natural gas will run out. The survivalist must be prepared to rely on alternatives (e.g., solar-powered devices, candles, woodstoves) for any extended emergency.

- Sanitation systems are often overlooked in emergency preparedness. Camp toilets and bleach should be part of every home survival stock. Home toilets can be flushed with buckets of water as long as the municipal sewage pumps are working. You may have to dig a pit toilet in your yard or empty waste buckets into a pit as a last resort. Although you will not have as much trash and garbage if the grid breaks down, you will not have anyone picking it up either. A safe way to burn trash and biological (food waste, etc.) garbage must be established. Remember that there will be no fire department coming if you do not do this safely.

- Using up several gallons of water per day will quickly exhaust your stored water supply. If you can install rain barrels on your residence, it is an excellent investment. Gathering rainwater, pond water, and water from nearby streams and lakes may be your only options. This water will probably be contaminated. Boiling water takes fuel that you may not have. Using bleach will work until your bleach supply runs out. Invest in a high-capacity water-filtration system.

- Keeping warm in cold weather will be a serious challenge during a long-term winter emergency. While modern homes are well insulated, they are too large to be kept warm once the central heating systems are inoperable. If you have a woodstove, fireplace, or camp heaters available, close off one room to heat with this source. Leave faucets running very slowly (if water is still on) to prevent freezing. If it is extremely cold, you may need to drain the entire water system to prevent serious damage to your pipes. Sleep in sleeping bags in the heated room. One of the best approaches is to put up a tent inside your home and live in it until conditions improve. It will be much easier to heat and light than a whole home would be.

- There is no such thing as alternative food. You simply must have enough real food stored and available to last for months or even a year or more. Hunting, fishing, and foraging will have limited potential since desperate and even violent non-survivalists will quickly loot, hunt, and fish everything dry. If you have already initiated survival gardening or even raise some chickens or goats you are way ahead, but you will need to defend these provisions. Skills like gardening, foraging, hunting, fishing, and canning will have great value if the grid goes down indefinitely. Restocking seeds and other survival food is a wise precaution.

- Since police, fire, and emergency medical services will be delayed or unavailable a survivalist must have appropriate firearms, fire extinguishers, and first aid equipment and training. In the case of extended disaster situations, survival might require advanced equipment and training.

Common short-term interruptions of utilities and services only requires basic preparedness and may create discomfort and inconvenience, but longer and more extensive interruptions may involve civil disorder, looting, mass evacuations, epidemics, and martial law. While the survivalist may be able to live off the grid, the unprepared and the non-survivalists will create additional challenges in many areas. If the grid totally collapses, survivalists must be able to survive the initial effects and side effects while transitioning to a new normal.

133   What can a survivalist do to avoid being a victim of street crime?

In many ways, the law-abiding citizen during a survival situation is in the same situation as a conventional army confronted by a guerrilla ambush. You are carrying out normal operations and are deployed and equipped for getting to work or buying groceries whereas the criminal has the initiative in selecting the time, place, and method of attack. Just like a guerrilla, a criminal will want to strike hard and fast and get away without being pressed or pinned down. The average street crime takes from four to six seconds from the time the victim realizes it's happening until the time the criminal is gone. In the streets of today's urban areas, a little paranoia is very good thinking. Whether you're walking or in your vehicle you should be thinking like you are on a combat patrol where you are the point man, the squad leader, and the rear guard all at the same time.

Deny the enemy a target

When possible, plan your route so as to avoid high-crime areas, empty parking lots, and dark alleys, and if you must move through such areas, plan to do it at times when it is light and most crowded. If someone wants to commit a crime against you, make them come to your turf.

Deny the enemy confidence

One thing a criminal does not want is a fight, so that person often looks for "soft" targets. A person walking along daydreaming, on a cell phone, or looking down at the pavement tells a potential criminal that this target is not alert and thus vulnerable. If you are marching along with purpose, scanning the area for threats, and with your head high, the criminal will probably look for someone else to attack. Your choice of clothing can help too. Someone wearing boots, a leather jacket, and a buck knife on his belt is a lot less likely to get jumped than someone wearing sandals, shorts, and a sweater. If you encounter a person or persons coming toward you, never look down, keep your head up and look past them. Remember downcast eyes convey, *I am submissive and I will do what you tell me to do*; never let anyone think that! Remember that all your potential attacker knows about you is what he sees so if you look like trouble he has to assume you could *be* trouble, and he does not want that.

Deny the enemy surprise

Remember that you are your own point man and the rear guard, so as you move scan the whole area to identify potentially dangerous spots and good ambush sites. From there you can plan your route to avoid what you can and make a reaction plan for those you can't avoid. Then as you move through the area, tune your senses for noises, shadows, and odors. Additionally be alert: there are other people along the route. What are they doing? Are they watching you? Can they intercept you? Are their actions normal, or do they seem to be waiting for something? Fulfill your rear guard duties by zigzagging slightly on the sidewalk and turning your head so you can get a good view of what's behind you. You should do this at least twice every block. Don't put yourself in the enemy's kill zone where he can surprise you. Walk on the outside of the sidewalk, or even in the street if necessary, so he has to come out of hiding (from alleys or doorways) to attack. If your scan picks up a suspicious person or persons ahead of you, cross to the other side of the street.

For your vehicle, be sure and buy a small stick-on convex mirror and install on your left rearview mirror. Carjackers will approach from your blind spot while you sit at a traffic light or in a parking lot. The extra mirror will help you spot them. A mirror or two in your trunk lid or liftgate may help you spot attackers who close in on you while you are loading or unloading groceries.

Deny the enemy the initiative

Rest assured that the criminal or gang has a plan. So you must have a plan as well. Your plan should be simple because it's often the simple plans that work best. Remember when you are being attacked, you only have four to six seconds, so you must know exactly what you are going to do, so you can react fast. Your plan can be *I will scream and kick like hell*, or *I will throw my bag and run the other way*, or *I will start yelling as loud as I can*. One idea is to have a money clip with a few dollars in it (the clip gives it weight) that you can throw in one direction while running in the other direction. Consider routes of escape (avoid dead ends) and potential safe havens such as open stores, well-lit areas, and gas stations. Inventory your weapons (everything you have can be a weapon) and how they can be used.

Deny the enemy privacy

Just like the guerrilla ambush, the criminal does not want to have the cavalry show up and pin him down, so stay where there are other people around. If you are about to board an elevator or a subway car, and don't like the looks of someone on board, don't get in. Far better to ride the next elevator or train than the next ambulance. When in doubt, listen to your instincts.

But if you do get into a confined space with a potential assailant, there are some things that you can do. If you are attacked in an elevator, do not push the emergency button, as it will stop the elevator; instead push all the floor buttons and prevent the attacker from pushing the emergency button. This way you have an escape opportunity every few seconds when the door opens.

In another scenario, never get in a car with a potential attacker. If you are in your car and a criminal points a gun at you, you can hit the gas and take your chances with traffic or get out of the car, but do not let them get into the car with you. If a potential attacker points a gun at you, run like hell. The chances that he will shoot at you are about fifty-fifty. But your chances if you get into the car with that person are slim to none. So whatever you do, don't get in the car. At home you should install motion-activated lights to cover your routes to the front door and garage. Be sure to cut down bushes and place mirrors around the front of your house to deny potential assailants anyplace to hide. Be sure to keep your vehicle locked and keep valuable items out of sight. Get in the habit of parking your vehicle in the garage. If you have an attached garage, be sure to keep the door from the garage to the house locked. This is a common route of entry for home invaders.

Defensive Weapons

Criminals generally act on instinct. Responsible citizens, on the other hand, will think about and analyze the consequences before using deadly force. In the seconds it takes for an intelligent citizen to compute the probability of being wrong, the assailant will kill or disarm him. If you elect to carry a gun or a knife, you should be absolutely sure that you know how to use it and that you will use it without hesitation. If you have doubts, then you are just carrying a weapon that could potentially be turned on you. No matter what else you are carrying, in most cases having pepper spray units is recommended. Pepper spray is especially useful as cans are simple to operate and nonlethal; therefore almost anyone will use them without hesitation. They are very effective, come in sizes that fit almost anywhere, and are legal in most

Modern concealed-carry devices come in a variety of designs including enclosed carries that fit on the belt and look like cell-phone cases, vests and jackets with built-in holsters, purses with quick access pockets, and belt pouches like the one above.

places. Pepper sprays have ranges of up to twenty feet and will put down an attacker or several attackers for several minutes. In the event that you do spray the wrong person, no lasting harm is done, and if it can be shown that you had good reason to fear harm, you probably won't face consequences. Keep one in the car, in your pocket or purse, and a bigger one for home.

You don't need to be Rambo to survive on the city streets but you must make plans, be equipped, and maintain a high level of awareness. Remember that predators always prey on the weakest and the slowest. In the urban (and suburban) jungle, the unaware and the unprepared will perish. Don't let it be you or those you love.

134 What is the foundation of having a strong will to survive?

A true survivalist has a well-founded will to survive based on a sense of personal worth to others. A survivalist or survivor thrives because they are self-motivating and self-defined, but not selfish. Those who give up are those who let others define their value and are influenced by their place (or lack of one) in society. A survivalist is never lost, never alone, and never without purpose, because they are confident and adaptable, without outside support. Survivors live by the mottos, "I am me," "I am here," and "I got this." Survivalists are motivated to survive and overcome hardship, pain, and struggle based on their understood value to the community, family, and society. Because of this, survivalists are generally healthier, stronger, and less worried than the unprepared, non-responsible denialists.

135 How can I make my home more secure?

As social and economic conditions deteriorate, all categories of crime will increase. Burglaries, home invasions, robberies, and assaults are more common than most people realize. Having all of your survival equipment stolen or being disabled in a robbery or home invasion is just as much a disaster as any storm. Actions that you can take to improve your homes security are listed below:

- Lock your doors. It sounds logical, but a good number of home invasions involve criminals just walking in. Criminals are opportunists. Potential thieves may go from door to door just trying the knob. If the door is locked, but they do not hear anyone inside, they will try knocking. If there is no answer, they may try the back or side door. If still no answer, they may just kick in the door and start taking things. If someone rattles your door, you say, "who is it?" and they run, call the police.
- Beware of the distraction scam. If someone comes to your door claiming to be a roofer, driveway coater, or utility worker, be wary. Do not leave your house, and do not let this person in.
- Beware of the utility worker scam. Someone claiming to be a utility worker could seek entry into your home to address a gas leak, water leak, or other issue, and once inside, rob you. Never let anyone in until you have seen their ID through your locked door and called the utility to confirm their identity.
- Surprisingly, most illegal home entries are through doors during daylight hours. All doors should be solid hardwood or steel with high-quality deadbolt locks. When a door is kicked in, it is usually the frame that breaks at the strike plate. If possible, have steel doorframes. Lock strike plates come with short screws that only engage the doorframe. A hard kick will almost always break the wood of the frame. Replace these screws with longer two- or three-inch stainless steel screws that go well into the adjoining wall studs.
- Install a peephole or have a security camera, so you do not have to open the door to establish who is there.
- If you have an attached garage, treat the door from the garage to the house as an exterior door. It should be strong with a heavy-duty deadbolt lock and it should be kept closed and locked. Home invasions are often made through attached garages.
- Be sure that your address numbers are big and easy to read from the street,

even at night. Small, hard-to-read numbers may cause delays in police and EMS responses.

- Remove or trim bushes and shrubs that could provide hiding places for criminals.
- Install motion-activated security lights.
- When on vacation, set interior lights and a radio on timers to go on and off at night. Stop mail and paper deliveries or have a trusted neighbor take them in.
- Use your garage for storing your vehicles, not your junk. Criminals just walk down streets at night checking for unlocked cars.
- Never leave valuables of any kind in plain sight in a vehicle. It's an invitation to break in even if it's locked.
- Dogs are great security aids, and even if you don't have one you can leave a large dog food and water dish outside the door to deter potential criminals.
- Never display so-called crime-deterrent signs, as these will advertise that you have guns. This makes your home a high-priority target for burglary when you're not home. This can also harm your self-defense claims if you do need to use deadly force.
- Do not post vacation plans on social media. Doing so opens you up to all kinds of crimes and scams.
- Do not put the boxes from high-end items such as televisions, generators, or appliances out by the street for garbage pickup. Tear the boxes up and place them inside the cans.
- Keep your garage door closed.
- Be sure that all valuables are secure and out of sight if you have guests or service providers in your home. Burglaries are often committed by those who have been in the home before.
- Try to avoid being too predictable in your habits. Coming and going at different times and from different directions will discourage criminals. Taking a walk at the same time on the same route every day is not good security.
- Stay alert every time you come home. Is there a suspicious vehicle nearby? Have you been followed? Is someone lurking in the shadows? Is your door ajar? If something doesn't look right or feel right, keep moving and get to a neighbor's house or a police station. If you discover that your door has been opened or you detect an intruder when you enter, get out immediately, and call or go for help.
- Be sure that you have an intruder action plan for your family.
- Case your house like a criminal. Does it look like the easiest house on the block to target? Are there good places to hide and access windows and doors? Is the car in the driveway locked or unlocked? Is it unoccupied for part of the day?

136 How can a survivalist prepare to survive a violent revolution?

While a revolution still seems improbable, America has become so splintered that the political systems and governmental agencies may be unable to prevent some segments of society from resorting to some forms of revolutionary activities in the future. Because of this uncertainty, some of the following can happen:

- Racial and religious groups may resort to terrorist activities, hostage taking, and sabotage.
- Mass demonstrations may turn into more organized militaristic action where cities are taken over, and police and National Guard units are overwhelmed. Radical groups might take over regional armories.
- Multiple states and/or cities could elect to assert levels of independence, or even secede from state or national government, resulting in massive disruption and conflict.
- Advocates of centralization and socialization and the supporters of greater decentralization and personal freedoms could continue to coalesce into strong opposing paramilitary forces.
- The government itself could become so oppressive and intrusive that part of the population comes to resist and revolt.

In reality, most revolutions involve a very small part of the population and a very limited area of major population centers, but the impact can be massive. Even a limited and failed revolution could result in a collapsed economy, martial law, and a more oppressive government. A large-scale revolution could destroy cities and infrastructure, and initiate confiscation, mass internments, and the end of most liberties. The survivalist's preparedness and defensive arrangements will be of great value during the chaotic conditions of any kind of insurrection.

Be aware of the political, economic, and social climate, especially as it pertains to your immediate relationships, community, and interests. Try to position yourself with the best chance of avoiding involvement. If you are not able to avoid involvement, plan to survive, and stay free regardless of who wins. Avoid commitment or overt support for potentially revolutionary or violent positions and groups. Stay discreet and flexible. A reputation for responsibility and capability in your community will be your most valuable asset. A strong and self-reliant population is the best insurance against such a destructive and divisive event.

137 What can a survivalist do to protect children?

Today's youth are set to face increasing levels of economic and social chaos, as well as more frequent and severe natural and man-made disasters in the coming decades. Helping our youth to survive physically, mentally, and morally is critical to the survival of a free society in the future. The following recommendations provide basic guidance and information for parents and guardians for surviving a variety of threat situations.

Home Accidents and Emergencies

Thousands of children are injured or die each year from preventable home accidents. Other children suffer from physical and emotional abuse from the very parents, relatives, and other adults who should be protecting them. It is the responsibility of adults to provide a safe environment, be aware of potentially hazardous conditions in the home. and act immediately when evidence of child abuse is observed. Establish clear and reasonable safety rules and emergency procedures for all family members.

Home Fires

Never leave young children at home alone. Children are often fascinated by fire and may accidentally start a blaze and try to put it out by themselves. Children are injured, trapped, and die like this every year. Never leave matches, lighters, or other ignition devices lying about where children can get to them. Teach children to get out of the house and call 911 or go to the neighbor's house if there is a fire. Adolescents can be taught to use a fire extinguisher and to evacuate younger children if you're not home.

Home Intruders and Invasions

Intruders may enter the home while the family is asleep or enter while no one is there. They may intend to abduct children, commit robbery, or commit other crimes. Parents must train the children on what to do.

If there is an intruder in the house at night, kids should know to quickly gather in the parents' room or designated safety spot and wait for the police. They should never go looking for the intruder. If they cannot get to the safety spot, they must have a place to hide.

If a forced entry is made by an intruder, the child may lock and barricade their rooms, escape out a back door or window, or hide in a cabinet or other location. If the child comes home may have been broken into, teach them not to go inside. They should get away from the house, call 911, and go to a neighbor immediately for help.

Children and Firearms

Firearms ownership is a serious responsibility. This is especially true in any home where children live or may visit. If you are not fully committed to keeping firearms out of the reach of children, then don't have them. Children have shot themselves, their siblings, and others with firearms that were "hidden" by parents. Most children are extremely good at searching and finding. In a drawer, under a cushion, on a high shelf, behind a cabinet—they will find it! All firearms should be kept in a securely locked gun box, and the keys must be very well hidden. Your self-defense gun(s) must be secured in a combination lockbox or with a trigger lock at home. Ammunition and firearms should be stored separately. Adolescents should be taught how to use firearms safely, but never permitted to handle them without adult supervision. Even if you do not have children at home, be sure to lock up all firearms when children will be visiting.

Other Hazards to Children

Tripping hazards are very dangerous for children, so keep stairs and walkways clear. Children can climb on or over railings and fall off porches, and through window screens. The installation of window and stairway guards and gates is recommended wherever such hazards exist. Small children have drowned in buckets full of water. Never leave children unattended in bathtubs or pools of any kind. Larger backyard swimming pools must be fenced and locked when not supervised. Poisons such as drain cleaners and paint thinners must be kept out of reach of children. The same applies to prescription and over-the-counter medications. Flammable liquids such as gasoline, lamp oil, and solvents that are as hazardous as drugs (huffed), poisons, and fire accelerants must be kept in secure locked cabinets. Obviously knives, saws, axes, and other sharp objects must be kept out of reach of younger children. The handles of pans of boiling or frying food must be kept inward so they cannot be grasped by children. The same goes for dangling cords on hot electrical appliances such as coffeemakers and broilers.

Knowing How to Call 911!

All children should be taught how to call 911 at the earliest possible age. They should be told to do so if anyone in the house is seriously injured or unconscious, or if there is an intruder or attempted break-in, a fire, or serious injury. Tell them to give their name and age, to describe the problem to the dispatcher, and to follow the instructions given by the dispatcher.

Dangers on the Streets

Sad to say, our streets are no longer safe for children. Child abductions, gang activities, drug use, and violence are not restricted to urban communities. Suburban and rural areas have their own variations on these dangers. Parents and young people living in so-called "safe neighborhoods" are inclined to become complacent, easy targets for criminals.

Recognition of Child Abuse (including bullying and cyberbullying)

Children may be molested or abused at home, at school, or in other places by adults or other children; such abuse may include sexual molestation, physical injury, emotional cruelty, or bullying. Since the sources of abuse may include parents and other caretakers, it is the responsibility of all adults to be alert for signs of abuse in children with whom they interact. Signs of abuse include: children who are never outside or allowed to play with others; children who show signs of frequent injury or seem fearful of adults; indications of malnutrition and illness; children that are unusually quiet and inactive. Of course, some injuries are just accidents and some behaviors are just mood swings, but multiple and ongoing signs of possible abuse should initiate further investigation and reporting. Be suspicious if your child talks about spending time with an older person or receiving gifts from or having secrets with an adult. Your children should be told not to go into private locations or take gifts from any adults without your permission. Listen, believe, and investigate when your children tell you about inappropriate touching or suspicious action by adults, even if it's a relative or someone you know.

Preventing Child Abduction

Small children are easy prey for child molesters and abductors. They may be lured into a nearby home by a sex offender or snatched outright off the street. Abductors are skilled at misleading children. They may say they need help finding a puppy, or they may say that a parent has been hurt and they will take the child to them. Abductors may just want the child to get close enough to be grabbed. They may ask for directions from their car or van and then pull them in when they get close. Children should know that adults do not ask children for help. They should stay out of reach of strangers at all times.

Be aware that most child abductors are not strangers. They can be family members or acquaintances from home or school. Teach your children never to go anywhere with anyone they do not know, but also not to go anywhere with any adult without your permission. Train them to firmly say "no" and scream, run, or fight. Remind them not get into a vehicle or take anything from strangers. Encourage them to stay in crowds and stay in groups, and avoid being alone and avoid being in empty places.

The police are not going to throw a lot of resources into locating a missing child unless it has been over twenty-four hours or there are other factors involved such as weather, disability, custody issues, threats of violence, or evidence of violence or abduction. Ninety-nine percent of missing children turn up within one to two days. After that, the chances of recovery become much less. Children over the age of consent cannot be forced to return, even if they are located by the police. If you are sure something is wrong, report it to the police and then start checking with the child's friends and at places where they hang out. If you can't locate the child within a day or you find information indicating abduction, molestation, injury, or illness, get back to the police immediately.

Recognition and Prevention of Bullying

Bullying can take many forms. Individuals or gangs may use intimidation or physical violence to force a child to join a gang, take drugs, or be involved in other high-risk activities. Children may choose to pick on a child because he or she is different, or does not conform. The internet and social media are also avenues for bullying. Cyberbullying is real and can cause lasting psychological harm in sensitive children and adolescents. Be alert for signs of injury, depression, or changes in behavior, such as skipping school or isolation that may indicate bullying. Children may be ashamed to tell you that they let someone intimidate or injure them or that they are afraid. The best defense against psychological bullying is the child's own sense of pride and self-worth. Being an important part of a family and knowing they have support and can talk about issues is critical. Any signs of physical injury or organized bullying should be reported to the police and/or school officials promptly.

Parental Awareness and Responsibility

Parents must be constantly observant of their children's behavior. Poor attendance at school or poor grades may indicate depression, drug usage, or association with gang members. Frequently coming home late or sneaking out should initiate investigation. Flashing gang signs, secretive behavior, or indications of drug usage require immediate intervention. You are responsible for ensuring that your children does not make serious, life-damaging choices. Adolescent brains are not fully developed, and young people lack the benefits of experience and observation necessary to make good decisions. You must be their guide and leader toward responsible and productive adulthood. You cannot just be their pal and hope for the best. Regardless of the situations or temptations, loved, confident, and self-reliant children are much less likely to do drugs, join gangs, run away, or commit suicide. They are survivors in emergencies and successful in life.

Preventing Accidental Injuries and Deaths

Young people are often overconfident and more prone to taking chances than adults. The possibility of being seriously injured or killed is not highly developed. Trying new things and pushing their luck is more normal than being careful and safe. Today we have smartphones to completely distract and screen young people from danger around them. Young people (and adults) are robbed, assaulted, struck by vehicles, and experience collisions and falls because they were unaware of their surroundings. These tragedies can and should be prevented. Devices that obstruct or distract from complete audio and visual awareness should be used only when a person is stationary and in a safe environment. Using such devices while biking, walking, skating, or driving must be strictly prohibited.

Even standing close to traffic, railroad tracks, or in a location that may attract criminals should be avoided. Be sure to provide your children with protective gear for whatever sports or activities they are involved in. Bicyclists should be provided with good-fitting helmets and high-visibility clothing. If they ride at night, they should have reflective clothing, and their bike should have reflectors as well as lights.

Avoiding and Surviving Shooting Incidents

While drive-by shootings and gang shoot-outs are more common in urban areas, they can happen anywhere without warning. Shooting incidents happen far more frequently where young people congregate. Victims are often gang members, but just as often they are just in the wrong place at the wrong time. The first priority in preventing your child from being involved in such incidents is to keep them out of gangs and keep them away from association with gang members. They also need to stay away from locations where gang members are likely to hang out. The community must provide alternative associations, activities, and locations. As always, you must have a continuing dialogue with your children about associations and activities. Teach your children to avoid association with anyone who carries a gun or brags about shooting someone. Children should be taught that if they hear a gunshot, do not go to see what's happening, but must they get down and take cover quickly. If they think there is going to be shooting, get away fast. Do not run toward or away from police, just stay down, show your empty hands, and follow their exact instructions.

Hazards at School

Young people are subject to a tremendous amount of hazards while in school. They spend much more time interacting with their peers than with their parents. What seems to be acceptable within their group may be high-risk behavior with potentially disastrous consequences. Their desire to fit in supersedes good judgment. They seek leadership and a sense of belonging. Saying no and being different take courage and determination. Home, family, and established values are their only defense. Additionally, kids need to feel comfortable talking to you. As a parent, it's your job to get them through school safely and without making poor decisions and associations. School hazards include, bullying, gang recruitment, drug pushers, assaults, and abuse. In recent years incidents of so-called "active shooters" have also been more frequent.

Active-Shooter Situation Survival for Youth

A child or young adult may encounter an active-shooter situation at school, in a public place, or even on the street. Young people must be encouraged to report anyone in school who talks about shooting, killing, revenge, or having guns or bombs. They should be trained to immediately report seeing a firearm being carried into the school by a student or an adult. At the first sign of a potential shooting incident or upon hearing shots fired, they should know what to do. The school may have a plan for a shooting incident, but in all cases, the child should know where to take cover if evacuation is not possible. Getting out of sight behind solid walls or appliances is the next-best option to escape. Barricading the door in a room is another way to stay safe. If these are not viable choices, then lying flat and playing dead may be their only chance. Running or just standing in place is an invitation to being a target in such situations.

Preventing Adolescent Drug Abuse

Most adolescents are highly susceptible to peer pressure and the need to fit in. This often clouds their judgment. It's just not enough to assume that a child is "too smart" to try drugs or join a gang.

You should also be diligent about what you keep around the house. Household chemicals such as paint thinner and adhesives can be huffed. Alcohol can be consumed. Prescription drugs and over-the-counter medications can be abused. Marijuana, heroin, cocaine, and a constantly changing variety of synthetic drugs are out there for your child to try. So don't wait. Discuss the dangers of drugs with children in elementary school and continue the discussion each year. Discuss the health and legal consequences and have examples from the news of how people deteriorated physically, committed crimes, ruined lives, or died just because they tried something.

Children and adolescents often follow examples of parents, relatives, and other adults. Parents who smoke, drink in access, use any form of drugs recreationally, or tolerate such behavior among friends or associates are encouraging drug experimentation and abuse regardless of what they tell their children. You must set the example before you can prevent this self-destructive behavior.

Surviving Disasters (home, school outdoors)

The frequency and severity of disasters and violent incidents is steadily increasing. Every family should be prepared to cope with emergencies without help if necessary. Parents owe it to their children to assure that there is water, food, shelter, basic first aid supplies, and other necessities on hand. An evacuation pack should be ready for adults and children as well. As children grow older their level of emergency responsibilities and their equipment should be improved.

School-age children should be taught basic first aid, including how to recognize signs and symptoms of heart attacks, strokes, hypothermia, hyperthermia, and insulin shock. They should be able to recognize severe versus minor bleeding and how to apply direct pressure and elevation to stop it. Older children should learn to administer CPR and apply tourniquets along with basic bandaging and splinting. Children must know to "stop, drop, and roll," if they are on fire and to quickly cool and cover burns.

Lost or Separated Children

Regardless of how vigilant a parent or guardian is, a child can become separated or lost. This may occur at a shopping mall, public event, or outdoors. Children should be instructed to stay in one place as soon as they realize they are lost or separated. Retracing your steps or going to the place you last saw them is the best chance for fast recovery. Children should also be instructed to seek out a police officer, security guard, event staff, or a store employee for help.

Storms, Tornadoes, Hurricanes, Power Outages

Children and adolescents need to know what to do if they are home alone or away from home when severe storms, earthquakes, floods, power outages, and other disasters occur. They should be instructed on how to escape, find shelter, get to help and survive until you can get to them. They should be given increased responsibilities in your family's emergency plans as they grow older.

Family Passwords and Code Words

The family should have a special code word to imply "I need help" and a password to use to imply, "it's me, a family member." You may want to have special action words to activate various emergency plans as well.

Survival Kits for Children and Teens

An important survival imperative states that "it's not what you have; it's what you have with you that counts." Having age-appropriate items to aid in emergency situations carried in pockets or packs can provide lifesaving support in emergencies as well as providing a sense of comfort and self-confidence. Having their own "survival items" and "survival kits" will develop a preparedness and self-reliant mind-set that will serve them well as they mature to adulthood.

Early childhood survival items include a whistle, Band-Aids, a miniature flashlight, and a child-size N95 respirator.* Some packaged, nonperishable (for emergency use only) candy can also impart some comfort. A card containing emergency contact information, the child's name, address, and contact phone numbers, and any medical conditions or required medications, should always be carried. This card should be sealed in plastic. Do not depend on cell phones for this!

---

*Fires, tornadoes, chemical incidents, and biological hazards all create airborne soot, dust, and mists that can be immediately harmful. It is important that children and adolescents have a means to protect themselves from these risks. Child-sized respirators can be purchased online. Buy enough to cover an extended (epidemic, etc.) situation and show the child how to properly fit them. Adolescents will be able to use adult-sized respirators.

As children grow older, more survival items can be added such as energy bars, light sticks, pepper spray, survival blankets, bandanas, and even tourniquets. More complete survival kits should be created for children and adolescents to take on outdoor activities and there should be a full evacuation pack of appropriate content, size, and weight for young family members as well.

About Knives and Children

Years ago, the possession of a pocketknife was a rite of passage for young boys. They were usually small one- or two-bladed knives. These were never used or considered to be weapons. Today carrying a knife of any sort to school is prohibited. Regardless, a pocket knife, Swiss Army knife, or multi-tool device is still an essential survival item for non-school pockets and kits, but should come with parental supervision and safety training.

Youth Interaction with Police

Young people must understand that police officers are sworn to enforce the laws and protect the public. Children should be introduced to police officers at an early age and come to see them as sources of safety and help. Violence of any kind is the last resort for a police officer, but when faced with a threat to themselves or others, they are obligated to act.

The police do not just go around shooting innocent people walking down the street. Although some police shootings are overreactions or accidents, they sometimes are situations precipitated by the victim's criminal activities and/or failure to promptly obey police commands. If a person appears to be armed, appears to be a threat to others, or fails to obey commands the police are justified to use deadly force. They are not allowed to simply let the offender run off. For an officer to fail to do everything within his or her power to detain the suspect is termed as a failure of duty, and the officer or officers are subject to disciplinary action and possible termination. They are not obligated to try to chase and tackle an offender that may well be faster and stronger than they are. They are obliged to stop the offender by the most effective means necessary while minimizing the risk of injury to themselves and others.

Children and adolescents must be taught the following rules by their parents and guardians in order to prevent tragic occurrences.

- Don't be involved in criminal activities.
- Don't do drugs.

- Don't hang around gangs or act and dress like a gang member.
- Don't run when the police say stop.
- Don't point things (any things) at the police.
- Stop and obey every police order immediately.
- Do not fight or struggle with officers.

As parents and guardians, you must not tolerate or enable children's participation in any kind of criminal, gang, or drug-related activities. Further, do not tolerate criminal activities or drug usage by friends and family members. Teach them the above rules for avoiding violent police/civilian confrontations. Teach them self-respect, respect for others, and respect for the law and make them safe, responsible, and productive citizens. That's your job.

138   What are the alert levels used by survivalists to classify threat conditions?

While being alert and observant of potential threats is the hallmark of good survival thinking, no one can be constantly at a state of maximum readiness. It is unreasonable to expect anyone to be at the same level of alertness while relaxing at home as they would be walking down a darkened street in the city. Many survivalist adopt a military-like, multilevel system to establish how ready they are to act based on their environment and potential threats. An example of this type of system is as follows:

Condition Green

All conditions are normal and safe. You are in a familiar and secure environment and there are no threatening conditions inside or immediately outside the location. Relax.

Condition Yellow

You are in a relatively safe and familiar environment such as your job, the road, or a store, but there are potential hazards such as street crime, accidents, weather conditions, strangers, or other concerns. You need to be aware of everything going on around you. Look, listen, and smell for hazards. This condition should also always apply to cases when you are in an unfamiliar environment such as hotels, airports, outdoor venues, and wilderness areas.

Condition Orange

The potential for a life-threatening occurrence is evident. Your location is a fire hazard or has too few exits, you are in a crowd, there are suspicious people ahead, and dangerous storms are possible. Or you just feel like something is off. This is the time to move to a safer location, acquire needed survival items, and make a mental plan for possible escape, shelter, defense, and survival.

Condition Red

You recognize that you are in immediate danger. Criminals start moving toward you, you smell smoke, you hear shooting, a weather warning is given, and signs of panic are evident. Because you anticipated the possibility of such dangers you immediately execute your plan using the survival skills you have learned and the survival items you have with you. You are therefore able to save yourself and those you care for most, and then can help others.

139   What kind of vehicle is best for a survivalist to have for evacuation from a disaster?

The ideal survival vehicle is a military Armored Personnel Carrier, or heavy-duty, four-wheel drive truck. Commercial four-wheel drive pickup trucks and large SUVs are also suitable, but such vehicles are expensive and usually impractical for everyday use. Fully equipped survival vehicles are bound to attract attention and take up room. Unless you can afford to have multiple, high-end vehicles, you will probably need to compromise by having one vehicle that has some survival functionality and can be quickly rigged for an escape; or by having another basic commuting vehicle and a second more capable vehicle that can be used for survival situations.

There are four primary considerations for your chosen survival and escape vehicle in order of priority:

1. **Reliability**: Your designated survival vehicle must be the one with the least mileage, best maintenance, and newest tires and battery. Its fuel tank should never be much below three-quarters full.

2. **Roominess:** You need to have room for the whole family and all of your survival gear and supplies. This means having a mid-sized SUV or pickup truck with a cap. Vans can be eliminated, as they are generally unstable and have low ground clearance. Keep in mind that you may actually have to live in the vehicle.

3. **Range:** Having too large a vehicle with poor gas mileage may be a problem when all of the fuel sources are unavailable. Part of your selection process should consider if you could expect to get to a safe location on one tank of fuel through traffic jams. Having the capacity to carry fuel cans safely should also be a consideration. Some trucks and SUV offer auxiliary fuel tanks.

4. **Ruggedness:** Reliability, room, and range must outrank ruggedness, but it is an important factor. Jeep-like vehicles, with four-wheel drive or all-wheel drive,* and high ground clearance are preferable. These features will help get through mud, snow, and rough terrain.

---

*The terms "four-wheel drive" and "all-wheel drive" are interchangeable. Both can be robust and effective for slippery conditions and rough terrain. The term "all-wheel drive" is usually used for larger SUVs and sedans, whereas "four-wheel drive" usually applies to trucks and larger SUVs with higher ground clearances.

Recommended Vehicle Equipment:

- Spare gas cans, with at least ten gallons of extra fuel
- A liquid transfer pump or siphoning tubing
- Towrope or chains
- Come-along winching device and cable
- Spotlight that runs off of the accessory plug
- Camouflage netting
- Carpeting strips (12" x 48") for traction
- Battery-powered air pump and tire repair kit
- Jumper cables and/or portable power pack
- Six to eight smoke bombs for escape and diversions
- Flares
- Fire extinguisher
- Bolt cutters to access closed roads and garages

The above list is what you should keep in that vehicle or can quickly load into it. It does not include all of your survival packs and supplies that you must have ready for easy and fast loading as well.

Accessories that can improve a vehicle's survival functionality when practical to install include:

- Electric winches
- Towing hooks
- Bumper guards
- Extra running lights and spotlights

Unless you live in an area where camouflaged painted vehicles are common, select dark shades of gray, tan, and brown.

Trailers offer a good option for survival preparedness. You can load up a small trailer with all of your survival needs and keep it in the garage, ready to go. Of course you do need to have a sufficiently robust towing vehicle with a hitch. Trailers can also be pre-positioned outside the danger zone to be picked up on your escape route. A small camping trailer or cargo trailer can be stored at a remote storage facility or secure yard. While a larger house trailer or camper bus may seem ideal, they may inhibit mobility and will require a bigger towing vehicle and lots of fuel.

140 Should survivalists establish hidden caches of survival supplies?

In many cases the survival equipment you can transport may be insufficient for the severity and duration of the threats and challenges you are facing. Once your vehicle is stopped or your survival pack supplies run out, you may need to have pre-positioned supplies on your route or at your final destination.

Having your survival pack and all your supplies in your home creates some risks. You may want to consider keeping your packs or a backup pack in a shed or detached garage. That way, if your home burns down, you still may have your pack.

If a disaster such as a flood, hurricane, or civil disorder seems to be approaching, you may want to temporarily shift some of your supplies to a safer area. Consider asking a friend or relative to hold a few packs or tote bins for you.

Caches established for serious disasters must be outside of the zone of chaos and destruction but accessible along your route or at a destination within a few days' travel. If you have close friends or relatives living in a safer and more remote location, they may be willing to store your additional supplies in a shed, detached garage, or basement for you. In a disaster, they will probably welcome the extra help and defensive capabilities you will bring. This is an excellent function of a survival group or networks.

Wilderness survival caches are usually buried in the woods or desert. They give the survivor the capacity to survive off the grid and out of sight, but are vulnerable to theft and damage.

No cache is of value if it cannot be located and accessed quickly. Finding a location off the beaten path, out of sight, and yet easy to access, can be challenging. Establish the location by triangulation and reference to permanent, visible landmarks such as buildings, large trees, or rock formations. You can also establish the spot using GPS locators, but be skilled in map and compass usage in case GPS is not available during a disaster. Avoid placement of caches in low or marshy ground where they are more apt to be damaged by water.

Cache containers must be absolutely watertight and corrosion proof. Large-diameter PVC pipes with threaded caps make good containers. Heavy-duty plastic military ammunition cans are also suitable. All contents should be placed in sealed, heavy-duty plastic bags. Weapons and other metal gear should be heavily greased. Cache locations should be inspected annually and dug up, inspected, and relocated every two to three years.

The contents of caches depends on the anticipated needs of the survivor beyond the first few days of a disaster, but could include:

- Blankets, sleeping bags, and shelters for winter survival that goes beyond what you can carry in your packs.
- Nonperishable food supplies to keep you going when your pack supplies run out.
- Stoves, lanterns, and fuel for light and heat.
- Ammunition for your carried survival weapons and maybe a backup weapon and ammunition in case yours is lost or unaccusable.
- An entire small survival pack with all water, shelter, food, defense, medical, and other needs, in case (worst case) you cannot get to your primary pack or it is lost.
- Recovery supplies such as seeds, tools, and trade goods.

Caches can be a significant advantage in a survival situation. Use your imagination to create locations, containers, and contents.

141 How important are health and physical conditioning to being a survivalist?

The answer should be obvious. Poor health and poor physical conditioning reduce your chances of surviving in every conceivable emergency. Reduced muscle tone, lung capacity, and heart health will severely limit your ability to run, carry equipment, fight, work, and lift. High blood pressure, diabetes, and other issues can be fatal under the stress of a disaster. Poor teeth can limit your diet, cause pain, and lead to infections. Being overweight and out of shape puts you at a disadvantage in any demanding situation. Dependency on any kind of commercial medication severely limits your survival chances in the long run. While we cannot always avoid illness, and we are bound to suffer some effects of aging, there is no excuse for allowing our physical condition to decline more than necessary. There is little point in packing a survival pack that you probably will not be able to carry, or learning survival skills that you will not be strong enough or tough enough to perform in an emergency. Depending on age, heredity, and early development, we all start with basic physical capacities, but we must do all we can to improve and enhance what we have. Some of those ways are:

- Walking is one of the most beneficial and easiest exercises. Never drive when you can walk. You should try to walk at least ten miles per week.
- Establish a habit of exercising at least three time per week. Build abdominal muscles, arm muscles, back muscles, and shoulder muscles that you may need in an emergency. Join a health club if you can or invest in some weights and other basic exercise gear. Push-ups, sit-ups, and various lifts and bends do not require expensive machinery. The self-discipline and determination required to sustain an exercise regimen is precisely the kind of mental ability required for survival.
- Stop smoking if you do. Dozens of ailments and limitations are caused by smoking and nicotine products. Most smokers can't keep up with most nonsmokers who are much older. There is no such thing as a smoking survivalist.
- Depending on one's metabolism, dieting may be necessary to manage one's weight. In a survival situation a few extra pounds may even be beneficial. Limit calories and exercise regularly to manage weight and cholesterol, while reducing fat and sugar intake as well.
- Be sure to maintain your teeth and get regular dental checkups and eye examinations. These services may not be available during long-term disasters.

- Get regular medical checkups, but try to avoid dependency on medications when diet, exercise, and healthy habits can suffice.
- Don't let age be an excuse for letting yourself go. If you lack the will to stay healthy, you probably lack what it takes to survive.

A survivalist does not have to be a physical fitness enthusiast or fanatical dieter, but must be committed to basic health and physical fitness as a fundamental necessity.

142   When did the survivalist movement begin?

Self-reliance and personal preparedness are fundamental American values that originated with the first colonists. The agrarian and pioneer culture of the 1700s and early 1800s made most people survivalists by nature until the Industrial Revolution shifted the masses toward dependency on centralized networks and regulated lifestyles. By the twentieth century, the majority of Americans had lost the capacity to do without systems that provided life necessities such as running water, electricity, automotive transportation, police protection, central heating, packaged foods, and other services.

The advent of nuclear weapons after World War II was the first cause for a limited number of Americans to consider the fragility of civilization. The vast majority of persons considered nuclear war to not be survivable and chose to ignore any level of preparedness or self-reliance, but a small percentage became survivalists and self-reliance advocates. From there, survivalists and survivalism became prominent in the 1980s at the height of the Cold War and many of the core philosophical foundations were established at that time. While the danger of nuclear war diminished somewhat after the collapse of the Soviet Union in the 1990s, the public began to acknowledge the weakness and vulnerabilities of their centralized and precarious support system. This realization generated the prepper movement That has become a recognized phenomenon. As the economy declines, climate extremes occurs, and social chaos increases, survivalism (or prepping) is becoming mainstream by necessity, and survivalists are grudgingly recognized as positive examples.

143 What is the rule of threes in survival and preparedness?

The rule of threes in survival states that you must always have three methods or devices available to meet every critical life need. The chances of losing or having a single system fail are fairly good under survival conditions. The odds of two methods failing are significantly lower, but having three devices, methods, or systems fail are very, very low. This is why NASA and the military use triple redundancy whenever possible. The table blow covers some alternative and backup methods:

Life Critical Need	Primary method	Secondary method	Tertiary method	Other Alternatives
Defense	Firearms	Knife	Survival bow	Pepper spray
Shelter	Home	Tent	Tarp or plastic sheets	Natural-material shelter
Water	Stored water	Water filter	Purification tablets or bleach	Solar purification Boiling
Food	Canned goods	Dehydrated foods	Energy bars	Foraging, trapping, etc.
Light	Flashlight	Lanterns	Candles	Glow sticks
Warmth	Sleeping bag	Space Emergency Blanket	Rescue blanket	Paper, leaves, etc.
Fire	Matches	Magnesium stick	Lighter	Flint and steel, batteries, etc.
First Aid	Full first aid kit	Mini first aid kit	Improvised bandages, etc.	First aid knowledge

The rule of threes also applies to survival plans and tactics. Have three ways of getting to a destination, three ways to survive any situation, and at least three plans for every anticipated survival challenge.

144   What if I make all these efforts to prepare and nothing bad happens?

Simply, most scientists, economists, historians, and anthropologists agree that civilization is moving toward a traumatic catastrophe of some kind in the not to distant future. No one is predicting a safe and benign tomorrow. While there are temporary and inspiring recoveries and progress in some areas, the overall trends in every aspect are downward. In the past when humanity ran out of resources and became desperate, they migrated to new areas, but now there is nowhere left to go. The philosopher Georg Hegel (1770–1831) postulated that civilization moved from epoch to epoch, destined for an end point. Karl Marx heard this idea and twisted it to mean that we were marching toward a utopian socialist society. While he was wrong about that particular end, Marx did also say that every system contained the seeds of its own destruction. In that he seems to have been correct. Destruction appears to be nearing. To fail to prepare is dangerous, irresponsible, and a betrayal of our children and our future. If nothing bad happens, you are still a stronger and more responsible citizen, but if anything catastrophic does develop that you're not prepared for, you will lose a great deal because of your very unwise gamble.

145 What should a survivalist keep in a disaster first aid kit?

First and foremost, stock up on your prescription medications. Hoard any antibiotics and painkillers while you can. Although most medications expire in two years, they are often effective for much longer, especially if vacuum packed and kept cool. You must have a basic first aid book to ensure that you can administer effective and safe medical procedures. The following is a partial list that could be expanded depending on your needs and skills.

1. 1 package of blood stoppers (Celox, QuikClot, and HemCon) powder or dressing
2. 1 tourniquet device
3. 1 eight-ounce tube of antibiotic ointment (e.g., Neosporin 9%)
4. 1 eight-ounce tube of hydrocortisone cream
5. 1 eight-ounce tube of tube burn ointment
6. 1 bar of antibacterial soap
7. 12 alcohol swabs
8. 1 bottle of nonprescription pain medication (e.g., Tylenol)
9. 1 bottle of nonprescription antacid
10. 1 bottle of nonprescription antidiuretic
11. 1 bottle of nonprescription laxative
12. 1 bottle of nonprescription cold and allergy medications
13. 1 three-ounce bottle of eye drops
14. 1 two-inch elastic bandage
15. 1 three-inch elastic bandage
16. 2 triangle (cravat) bandage/sling
17. 24 assorted small bandages (Band-Aids)
18. 20 butterfly bandages
19. 12 2x2" gauze pads
20. 12 3x3" gauze pads
21. 12 4x4" gauze pads
22. 12 safety pins (large)
23. 1 pair of EMT shears
24. Assorted tweezers and forceps
25. 1 pair of splinter forceps and/or tweezers
26. 4 single-edged razor blades or scalpel blades with blade holder

27. 1 toothache kit (available at drugstores)
28. 6 pairs of latex gloves
29. 6 N95 respirators
30. 2 CPR masks
31. 1 roll of 1" self-adhering tape
32. 1 roll of 2" self-adhering tape
33. 1 roll of .5" medical tape
34. First aid instruction book

If you have advanced medical training you may have a lot more supplies including surgical kits and suturing kits. Starting with an off-the-shelf military surplus kit and then adding supplies is a fast way to build your kit.

146 What should a survivalist do to survive a home invasion?

As economic and social conditions deteriorate, home invasions will become more common. Nice homes in nice communities are increasingly the targets of these violent crimes. In the case of economic collapse, once stores are looted and the relief agencies are exhausted, the desperate and unprepared will turn to home invasions on a massive scale. The suggestions below apply to home invasions during "normal" times when the police are available. More aggressive "home defense" measures may be necessary during a large-scale and extended civil disorder situation.

Intruder Prevention and Survival

- Don't hesitate to call the police at the first sign of attempted entry. Any hesitation or procrastination only gives the criminals time to find a way in.
- Do not open your doors to strangers or let them lure you outside.
- Always lock your doors, even if you are going just a short distance. Lots of burglaries are facilitated by unlocked doors.
- Attached garages are a prime access point for burglars and home invaders. Residents tend to regard the door from the garage to the home as an interior door, but the garage door is often open or is far less secure. Have the same deadbolt locks on the garage access door. Keep the vehicle door closed when not entering or exiting and always lock the garage-to-house door.
- Potential home invaders and burglars may watch your home to see when you are out and when you come in or they may follow you from work or a place you frequent. Varying your schedule and routes can help. Be alert for anyone casing your home or following you.
- Home invasions or break-ins are often crimes of opportunity. There are people who just go around knocking on doors and trying the handles. If no one answers they try the other doors. If no one seems to be home, intruders break in. This may start as just a burglary, but if it turns out that someone is home or comes home, you could have a hostage or murder situation. Lock the doors. Call police if suspicious people are checking window and doors.
- Never enter your home or anyplace if you suspect it has been broken into. If you enter and see signs of an intruder, get out immediately and call police. Do not go looking for the intruder!
- Look around before entering your home. An intruder can slip in behind you

as you are driving into your garage or sneak up behind you as you unlock your front door. This is often how a home invasion starts.

- If taken hostage on the street, avoid letting them take you to your home.
- There is no doubt that the first thing the intruders will do is take your cell phones and disconnect the landlines. A few extra cell phones hidden about may come in handy. Remember that even out of service cell phones can call 911.
- Have a code word or phrase worked out with your family to let them know you are being held hostage. The invaders may want you to call a family member or answer a call. This would be a chance to get help without tipping off the intruders.
- If you don't have children, you may want to consider hiding a few firearms where you can get to them quickly. In addition to the bedside drawer, the living room and kitchen are good places to hide weapons.
- Once you are under the control of the intruders, your options are greatly reduced. In most cases intruders will injure or kill victims. If multiple family members are present, running in different directions and breaking through windows to escape is better than waiting for execution. Do this before you are tied up.
- If you do find yourself this situation, remember that this is your territory. You have some advantages in knowing where things are and places to hide or escape. Think scenarios through ahead of time.
- Home security systems are great, but if the intruders know about them, they can disable or disarm them. Having firearms at home can save your life, but advertising the fact gives away much of the advantage and may even invite burglars when you are not home.

147 What should I do if the intruder enters while I am asleep?

If you awaken to the sound of someone breaking into your home, you must act quickly and carefully before the intruder gets to you and realizes that you are awake. Hopefully you have placed your cell phone on the bedside table and weapons and a flashlight in your bedside drawer. Your actions should include the following:

- If you can do so quietly, close and lock your bedroom door. This will buy you a bit of time and make it harder to be heard as you call the police.
- Immediately dial 911. Tell them that an intruder or intruders are in your home. Also give them your location and inform them of where other family members are located within the home, and note whether you are armed or unarmed. Stay on the line and follow instructions.
- Do not go looking for the intruder. Take up a defensive position that blocks access to you and your family and offers concealment. Wait for the police.
- If the intruder approaches, you are not obliged to give them a warning before taking action, but you want to be sure it is actually an intruder (not a family member or the police). Of course, the preferred outcome is a retreating intruder caught by police, not violence, in your home.
- If the intruder ignores the warning and/or continues toward you and your family, you are justified in shooting. Be sure you are positioned so that shots will not endanger other family members in adjoining rooms.
- Once the police arrive, put down your firearm and turn on interior lights. You don't want the police to confuse you with the criminal.
- Regardless of the circumstances of a shooting, you must obey all police instructions and do not say anything until you have a lawyer present.

148 Should a survivalist get involved in community safety and emergency preparedness organizations?

The stronger and better prepared your community is, the safer you are. If your town or county has a Crime Watch, Civilian Emergency Response Team (CERTS), a Volunteers in Police Service (VIPS) program, or other programs to involve citizens in crime prevention, safety, and emergency response, it is in your best interest to support and participate in such programs. Encouraging local officials to initiate civilian support programs and sponsor preparedness seminars and fairs can strengthen your community and provide another layer of protection and support during a disaster. Participants in such programs usually receive training and inside information beyond what uninvolved citizens will get. Being officially certified usually provides access to or passage through areas denied to the public during an emergency. Volunteers for these organizations are usually subject to screening and are held to higher standards of conduct and responsibility than ordinary citizens.

149 What are the moral obligations of a survivalist in helping his or her unprepared neighbors?

Taking time to learn survival skills and spending some of your money on survival supplies, puts you on the moral high ground. By completing these tasks, you have done your duty as a responsible citizen. Since you are not a danger or a burden to the community, you have already helped others, but you also have the opportunity and the choice to provide reasonable assistance to deserving neighbors. You are not morally obligated to put yourself or your family in jeopardy to help those who have chosen not to prepare.

Making hard decisions will be easier if you have offered to help neighbors and friends get prepared beforehand. Providing literature, sponsoring preparedness programs in your community, and advocating preparedness will make it easier to say "no" when you must say "no." If you truly feel that someone you know cannot be prepared, consider putting together some supplies and a pack for them. Whenever you do provide supplies to others, it is important to state that you have limits. Ultimately you have to make decisions on a case-by-case basis. Some suggestions on dealing with certain situations are listed below:

- In some instances people who did prepare and are good neighbors will still be in need. They deserve your compassion and help.
- You may have already created a network of supportive neighbors or friends. If they have done their part, then you must reciprocate.
- Those who are helpless, nonaggressive, or are refugees can be aided according to your abilities without endangering yourself.
- Those who have totally ignored preparedness, belittled survivalists, and have been selfish in the past do not deserve any support.
- Those who are threatening, violent, and aggressive must be turned away and resisted. Any show of weakness or compassion will only invite assault and looting.

Disasters and large-scale catastrophes are opportunities for the survivalist to be compassionate and helpful to others in time of need. You are not obliged to become a victim yourself. You cannot be your neighbor's keeper if you are unable to help yourself.

150   What questions should a survivalist ask him- or herself?

A questioning attitude is the hallmark of an intelligent individual and an essential element in survival thinking. The answers to the previous 149 questions should have provided you with essential survival information, established sound philosophical guidelines, and strengthened your abilities to cope with the material, physical, and psychological challenges of both rapid and slow-developing disasters. Ultimately there are important questions that the survivalist must ask him- or herself. A few of those self-examining questions are listed below.

- What is my mission in life? Knowing and defining one's reasons for living is the foundation of a strong will to survive and a guide for preparedness and survival actions.
- What are my priorities in daily life and in preparedness that will make be stronger and more self-reliant?
- What habits, associations, and dependencies do I have that I should discontinue in order to be healthier, freer, and better prepared?
- What are my values and my responsibilities to the future?
- Am I truly committed to survival, self-reliance, and independence, or am I reluctant to accept the challenges of being different?
- What am I going to do about the future of my family, community, and nation as I face both limited and possibly global catastrophic events?

We Are Survivalists

"He who fails to prepare for the night, fails to prepare for the dawn."

I am a survivalist, and by nature a survivalist is an optimist. I do not have a pessimistic bone in my body. If what I just said sounds odd to you, then you are not yet a survivalist and you do not understand the modern survivalist at all. It is very difficult to communicate to the public the concept of an optimistic, hopeful survivalist.

A fireman is a fireman, not because he believes everything will burn, but because he believes much can be saved. Doctors don't believe in death—they believe in life. Similarly, a survivalist is not a survivalist because he believes that everything will be destroyed and everyone will die, but because he believes that life and freedom can be saved if people are prepared. A fireman does not start fires, a doctor does not make diseases, and a survivalist does not make disaster. Crime, disease, war, revolution, tyranny, fire, flood, famine, and economic upheavals are the results of Mother Nature and the nature of man, and are not always within the power of anyone to prevent.

We all know that the sun will set each day, leaving us in the darkness, and we all know that warm summers give way to cold winters. But though we know we cannot stop the sun from setting or the cold winds from coming, does this make us pessimistic? I think not! So then, why are survivalists called pessimists when they make ready to face events that are just as much part of history and nature as the sunset or the changing of the seasons.

Another misconception about survivalists is that they are predicting world catastrophes. On the contrary, survivalists are the optimistic minority who are predicting survival. It is difficult to find any respected historian, economist, political scientist, sociologist, or military strategist who will predict that disasters are not inevitable; yet we survivalists dare to be optimistic about the future. We survivalists do not need to predict the probability of disaster any more than we need to predict the sun setting. Those who criticize survivalists are like those persons who refuse to look at the calendar, in the hope that through self-imposed ignorance they can keep from aging another year. Denial will not stop the inevitable from coming.

Sometimes survivalists are told that, "You will be disappointed if we don't have a world cataclysm"; this is another accusation that is totally ridiculous. We survivalists have loved ones that we do not want to see hurt or killed. We have homes and property we do not want to see lost or destroyed. We are not so foolish as to think that just because we are survivalists that disasters would not cause us to experience danger, loss, hunger, injury, cold, despair, and death. We do not want bad things to happen to good people; we want good people to be able to survive and stay free when those things do happen.

As survivalists, we spend time and money to improve our chances for survival and recovery in the event of a disaster, but we would celebrate if we could be assured that we had wasted our time. Contrary to popular belief, we survivalists will not be disappointed if there are no disasters to survive, any more than the Red Cross is disappointed when there are no emergencies, or the man who buys fire insurance is disappointed when his house fails to burn down. It may be said that the survivalist would much prefer the pleasant, but unlikely, surprise of being wrong than the rude awakening that the nonsurvivalist will face if he is wrong and thus unprepared.

Ultimately, the survivalist cannot lose because his survival preparations will be of value regardless of what the future has in store. In times of crisis, those who have not prepared to turn *to* each other are much more likely to turn *on* each other. It is most regrettable indeed that many people still consider survivalists as a threat and regard them with suspicion and even hostility. This attitude is logically indefensible and is rooted in the non-survivalist's own sense of fear and guilt. Subconsciously, the non-survivalist may hate the survivalist for reminding him of how fragile his lifestyle is.

So, let's get the facts right. The most dangerous people in today's world are the non-survivalists. Every person who has failed to make provisions for surviving without food, water, fuel, and other essentials from the outside world is potentially a mortal danger to his neighbors. What will a man do when he and his family are cold, hungry, thirsty, and sick? He may ask his neighbors for help, but when they have no extra fuel, food, water, or medication to give, will he just go back home to die with his loved ones? What do you think he will do?

Survivalists who stock up on food and other supplies do a great service to society because what we now buy is replaced on the shelves, so there will be that much more available in times of crisis. When disaster strikes, survivalists won't be the ones looting and killing for food. We survivalists won't be a burden on the medical facilities or a danger to the police. We will be able to turn to each other and we will not need to turn on anyone. We will be in a position to help our neighbors and our community without endangering the safety and freedom of our families. Survival preparedness should be regarded as a social obligation, one that every responsible individual owes to his family, community and nation. The nonsurvivalist is a poor and irresponsible citizen.

The reality is that survivalists are optimistic, self-reliant individuals who cannot help but see the imperative of preparing for the worst events, while at the same time working and hoping for a safer and freer future. Today's survivalist is an asset to the community and should be proud to say, "I am a survivalist."

Author's Note: A version of "We Are Survivalists" was first published in *Directions*, a newsletter published by Live Free in the early 1980s. It was written in response to the many misrepresentations and misconceptions then being established by the news media. The article has been reprinted many times in survival/self-reliance publications all over the world. This issue has been edited to reflect modern concerns. It still serves as one of the best explanations of the philosophy and position of true survivalism and of the Live Free organization that has been its oldest and strongest advocate.

About the Author

James C. Jones was born on the South Side of Chicago at the beginning of World War II. An impoverished and chaotic childhood made him a natural survivalist from a very early age. He put together his own survival pack at age twelve and often spent time in the woodlands and swamps that then adjoined the city. Working two jobs while living in one room and attending high school added more real-world survival experiences to his arsenal. Starting as a technician at a large chemical manufacturing complex after school, his passion for safety lead him to become an award-winning safety manager. While acquiring certifications in emergency medicine, hazardous chemical handling, safety management, and training management related to his job, he energetically pursued survival-related activities including rock climbing, caving, rafting, horseback riding, and survival camping. He founded Live Free USA in the late 1960s and helped it evolve from an outdoor survival club into a national preparedness and self-reliance education organization. During the 1970s and 1980s, he was a leading voice in defending and defining responsible survivalism on national television and radio.

Mr. Jones has developed and conducted hundreds of survival training events and seminars over the past forty years and has written hundreds of articles for Live Free's membership newsletter *American Survivor*. He is now retired and living in Indiana, but currently writes articles for several national preparedness- and survival-related publications, while continuing to teach a variety of survival courses and make presentations at major preparedness expositions. His books include *Total Survival* and *Advanced Survival*. Both books are published by Skyhorse Publishing. He may be contacted at survivorjj@aol.com.